Whatever happened to Adam?

Stories about disabled people who
were adopted or fostered

ONE WEEK LOAN

Whatever happened To Adam?

Stories about disabled people who were adopted or fostered

Hedi Argent

B *ritish*
A *gencies*
for **A** *doption*
and **F** *ostering*

Published by
British Agencies for Adoption & Fostering
(BAAF)
Skyline House
200 Union Street
London SE1 0LX

Registered Charity 275689

© Hedi Argent 1998

ISBN 1 873868 56 1

British Library Cataloguing in Publication
Data
A catalogue record for this book is available
from the British Library

Editorial project management by Shaila Shah,
BAAF
Cover photograph of Jean and Adam by
Joanne O'Brien
Designed by Andrew Haig & Associates
Typeset by Avon Dataset Ltd, Bidford on Avon
Printed by Russell Press (TU) Nottingham

Acknowledgements

First of all I want to express my deep gratitude to all of the families who have contributed to this book.

Then I would like to thank Hilary Alton for her help in setting up the project, for her continuing advice and support and for her interviews with two of the families.

I am grateful to Phillida Sawbridge for her helpful comments and suggestions at various stages of this book and to Judith Stone and Marjorie Morrison for reading the final manuscript, to Shaila Shah, my encouraging editor, and to Susanne Clarke, her patient editorial assistant.

Finally, I am indebted to Souvenir Press for allowing an amended excerpt from *Find me a Family* to be included in Chapter 3 and to Macdonald Queen Anne Press for giving permission to quote from *Matthew, My Son's Struggle*.

The people who told their stories chose to use their own and their children's forenames. Family names and place names have been omitted in order to preserve privacy. Only one young person's name has been changed to protect his birth family; two younger foster children and two newly adopted children who are mentioned in the text could not be named for legal reasons.

A Glossary of Disabilities and Explanatory Notes about PFC agency practice, other organisations and adoption procedures mentioned in the text, will be found at the end of the book.

Foreword

This is a splendid book. It tells the stories of some extraordinary families and their children. For the first time, we hear from families who adopted or fostered children with severe disabilities many years ago. What was it really like? How did the children grow up? How independent did the young people become? And how do they themselves feel about it? In this remarkable collection Hedi Argent vividly describes their experiences and family histories.

This book is also to be much valued because it is a timely reminder of the inherent worth of alternative families for some very needy children and the joys as well as the sorrows experienced by those rare people who choose to adopt or foster a child with special, indeed exceptional, needs.

Many of the children Hedi Argent writes about were placed with families during the very early years of Parents for Children (PFC) when the agency was seen to be pioneering the placement of children who had previously been described as 'not fit for adoption'. This "experiment" resulted in hundreds of children moving out of institutions and into families.

PFC freely gave advice and information to other agencies about how to make the seemingly impossible possible. What PFC was less successful in imparting was the need for drive, energy, meticulous attention to detail, superb teamwork, first class administrative support and a fair degree of good luck in order to achieve permanence for a child.

Sadly, the idea that every child could be found a family took hold without the supporting knowledge that for some children, particularly the older child who has had a difficult early life, the only way to achieve a stable placement is to invest in highly trained and well supervised professionals who can offer friendly, informed, and easily accessible services to the adoptive or foster family when they need it and as often as they need it. It is my belief that this division between the concept on the one hand and the necessary skills on the other has led to the current questioning of whether family placement for some children is the right choice to make.

Many of the children referred to PFC now have had far too many placement breakdowns and they are more emotionally than physically or intellectually impaired. Foster placement after foster placement has disrupted. Whereas in the past PFC would have regarded the child who had spent several years in a Children's Home as unfortunate and the foster child as fortunate, we cannot say the same today. The child we worked with in the past who had had a stable period of residential care was institutionalised, yes, but by no means as angry or disturbed as the children we work with now who have had far too many moves. Little wonder that powerful voices are raised against fostering and adoption. However, it would be tragic if the tangible benefits that family life can offer to a child are to be lost because the art of family placement is improperly understood and practised.

We know that family placement can work and does work for some very needy children. But we cannot ask people to undertake that task alone. Family placement workers must care passionately about the task and about the child. So must the family. They need to know all there is to know about the child's history. They need to know that whatever their task in the months and years to come will be done with the support of others. If the families get the right help – short break or respite services, access to experts they can call upon, experienced families to link with, and highly skilled social workers to inform, support and offer praise in the course of this lifelong experience – there will be joy to outweigh the cost.

We are asking families to make lifelong commitments and many of them have done so admirably. This book is a testament to that experience and amply demonstrates the enormous difference that such commitment can make to a child's life. It is my hope that in another two decades there will be a further generation of children and families who have an extraordinary story to tell of their journeys and a Hedi Argent to tell them.

Karen Irving
Director, Parents for Children
May 1998

Introduction

No-one knows what it will really be like until they do it.

No amount of preparation could have prepared us for what was coming.

You know how it's been for somebody else – but it's always somebody else, not you.

Nearly all the families who contributed to this book had something similar to say and yet each of the families is quite unlike any of the others. What they all have in common is that they have adopted or fostered children with disabilities, that they are committed to their children and that they appear to move mountains in order to secure what their children need. I think most readers will agree that their stories are extraordinary; some may wonder how such an unusual collection of people came to work with an adoption agency called Parents for Children.

Twent-one years ago, in 1976, Parents for Children (PFC) was launched as a pioneering specialist agency to test out whether older and severely disabled children could be placed with permanent alternative families. The stories in this book provide part of the answer. PFC developed a supportive and democratic way of working which appealed to families. A great deal was expected of them during the assessment process but that is not what the families remember – they remember the welcome, the trust, the honesty and the dire warnings about how hard it was all going to be.

As it was 20 years since the first children with disabilities were placed by PFC, and they would now all be between 20 and 30 years old, it seemed important to find out what had happened to them and their families. The urgent question for other prospective carers, for social workers, for specialist agencies and for everyone interested in disabled young people is: what degree of independence did they achieve and what does independence mean when impairment prevents even the simplest

1

act of self-help? As one mother says: 'Margaret sits and smiles unable to swipe a fly away.'

The number 20 became attractive, and the tales of 20 profoundly disabled sons and daughters, at least 20 years old, became the aim. It would have sounded neat to say that they were also placed 20 years ago but that would not have been true. It took more than a year to place 20 children and not all of the earliest placements have been included here. Decisions had to be made about representing a variety of families and children with different disabilities and disabling conditions. Also, some guidelines had to be observed in order to reflect a wide spectrum of experience and family life. Single, divorced, married and re-married, unmarried but in a partnership, widowed and disabled families have been included. All the young people who were followed up were placed before 1985; healthy babies with Down's Syndrome who dominated the early referrals to PFC were excluded in favour of older children with Down's Syndrome who had additional disabilities; the success or disruption of a placement or the death of a child or young person did not influence the choice; when two children had very similar impairments, the child who had been in placement longest was chosen. There is doubtless more than one other volume to be written about the young people who have been left out this time; for instance, all the adopted infants with Down's Syndrome have surely grown up to become independent to some degree; have they become more or less independent than their peers who stayed with their birth parents? This and many other questions remain to be asked and answered, but in the meantime, 14 families and their 20 adult disabled children have offered stories which are very special.

The contributors were contacted through a long established network of PFC families and original PFC workers. Fifteen families were approached, 14 responded and went on to tell their tales. Luckily it worked out that they had fostered or adopted exactly 20 children between them.

This is not a research study or a systematic enquiry into any one area of placement outcomes. Although there was a common framework of questions and the focus of interviews was on the young peoples' moves towards independence, families told their stories in their own way and emphasised what was important to them. They speak here with their own voices, only occasionally prompted by the interviewer whose comments have been kept to a minimum. Most of what they said was taken down in note form; some of each interview was recorded. The interviews took a long working day in the families' homes, interspersed by lunch and tea in a pub or a restaurant.

It was difficult to decide how far to push the interviews with the young people themselves. Some could participate to an impressive extent; some preferred to sit and listen without saying very much. A few were interviewed quite separately away from their home, a few who could not hear or understand were not interviewed at all. Other members of the family were invited to have their say; sometimes their views run through the story and sometimes they were added at the end after they had read the main narrative.

First drafts were sent to all contributors; they were able to amend, cut or expand as they wished. Final drafts went out accompanied by a Form of Agreement which they were asked to sign to release the material for publication. Throughout the process all the families were interested and enormously creative. It has been a joy to work with them again after so long a time and an honour to be allowed to hear of their trials and sorrows as well as of their triumphs and rewards. It has been a privilege to meet the young women and men and to gain some understanding of how life has been for them.

A great deal has changed in child care and adoption since these 20 young people were placed. Increased levels of contact with birth families, closer attention to ethnicity, culture and religion and their importance in identity formation, and an increased awareness of sexual abuse and its impact have all shaped practice and policy. Disabled children are more usually fostered now while they wait for a permanent placement, whereas all but one of the children in this book were living in institutions before they moved to their families. On the whole, families take changes more easily in their stride than social workers: they are less constricted by fashion or the official line and more in touch with children's needs and birth parents' feelings. Most of them mention their attempts to make contact with birth families for their children's sakes and often against the advice of social workers. Whatever else has changed in family placement work and will change again in the future, one thing is constant and certain: there are people who want to adopt or permanently foster children with disabilities. They may have personal or professional experience of disability or they may welcome the challenge of doing something extra; they may have deeply-held beliefs which give them the strength to do it or they may have special sympathy for disability because they themselves are socially disadvantaged. Or they may simply stretch that bit further to meet the needs of a particular child – not in spite of the disability but because of it. This book is about them, for them, and is dedicated to them.

Hedi Argent
May 1998

1 If I can't speak for him, who can?
Jean and Adam

Finding out

I first saw a picture of Adam on a PFC photosheet in 1978. He was beautiful. He was five years old, he was blind, he was brain damaged, he had hydrocephaly and epilepsy. The description said he couldn't walk or talk and no-one could tell whether he ever would.

I'd been preparing to adopt for almost a year. Ever since I found out from an article in *Nursery World* that you didn't have to be married. I was 35, a nursery nurse, and I wanted to look after my own children instead of other people's. I'd always wanted to adopt from when I was a little girl; I used to play adoption with my dolls. I don't know why. I'd sit and look at the pictures Barnado's sent – to encourage you to send money I suppose – and I don't know how I thought of adoption but I did. I wanted to get married and to adopt my children.

I never thought about disability till I saw all the photos of disabled children who needed families. I was staggered. First I was really stuck on another disabled child from PFC but I had to accept that this boy needed a dad. When the photo-sheet of Adam came my friend said: 'Jean, what about him?' But I said: 'Oh no! He's so cute. Everyone will be after him.' I was looking for a child nobody wanted.

Then I was invited to an Activity Day to meet some of the children. Right up to the day before I didn't know if I'd go. Then I thought: 'I've got nothing else to do, I might as well.' I remember it like it was yesterday. There were seven children and seven families. And they said: 'When Adam comes we'd like you to sit with him and give him lunch.' I thought: 'What am I going to do with him?' I wasn't too happy about it. Adam was the last one to arrive and they brought him over to me in his wheelchair and left him with me. Oh my goodness! So I picked him up and put him on my lap and he got hold of my hand and he moved it to the table and I gave him some food. He put it in his mouth and I looked at him and I said: 'Oh he's lovely.' That was it really; I was just gone. After lunch I sat with him on the floor and I wouldn't let anyone come near

5

him. One of the fathers came and said: 'Who's this then?' and I put my arms round Adam and said: 'It's Adam and he's very disabled.' He was mine; I didn't want anyone else to look at him.

When I got home that night I said to my flat mate: 'I know it sounds silly but I've really fallen in love. It's that little boy, Adam.' And I sat down and wrote a letter to PFC to say I wanted him and I took it to the post box. At nine o'clock on Monday morning I rang up to make sure it had arrived. I was desperate. I was that worried that it would get lost in the post and someone else would get Adam. I thought how could anyone not want him. And the fact that he had all these disabilities – it didn't matter. It isn't that I didn't know about them – I just didn't see them. At this point what I saw was Adam. This little plump boy with red curly hair who smiled a lot.

When I came up to PFC I was shaking. I thought if they say 'no' I'll faint, I know I will. Then I saw Adam's worker and she said: 'So you want to have Adam?' and she came in with all his photos and stuff to tell me more about him. I went home high. I've tried to think about it since and it was like someone who hasn't been able to have any children suddenly becoming pregnant.

No-one thought it was really going to happen. My mother was against it; she said: 'You'll never get married if you do this.' When she met Adam that changed because everyone thought he was wonderful. Some of my friends worried about how I would manage because he was quite plump and he'd get too heavy for me to lift – but as it turned out he got thinner as he got older. He's 24 now and about as tall as a 14-year-old and very slim.

All the preparation I had for Adam was excellent but I thought to myself: 'It doesn't matter what you're saying, I want to be Adam's mother.' I don't think I heard half of it. His disability was an unknown quantity anyway. He was blind and brain damaged and, I used to say to people, 'he can't walk or talk as yet'. It wasn't till later I learned Adam had a genetic disability. It was when his younger brother, who was fostered, was seen at Great Ormond Street Hospital. He was the same as Adam but not as bad because he was treated earlier with the shunt for the hydrocephaly. They said it was a "one off" genetic condition.

I met his mother before I had Adam. She was a nice woman and she really cared about Adam – she used to visit him regularly in the hospital where he lived. She asked me if I was being pushed into this and I told her I wasn't. After Adam had been adopted I asked the local authority to contact her but they wouldn't because she'd had a new baby and they didn't want to upset her. But I don't think that was right; they didn't give her a chance. I knew she loved him and would like to see how happy he was. Adam's older brother wanted to keep in touch and I agreed to that but in the end he didn't. After ten years I had a letter from him – he was 19 then – he'd always thought about Adam, he said, and wanted to know how he was getting on. I put a photo album together for him and sent it with a long letter but I never heard again. I did write two more times and said I'd be pleased for anyone from the family to visit Adam.

When I was getting to know Adam, he was living in this subnormality hospital (as it was called then) and some people there didn't think I should have him, being single. But the specialist was very helpful and supportive. It took six months to convince them that I was totally committed and could manage him. I was going to see Adam every Saturday and again on Sunday. And when I had annual leave I'd spend all my time going up there. It took an hour each way on the train. I used to sit on his bed at the hospital – I was still shy – and I used to point with his hand and say: 'Adam, Mama,' and hope no-one was watching.

I had to sort out schooling and housing and all the money before Adam could live with me. There was no adoption allowance then. It was difficult because I'd been used to earning but I never bothered much about money. When I had it I spent it and when I got Adam I managed on social security plus the disability and child benefits.

I wrote to every housing association in London and only got one reply, from Peabody's; PFC wrote that I was adopting Adam and they offered me a flat in South London.

When I brought Adam home to the new flat for the first time, I couldn't bear to take him back again to the hospital. So we got schooling and everything sorted out at the last minute and I just took Adam back to say good-bye. It was six months from when I first saw him.

Getting going

In the beginning it wasn't good. He had fits. He wouldn't use the toilet or eat. He wouldn't even drink. He only wanted to stay in bed and he cried a lot. I was getting beside myself. I thought: 'Either he's ill or he doesn't like it here.' One day I sat him up and said: 'What's wrong Adam?' and he picked up a plastic beaker, one of those that fit into each other, and he started to pretend drink. So I rushed out and got him a drink and he never looked back. He started eating and playing and using the toilet again. To this day I don't know whether he was getting ill or there was something wrong with his shunt but really I think it was just leaving the hospital after three years. When I used to take him out he'd put his hands over his ears for the traffic noises.

When Adam came to me he was in a wheelchair but I didn't think that was right. He wasn't comfortable. So I got him a "Major Buggy" to go out and he liked it better. Then when he got too big for it, I still wouldn't accept a wheelchair. Social services said I was in denial about his disabilities but I wasn't; he wasn't comfortable in a wheelchair and I just wanted the best for him. I'd heard about a Swedish push chair suitable for disabled children. PFC raised the money for it because I couldn't get it on the National Health. That was wonderful, Adam loved it. Later, when he grew out of that, I got the bigger size and I raised the money myself. He didn't go in a wheelchair till he was 12 – then he could cope with it. Now they adapt his wheelchairs to slope back but you have to fight for it!

I'd decided life wasn't going to be any different with Adam but of course that was ridiculous. We did go on doing things like getting on buses and going places and visiting friends and going to church, but it was the change in me that was most noticeable. I used to be a very laid back person and I became obsessed with Adam's health and appetite and whether he was warm enough. I watched his every move and expression – I suppose I just became a parent.

In those days it was mostly him and me. He thrived on the attention – he'd had some good care in the hospital but he'd never had anyone all to himself before. I didn't trust anyone else with him. I didn't even want him to go to school. I kept him at home more than I should and I got into trouble for that. In the end I agreed he had to go to school and he liked going. He's always been very popular with the teachers and the other children.

It was difficult at first for Adam to get used to the new environment. What I did was to teach him to move about. I didn't have much furniture and I used to lie him down on the floor and I'd throw Smarties all round him to encourage him to explore. Then he used to have a basket of toys he liked. He'd play with them on the bedroom floor before I put him to bed. Once, when I'd maybe had him for a year, I left him to play and when I came back he'd put himself to bed and gone to sleep. That was really a moment because he'd done something for himself.

At first he wasn't keen on physical contact – not too many cuddles. So what I started doing – we have floor cushions – was to lie down in front of the fire with him, talking to him, singing and being close. He went from not liking cuddles to wanting them all the time. He really loved listening to music. I used to find out what he liked by watching him.

Communication was never a problem. It didn't take long for me to know what Adam wanted; just by his eyes, by looking at him I could tell if he was happy. And he pushes you to where he wants to go. He can walk if you face him and hold both his hands so that he can kind of guide you backwards. They tried to teach him sign language at school but he didn't take to it. He doesn't use any signs for any particular thing. It's just: 'Do you want a biscuit?' – hand up means 'yes', or 'Do you want the toilet?' – hand up means 'yes.' And that's as far as it goes.

Two years after he came, Adam suddenly had a sleep problem. He just would not go to bed. So in the end he'd fall asleep on the settee, but as soon as I picked him up, he'd wake and refuse to go to bed. So I left him and slept in the sitting room with him. And he'd be up again at three in the morning wanting to play with his toys. His sleep pattern was completely up the creek and I was beside myself. I heard through the school about this psychologist – he was really into sleep – that was his thing. This man was absolutely wonderful. He came to see me and he said: 'Adam is ruling the roost here, and it's just not on.' It was me he was watching, more than Adam. He made out a programme for me and eventually I did get Adam to bed on time. But it took nearly a year before I could leave him to go to sleep on his own. The psychologist planned it all out step by step for me and it worked. That was the most difficult time I ever had with Adam but, even then, I got the help I needed.

I was never much into support groups. I did go to one for a while but I got all the support I wanted from my mother, my friends, the Church of Christian Fellowship, PFC and the school. As far as social services goes, I find it varies from area to area. Some are more on the ball than others. It could be to do with funding or whether they're geared to people with disabilities. Some local authority social workers are really excellent but on the whole I wish they'd listen more to what the parents say.

I've always shared a room with Adam. He has fits in the night and he has to go to the toilet. He might have got out by himself and stayed wet on the floor all night. It was easier for me to sleep in his room. I did try an intercom – that was worse because I was getting up at every noise. I had a lot of professional criticism, especially as he got older, but it was so sick that anyone could think there was anything wrong with it. They just didn't understand Adam's needs. Everything seems to be geared to sexual problems and abuse but what Adam needs is constant attention.

As time went on, Adam improved. He started to feed himself and he started to crawl. I thought in time he would walk and I used to stand him up against the wall and say: 'Come on Adam, walk to me.' I feel quite horrified when I remember. It took years for me to accept that he would never walk unaided. He did begin to talk at one point but he stopped as quick as he started. How could a boy who couldn't talk wake up one morning and shout: 'Mama!' then go on and say words and sentences within days and then just stop again? Occasionally he still says something that sounds like a word.

When Adam was 14, he went through a bad patch. He was having temper tantrums, screaming every time the door bell went and he seemed to become a different person. He was really hard to handle all the time. It was gross. I took him up to Great Ormond Street but they couldn't find anything. Then I rang the psychologist again. We found out he was sprouting pubic hair! I couldn't believe it. He was going through puberty and it was his way of dealing with it, that's all. Once I knew there was nothing wrong with him I could cope.

*   *   *

Digging in

Jean is now the mother of five adopted children and she has fostered numerous others, starting when Adam had been with her for three years.

*   *   *

Jean

Adam was used to having other children around by the time I took Tanya for adoption. She was six when she came and Adam was ten. I was looking for another child I could love like Adam – I was disappointed in me and in her that it couldn't happen. But I have come to care for Tanya in a different way. She's never paid any attention to Adam but if she sits next to him he likes to touch her hand.

*   *   *

Tanya is autistic and has severe learning disabilities. She has been very difficult to bring up. Now, at 18, she still lives in an incomprehensible world of her own. Her obsessive behaviour makes Jean's friends apprehensive about looking after her. Tanya is the only one of Jean's adopted children who does not have a named guardian in the event of becoming an orphan. Sometimes Jean wonders whether she has harmed Tanya by trying to make her live in the real world but after a particularly distressing bout of disturbed behaviour, I saw Tanya put her arms around Jean and give her a real hug.

Later, two half-sisters were adopted – the older one has already left home and has made Jean a grandmother. The last to be added to the family is a boy of 11 with a learning disability.

*   *   *

Jean

I've sometimes worried about the effect on Adam because little ones will climb on him or rush past him and he can feel the vibrations. But he

11

seems to like it as long as it's a pleasant atmosphere. He is very sensitive and responds to happy activity all around him.

*   *   *

As Jean had more children, so she needed more space. She applied for a transfer to a five bed flat but they gave her a bright new house, suitable for disabled people, with only four bedrooms. 'If I'd had five, I'd probably have taken more children,' she says.

*   *   *

Jean

Adam took the move in his stride. He had to orientate himself about where everything was but it didn't take him long and he didn't get upset by it although we'd been in the other place for 12 years.

When Adam became an adult, he remained short and he lost weight. I thought he was dying but it was all to do with his development. He developed sexually and began to masturbate and bring himself to climax. He doesn't do it as much now as he did in his late teens. I've taught him to do it in his bed, not in the living room.

Before Adam left school at 18, he went to college a few times on day release. I thought: 'How are they going to cope?' But I let them get on with it. They had to get him up three flights of stairs and it took half the morning. In the end they said because of funding they had to cut down. Adam had to have a one-to-one helper and they couldn't provide one.

Since Adam left school he's had a lot of help from community care – more than I wanted really. I went along with it, up to a certain point, to keep everyone happy. If you keep professionals happy, then they leave you alone after that. For instance, Adam loves his bath. He likes to lie in it for a long time. I can lift him in and out quite easily but other people always think it's more of a problem than I do. When he was 13, the occupational therapist tried him with a bath lift. But Adam wouldn't use it. They said I should have tried harder to get him used to it but he hated it and I asked them to take it away. Then when he was an adult, they said again that he had to have bath aids. I said: 'He doesn't like anything like that,' and they said: 'That's too bad,' and kept coming up with new ideas and I kept saying 'no'. Then they said: 'Let's teach Adam to get in and out on his own.' I said: 'What? With his clothes on and no water in the bath?' But she got him and she put his arms across the bath onto the wall and she's saying: 'Go on Adam, into the bath.' Of course he didn't, it was silly. I wouldn't let her go near Adam after that and we didn't have any bath aids. But that same worker was very helpful when it came to getting a new wheelchair. Unless a mother is completely off the wall, she knows what her child needs and doesn't need. Like an electric wheelchair; someone once thought that Adam should have one, but I thought whatever do they think he's going to do with it?

I told them I didn't mind Adam being home all the time. I didn't push for a Day Centre so it was three years before they found him a place. Now he goes twice a week and he loves it. He's the favourite. I tell him: 'Everyone thinks you're special.' He also goes to an independence project twice a week but he never will be; he won't even become partly independent. They keep him occupied and he needs other people, and his worker is a man, which is good.

First time Adam went away from home, he was on the project and he was 21. They were going for three days to Butlin's in Brighton. It took me a while to decide to let him go. I have a friend near Brighton and I wanted to go and stay there and follow them around but my other children said: 'No you don't.' So I gave the carers a long list like: 'If you stop on the promenade, don't forget to put the brake on the chair in case it rolls into the sea.' I was in such a state I couldn't do my shopping. I thought I was going to throw up. Everyone said I'd be able to get a good sleep because I wouldn't have to get up in the night but I couldn't sleep at all. I made them phone me up every evening to say he was OK. They showed me photos after and he was smiling on every one of them.

It was the same with respite care. I never asked for it so it wasn't offered until he was an adult. I was at a meeting for Tanya when they said: 'Why doesn't Adam come into adult respite?' The more I thought about it, the less I wanted to send him, but we tried it out for one night and he was fine. Then he started going once a month for a few days or for a weekend. Sometimes they can take both my disabled children together and my oldest daughter takes the others and I go off and stay in a hotel – it's wonderful. Friends say I should have done it years ago but I never wanted to.

I know Adam hasn't got all the benefits he's entitled to. He should have the Disability Benefit – I've got the forms but I hate filling them in, I've half done it. And I should have applied for Income Support when he left school but by the time I got around to it, it had all changed. I've had conflicting advice about social security and we've had some hard times, but now I've got a Welfare Rights Officer to sort things out.

I feel totally responsible for Adam. I think I'll outlive him but if I don't I've made arrangements for him. He's changed a lot. He likes best to have his bath and to stay in bed. I let him stay as long as he wants when he doesn't have to go anywhere. He doesn't play like he did when he was small. The other children talk to him and he sits on the settee and looks happy. He only has to hear the biscuit tin and his hand goes up for 'yes'. They like feeding him. He is a very gentle and quiet young man.

On the whole I think I've got what I wanted for Adam and what I think he needed. The only thing I'd like and haven't got is my own personal hydrotherapy pool. I used to take him once a week to the pool in the hospital but the therapist said he didn't need it as much as some other people and there wasn't the funding for him. He was enjoying it though, and I'd like him to have it again.

Holding on

Fostering was never an option for me. Adam is like my own and I forget he isn't. I see family similarities and have to remind myself he's adopted. It sounds weird but I don't forget his birth family either. I talk to Adam a lot. What I say is: 'Your first Mum doesn't know what she missed. I'm glad she gave you up for my sake, but I'm sad for her.' I wonder now whether she'd want to know that Adam doesn't have long to live.

Every time Adam went in to hospital to have his shunt renewed they'd do tests before the operation and there was always a problem with his kidneys. Last year when he went in, he'd had a particularly bad fit. We were on holiday in a caravan at the time and talk about panic – he looked as though he was going. By the time we got him to the local casualty he'd recovered and they didn't even examine him, just asked a few questions and sent us back to the caravan. I wondered what they'd have done if he hadn't been disabled. Anyway, when we got home, they kept him in hospital for a week. I spent nearly all day with him and did everything for him. When they'd done the tests, they asked if I'd like to see the renal consultant. I saw the Registrar in the end. He came into the ward and he said: 'Maybe we can find somewhere quiet to chat.' As I was trotting after him I thought: 'I've watched all these medical programmes on TV I know what that means.' So we go into this little room, with a nurse, and he says: 'Sit down' and 'What would you like to ask me?'

He showed me an Xray of Adam's kidneys and said they were shrinking. I said: 'Does that mean he'll go into kidney failure altogether?'

He said: 'Yes, and you will probably want to know how long it will take.'

I said: 'Can you tell me that?'

He said it would be not less than two years, he thought, and perhaps up to five. I was so relieved he didn't say: 'Six months to a year' that I said: 'Oh that's fine, I'll think about it when it happens.' I could see on their faces, the way they looked at each other, 'She's in denial again'.

He wanted to talk about the options; to write them down in the records. They wouldn't do a transplant – I knew that. They wouldn't offer dialysis but he said they could give some treatment which would be distressing to Adam, and I said no to that. The surgeon had already talked to the Sister on the ward who knew Adam and agreed with me. I asked him how I would know when Adam was getting ill. He said Adam would slow down generally and not be able to go to the toilet. He told me that people with kidney complaints often have a peaceful end; one of my friends has confirmed that. I feel better now because I was so worried Adam would be in pain and I wouldn't be able to help him. The other children all know. I'm trying to teach them to make the most of the present, like I do.

I'm 53 now. I sometimes wonder if I would have had all my aches and pains if I hadn't had Adam. I have sciatica and carpel tunnel syndrome, which means in the morning my hands are numb and I get all pins and needles. That's why I thought I had muscular sclerosis (MS) and my GP referred me to a specialist, but he said to me: 'I bet you think you've got MS but you haven't. It's wear and tear in your body.' You need a fair amount of physical strength to look after someone like Adam. And it depends on what kind of person you are. I'm emotional; that adds to the wear and tear. To anyone thinking of adopting or fostering a child like

Adam now, I'd say if it's something they definitely want to do, they're half way there, but if they're in two minds about it, I'd tell them to think very carefully.

*   *   *

While Jean was finishing her story, she was sitting on the settee with Adam. She looks much younger than she is. Adam's red curls have been cut into an adult style but he retains the angelic smile of his childhood. He is calm and relaxed; a genial presence in the busy household. Every now and again he turns to Jean and gives her a hug. Jean believes she knows what Adam thinks and feels; she has told his story. But, I ask her, can she speak for him? 'I have to. If I can't speak for him, who can? And no-one is going to take any notice of him otherwise.'

2 It's not the big things that matter most
Chris, Tony, Claude and Robert

'Don't forget to find me a family,' Robert used to say to his PFC worker every time she came to see him in the residential nursery where he was still living when he was eight. Robert, who has Noonan Syndrome, got his family: a mother and father and Claude, a younger adopted brother who has adrenal hyperplasia. Much later Corena, a 12-year-old sister with severe learning difficulties, also joined the family. Corena is still at school. This is her brothers' story.

Who we are
Claude
My name is Claude. I'm 20. I'm not that special – I just have to take tablets all the time.

Mummy used to come to bath me in the Nursery before I was adopted. And I was sick all over Daddy because he bounced me up and down just after I had my tea. Daddy used to work in the same hospital I was born in. He was there when I was born but we didn't know. I remember you picked me up in a red Avenger with a black roof – oh no – that's when we picked up Robert. I nearly killed Robert on his first visit. I threw a car transporter at his head. Then he hit my fingers when I was holding on to the top bunk; I fell down and he thought I was dead. But I paid him back on several occasions, didn't I Mummy? Robert's alright. We get on now. I might be younger but I'm bigger. Robert is special; he's had more operations than most – I worried about him when I was little, but not any more.

I don't think much about my first family. Not at all actually. I've got too much to think about with this family! I've got a book with it all in but I'm not interested. I've got parents and a family and a brother. It's been great. Well, at least sometimes (laughter – Claude has a great sense of humour and laughs a lot). If there was someone like me, they should be adopted like me.

I work for an agency – street cleaning and on the dust carts. I'd like to own my business one day. A car valet business. I've done it before, it's very easy, it's good money. I wouldn't quit work; I'd get someone else to run the business for me. That's how I'd do it. At least if your business goes bust you're not unemployed then and you haven't lost everything. And I'd go to college to stop Mummy moaning at me about reading and writing.

I'm just waiting to win something so that I can disappear and then Mummy's shopping bill will be cut in half (more laughter). I do the lottery on Saturdays and mid-week. I'm a Manchester United supporter and I'd like the proper new strip for my birthday, not the one you can get in the market. There's a shop near where Robert lives.

(At this point there is a lot of noise from two large dogs who have been shut into one of the bedrooms.)

Why did you shut the dogs out? You may as well get the dogs – they're family.

Chris

I'm Chris. I was born and bred in West London where we still live. I lost my Dad when I was three, so my Mum and I were always very close. But she had to work and I was mainly brought up by my grandmother until I was six – I had a very good relationship with her as well. I went to boarding school when I was seven and stayed until I was 16. My father was a Mason and they make provision for the children's education. When he died, it obviously seemed the best thing to do – the boarding school was a good one and it was free. I did get used to it in the end but I swore that I would never send a child of mine to a boarding school.

My Mum got married again when I was 13. My stepfather was 20 years older than her and, to be honest, more Victorian, but I got on reasonably well with him. And it was nice because I could go home for the holidays, whereas when Mum was working, I had to stay with her friends.

I did an NNEB (Nursery Nursing Examination Board) course when I left school and I've been a nursery nurse ever since, although I didn't work when the children were little. Now I work in the nursery department of our local school; I've always been able to fit in with school holidays.

Tony

My name is Tony. I am now 50 years old. I'm originally from the North of England. I came to London when I was about 18, searching for that elusive street paved with gold – I'm still looking for it, aren't I? I got married very young and had two children but sadly it didn't work out. Chris and I met 27 years ago. Where did we meet? Oh yes, it was at a party – I went there with another girl, but Chris and I started going out together and eventually we got married. We had our silver wedding anniversary last year.

I was brought up in Children's Homes from the age of three and I lost an eye in an accident. I know what some of these children in care go through, in terms of not having parents. My own parents split up and I was left behind, as it were.

My hobbies are archery, although I don't have much time for it now, and making videos since Chris gave me a nice, new camcorder for my birthday – we've got some wonderful holiday shots. We go camping in France, Italy and Spain with the family. Chris and I have only been away once on our own in 20 years.

I'm an assistant office manager for a large complex which houses nearly 100 companies; I also run a small company making patchwork templates.

*   *   *

Robert has his own place now in a nearby suburb of London. He was not present when Chris and Tony and Claude told their story; he adds his own part later.

Chris and Tony speak with one voice about most things. Their comments intermingle to form one narrative.

*   *   *

Why we adopted
Chris and Tony

After we'd been married for a time, we were trying for children but didn't have any. We both had tests and it was found that Chris couldn't bear children.

I have a chromosome disorder which means I can't have children and

I'm small. I never had much advice. It was there and that was it. I don't ever remember anyone saying they could or couldn't do anything about this, or, 'What do you feel about this?' or 'I'm sorry about this'. When we had the fertility tests I was livid. I walked into the waiting room and the nurse said: 'Oh hello, are you the one with the chromosomes?' That was very hurtful; to be made to feel a freak. If I could go back in time now, I'd know what to say and to ask for more information and an explanation. But having said that – you can't go back – and I'm quite happy with what I've got.

We always wanted children and talked about adoption. We applied to the local authority but were turned down because of our health and history. That was very upsetting. Then we heard about PFC from a young temp who was working in our office. She passed the agency on her way into work. We rang up and were told straight away that all the children had a disability. To be perfectly honest, we'd never thought about adopting children with disabilities at that stage. But as soon as we did think about it, it seemed like an extremely good idea. Why ever not? They needed families as much as other children, if not more, and we felt we had things from our own backgrounds to offer children with disabilities. I remember we crept up to the door at PFC expecting to meet a brick wall like at the local authority; instead we were welcomed in. We were made to work hard to prepare ourselves for adoption but we never looked back.

We came with an open mind to hear about the children and we started to get the photosheets with the children who needed families. Claude leapt out at us from the page. We both felt the same. He was one year old and he had adrenal hyperplasia and was said to have cerebral palsy and severe learning difficulties. There was a question of his survival. We thought we'd see a weak baby lying on a rug not doing anything at all. We picked him up and he tried to stand on my lap! We got to know him while he was still in the Nursery where he'd always lived. His mother came from Mauritius. She was only 16; she wouldn't say anything about the father except that it was a holiday affair – there's always been a bit of a mystery about that. She wanted to have Claude adopted; she didn't want to meet us or to have any contact. We didn't know he had the same birthday as

Tony until the day we were introduced. What a birthday present!

We'd read about Robert even before we became interested in Claude, but we were told right away that he was already being discussed with someone else. He never went to live with them, but they visited him and then didn't come back. That made a deep impression on Robert. I think he thought we'd do the same thing.

Suddenly Robert was back on the photosheets and we rang up and said: 'We know you think it's going to be too soon . . .' But they didn't, and Robert came to us more or less a year after Claude. Because of the rejection he'd had, they wanted to get him settled in his new family as quickly as possible. It rather amazed us – the speed. Robert was testing us from the word go. The second time we visited he totally ignored us. He was scared of letting himself go. Only at the end of the visit he came up to us and said: 'Are you coming back to see me again?'

When we applied to have Corena ten years later, we thought they'd say we had enough. But again they didn't. We never considered fostering. We went in with the idea of adoption because we wanted it to be permanent and we wanted the children to feel they belonged. It's more difficult for adoptive parents nowadays. It's more slanted to the child – which it should be – and to the birth parents; which leaves adoptive parents in the middle. We always understood, with Robert, that there could be contact in the future, but he was our child and it wasn't until he himself started talking about it in his teens that it really meant anything.

What we expected

We knew Claude had to have all these medicines – in the beginning it was injections – and we had to learn how to do it. It was frightening in some ways. Tony was better at it than I was. If Claude hadn't had his medicine, he'd have grown too much and eventually he'd have died – it's as simple as that. He still couldn't live without it. It was a question of trial and error. We had to wait and see – nobody seemed to know. Things were put in a pessimistic way so that we should expect the worst. We were warned that Claude would never learn to walk or to speak. When you have a child for adoption, you have to take him to the Health Centre to register him with a doctor. The doctor in charge wanted to put Claude straight away on the disabled register and put his name down for a special school, at which point Chris drew herself up to her full four foot and ten inches and said: 'Certainly not.' He went to an ordinary nursery school, he learned to walk at a normal age and he reached most of his developmental milestones. The consultant at the hospital was very helpful. He looked after both boys until they became adults; he was a paediatric specialist in growth and hormonal disorders.

We were overwhelmed by Claude, we were; we bonded with him at once and he took to us in the same way. He was completely our child. Even the dog knew it. We had Sam then, a very jealous dog. If Chris sat on my lap he'd pull her sleeve until she got down. The first day we had Claude home, Sam tried to edge him off my lap – Claude turned round and grabbed him by the nose and there was never a problem after that. The only time Claude was upset in the early days was when we went on holiday the first time and he got out of his routine.

Claude had just started to walk – two little steps at a time – when we went to the adoption hearing. The judge seemed surprised and said: 'Is he going to make it?' And we both thought: 'Yes, of course he is!'

We expected it to be more difficult with Robert at the beginning because of his age. He was eight when he came to us. It was a bit harder because we didn't know if Robert was going to like us. I thought: 'What happens if he doesn't like me?' And when he first came he didn't know how to show affection. He would try to kiss us on the lips and we had to explain that's what mummies and daddies do. And he was very wary of men. All the staff at the Nursery were women. But I could relate to that. All the staff in the Children's Homes where I was brought up were women.

Robert was distrustful. He wasn't used to being with a family that wouldn't give up and he was very institutionalised. We were prepared for that. He thought everything should happen at a certain time. He'd say: 'When's break time?' Or he'd drop his clothes on the floor and say: 'Aren't mothers supposed to pick them up?' Boy, was he in for a shock in this house! Also he had no idea of what went on in families. He made friends with the boy next door and couldn't understand why we wouldn't let him go in and play with Adam at six o'clock on a Sunday morning. And he'd never seen people rowing and making up. He told us later that if we ever had an argument, he was scared that the family would break up. To this day he doesn't like anyone arguing or raising their voice. Getting to love Robert was gradual and Robert's personality, which is open and loyal, made it easy in the end.

Some of the things Robert came up with had nothing to do with adoption or disability. They were more like you would expect from any child. When he stole 50 pence from us it turned out he didn't like his teacher. He also smothered himself with white baby powder to make us think he was ill so he wouldn't have to go to school. Robert has been easy in a lot of ways. He made himself at home quite quickly. He's given us very few non-medical problems. He's able to talk – and boy does he talk – he's really good at expressing his feelings. He always did well at his special school; he came top of his class. Because of his size people tend to mother him, which he liked when he was young but finds irritating now.

We didn't know exactly what to expect of Robert's disability because the syndrome varies. It was called male Turner Syndrome at the time but Noonan Syndrome is the proper name. We did know Robert had a heart problem and learning difficulties and restricted growth. We knew he would have to have plastic surgery for his eyelids which interfered with his sight.

We were prepared for jealousy between the two boys and we got it. Claude threw his cars at Robert and we had to take away the metal ones. Robert went for Claude with a stick. We expected a lot of both of them. It's one thing to explain that Mummy is having a baby, it's another to bring in an older child who needs a lot of attention because of his disabilities and what's gone on before in his life. A two-year-old can't understand that; Robert, on the other hand, had to have a baby around from the start.

Now they're brothers. Claude finds it easier to talk to Robert than to anyone else. They'll go out together for a burger or to the Manchester United shop. People are rather astounded when they see the two of them and are told they're brothers and Claude is the younger. Robert looks fair in spite of being half Italian, and so young on account of his size, and Claude is a very dark and tall young man.

When we adopted our children, we expected to conduct our lives normally like everyone else, and we still do. It's other people who see us as mad or marvellous – that's quite flattering sometimes but it can be embarrassing. We knew there'd be hospital visits and things like that which you wouldn't get in an ordinary family, but as a family we work with all the usual family ups and downs.

What we did not expect
In spite of the warnings we felt Claude was an ordinary child except for his medical condition. But then we hit problems when he went into the reception class at school. There were behaviour problems, he didn't seem to be learning and his language was limited. He had low self-esteem – his disability makes him hairy all over and his teeth were orange from the medication. Then he developed a skin complaint – he'd come up in great big blisters and when they burst they went into a scab and scars. He used to get teased a lot about it. The school was unsympathetic, they just would not look at what was behind his behaviour problems. The doctor didn't help either – he asked if we were leaving Claude near anything too hot! We thought we were going to be done for child abuse when they didn't believe our description of the blisters. It was seven years later that they discovered he had Gunters. It's so rare that the specialist was very excited to find it. But nobody listened to us for all those years and we never got an apology. No-one ever said: 'You were quite right.' After that they used Claude when the medical students took their exams. They used to give him a big model car for doing it.

We've always felt that learning wise there is something that's never been diagnosed. Claude doesn't have general learning difficulties but he has blocks. So much of it is psychological. He transferred to a special school when he was eight. He was happier there. Then we moved to another town where he was also happy in a special school. When we moved back to our old area we had to push very hard, including writing to our MP, to get Claude back to the same school. But the Headteacher had changed and Claude never really settled down again. When we went up for his review the psychologist told us that Claude was sitting in the classroom with a coat over his head. Apparently there'd been a lot of teasing and name calling like: 'hairy'. We were really worried at that stage because he started doing it at home and when we took him out. He'd sit on the bus with a coat over his head. We didn't know what was what. I used to have nightmares about not being able to put my finger on what was wrong. There were all these complaints from school and it affected our relationship with Claude at home. There was the constant question: 'Am I a bad mother?' We got fed up with it and we all went for counselling at the Child Guidance Clinic. We had a couple of sessions – they said there was nothing the family could do – he simply had to change schools. He did. He went to a school for mainly physically disabled children and it did him a lot of good. He got over his psychological problems, especially when he could start to shave. For his last year, from 15–16, he was integrated into a mainstream school with a one-to-one helper. But he wanted to leave. He'd had enough. School was never his thing.

Then we didn't expect the change in adoption: how people think it's wrong for white parents to bring up children from ethnic minorities. We do think it's totally right for children to be placed with their own ethnic group whenever possible, but not if they have to wait needlessly for a family. With Claude, we've been lucky, we live in a mixed area. Even so, there have been times when it's been difficult for him. When he had the skin complaint, he said: 'It wouldn't happen if I was white.' We kept explaining to him: 'It makes no difference if you're white, brown or sky blue pink.' One Mother's Day I saw a piece in *Nursery World* and I sat down there and then and wept. A social worker had written an article saying that white people adopted black children because they wanted to have power over them. I don't think I've ever been crosser or more upset than I was at that moment. We talk to Claude about Mauritius and show him pictures. We'd love to go there if we could afford it. I think Claude sees himself exactly as he is: he is Claude and he is brown. That's who he is.

With Robert being older, most of what they said about him was correct. It was medical things that were unexpected. We've spent more time in hospital with Robert than with our other two put together. And quite understandably he was difficult when hospital was coming up – nothing aggressive – just difficult: he wanted a boiled egg and when it was put in front of him he wanted it scrambled.

*   *   *

Chris and Tony were not prepared for the complications of medical authorisation when they took Robert. He had to have surgery on both eyes before he was legally adopted. So the birth parents, who had not seen him since he was a baby, were asked for their consent. The eyes were done one at a time with a month in between. At the last moment, when Robert was already on his way to the operating theatre for the second time, it was discovered that the consent did not cover two operations. Chris and Tony could do nothing; they had to take Robert home and deal with his bewilderment.

*   *   *

Chris and Tony
Later, when he went in for another operation, we were told his heart was worse than expected and that he had to have heart surgery. That was the worst time we've had. Robert used to say to us: 'Will you promise I won't have another op?' And we used to have to answer: 'We can't promise that. No-one knows about the future.'

*   *   *

Chris and Tony were surprised to find a lack of sensitivity about Robert's disability.

*   *   *

A doctor said to us – we were being assessed for attendance allowance for Robert – 'Why did you adopt this rather invalid child if you can't afford to keep him?' Robert was sitting in the room at the time which made it worse. He said to the doctor: 'Because nobody else wanted me.' At that point we told the doctor to get out of our house. We didn't get the attendance allowance and we never applied for it again.

We had to show people that Robert was not just a little fellow with Noonan Syndrome. Robert isn't an interesting case; he's Robert. They used to strip him and take photographs every time we took him to the hospital for a check-up. In the end we said: 'No, we don't want any more; he doesn't want any more.' We know they need to do research to find out how to help other children, but at the same time they should treat people as people and not as cases. They never asked about the photographs, they just did it. We said: 'Ask him, does he want it done?' Robert said he didn't. Fine, that was it, no more. These children are children first, the disability comes after.

How we adjusted

In a lot of ways adopting disabled children cemented our marriage. We've had to get through such a lot – it either brings you closer together or it pushes you apart. It does put so much pressure on you thinking about the needs of the children that it wouldn't surprise me if Tony had felt left out at times. (Tony said he had never felt left out.)

We lost one wage and we had to make do without adoption allowances for the boys. There weren't any at the time. It was a hell of a shock not to be able to spend money like we were used to. A lot of the adjustments were the usual ones when you first have children. Finding a routine and meeting new friends away from work. I missed work at first.

We also had to become medically skilled. We had to give injections and be responsible for a baby's life. The first time we left Chris's mother to baby-sit she was very nervous – the only time I ever knew her to be nervous of anything. We went out to dinner in a restaurant and we rang her to see if everything was alright. She said Claude was coughing and asked us to come home immediately. Our meal was in front of us and the wine had just arrived! We had to get up and leave.

It was hard for my mother to accept the idea of adopting disabled children, but once she got over the initial shock she grew very fond of them and used to call Claude and Robert 'my boys'. She was anxious for us the first time and the second, but by the time we took Corena she'd given up on us. She'd always said that she didn't want her grandchildren to call her "nanna" – she wanted to be "gran" or "grandma" – but they all called her "nanna" and she liked it.

The biggest adjustment we had to make was when Robert wanted to trace his birth family when he was 17. We'd always promised we would help him if he wanted to find them and round about that time the law changed to make it easier. We were worried in case he got hurt again by being rejected. As it turned out we didn't have to do anything because PFC spoke to Robert about it and it went on from there. Only Robert didn't wait for PFC to prepare the way for him – he got his father's phone number and jumped the gun.

His birth parents were divorced, a younger sister of the marriage was living with his father. Both his birth parents had remarried. They didn't even know that Robert had survived. They'd been afraid to ask. They were nervous about seeing him. They did all meet and Robert got very intense and there was such a lot of talk about it that we got very emotional ourselves. We felt we'd been through so much with him and at the end where did that leave us? His father is well off, he owns a restaurant, and can offer him things we can't. But I have to say that Robert gave us all the reassurance we needed. He said: 'You're still my Mum and Dad but I had to find out who I looked like and where I came from and why I was put in a Home.' And Robert arranged for us all to get together at the restaurant for our wedding anniversary. We're OK now. We've come through it. Both sides have coped with Robert finding his birth family. I think we've all benefited from it. Robert might never have settled down completely without it. There's still a certain amount of: 'Why me? If I weren't like I am none of this would have happened to me,' but he's come to terms with it more. Robert sees his father only occasionally now and his mother even less. He calls them by their first names. He is more in touch with his sister – she came to our silver wedding party last year. She says she is quite comfortable with us and we all like her.

We thought when Robert made his contact that it would be a good opportunity to open up the subject with Claude again. But he doesn't want to know. His reaction always is: 'I've got one set of parents, I don't want any more.' He does find it difficult to express his feelings.

Which opportunities and choices
Robert had to leave school when he was 16; they didn't keep them longer than that. The Careers Officer was most unhelpful. What she had to say could have been written down on a post-card. Whatever Robert asked, the answer was: 'You're too small'.

Robert went to college on a catering course but he couldn't keep up with the theory. Then they put him on a Youth Training Scheme (YTS) and he was placed in a Day Nursery. They only took him because one of the staff was away and then they dismissed him for gross misconduct. Robert had been put to sweeping out the yard and was wearing his earphones. It was against the rules and he'd been warned once. The next day the girl he was replacing came back from holiday. After that he worked in restaurants. His health problems affect his work. He now has sclerosis of the spine which interferes with his breathing. He passed out one day at work. They have had to put a metal rod in to support the spine. Also his toes still need straightening. All the hospitalisations make it hard to hold on to a job.

Claude attended a special college course for independence and vocational training after he left school. He found it too difficult. YTS then placed him in a garage, doing car valeting. We were getting concerned because he didn't have any proper pay slips. We told him to ask and the following week they told him not to come back. He was owed holiday money and he wasn't given a P45. We never managed to get it sorted out for him. When we complained at the Job Centre they weren't at all interested. We don't think much of YTS. Not as far as young people with disabilities are concerned; they just seem to use them.

For the last two years Claude has been working for a couple of agencies – doing road sweeping work and that sort of thing. Unskilled work they call it. He gets himself up at 4.30 in the morning and he's pleased with his wage, but it's below the minimum. He is independent – only we have to mop up the bathroom every single morning after he's gone and he couldn't be quiet if he tried.

We can advocate for the boys to a certain extent but we're not career experts. There are probably things they could do and would be suitable for that we don't know about. They have both been through so much that there should be an opening for them to help others. Claude blossomed when he went, as part of his college course, to a boarding school for physically disabled children. They need someone to really advise them. When Robert asks me about what he could do, I don't know what to say beyond: 'You're a good listener.' He tried for a counselling course but he didn't get on. So far no-one has been able to suggest anything about work or leading them towards further education. Claude ought to improve his basic reading and writing skills but he needs the motivation to do it. It's a worry; we can see him drifting. Robert wanted to be a chef – I don't think he knows what he wants to do now.

When the family changed

When I was made redundant everything changed. Our house was nearly repossessed. We learnt a lot from it and we'd handle it better now, but we were devastated at the time. That was the worst period we've ever been through. We two could have managed in a bed-sit, but for our children routine was so important. We had to move out of London and we felt guilty for disrupting them, although they didn't really seem to suffer. There was a lot of pressure on us but we supported each other. We were aware that if we started getting at each other it would be worse for the boys. We only had the two of them then. I got another job after six months.

When my gran died Claude was upset. She was very ill in hospital and he broke down when he saw her. Robert didn't know her so well. But when my mother was dying they both understood. It was very stressful for all of us when we found out she was ill. We visited her often but she didn't want to come and live with us – we were always asking her. Claude and Robert were very close to her. Robert in particular used to talk to her a lot. The whole family grieved when she died and they were part of that.

We thought we'd never survive the course when Corena joined the family. She was 11, Claude was 12 and Robert was 18. Claude and Corena were at each other's throats from morning till night. It started at breakfast and it never stopped – and I do mean never. We had to make rules: the dining table and the living room were fight-free zones. It was about everything and anything. They only had to look at each other. He'd wind her up and she was easily wound up. Robert shut himself away in his room for most of the time. Slowly, after the first summer holidays, it simmered down. Now the two of them live in a state of mutual tolerance for most of the time. They close ranks if there is an outside threat. When the boy next door calls Corena names, Claude says: 'Don't you say that about my sister.' He wouldn't let her be hurt.

It was a big change when Robert decided to leave home. Not just leave home but the distance as well – a couple of hundred miles. He got friendly with an older woman he worked with and when she went back to Sheffield to live, he decided to leave home and move to Sheffield as well. He was only 18. We pointed out that Sheffield had the highest rate of unemployment in the country, but Robert, because of his size, has to prove himself. He wanted to spread his wings and to show he was independent. We worried about how he would cope.

He was vulnerable in a strange city. He stayed with his friend and her husband for a couple of weeks and then he went to the YMCA. When he got a job in a Caribbean restaurant he rented a private flat. We found the separation very hard. It would have been easier if he'd said: 'I'll find a flat around here.' We weren't near enough to help him if he needed it. Robert moved around a bit before he settled much closer to home – he lives on his own now, the same side of London as us. He comes home when he feels like it, which is a lot of weekends. He's not working at the moment because he's waiting for another operation on his feet. He lives on invalidity and housing benefits. He manages his own finances with a little booster from home. He gets nothing from social services and wouldn't want to. He didn't like having to see a social worker to sort out his allowances.

Claude doesn't want to leave home; he lacks the confidence. He knows he'd have to spend a lot more money in terms of rent and food. We'll have to eject him if we ever want him to go. It would be very good for him to stand on his own two feet but we would never make any of them leave home. Claude is maturing more slowly than other youngsters of his age, but his position in the family is changing. He can be left to look after Corena or to stay in the house; he is working and he is responsible for his own medication. We were absolutely determined he'd be independent in that way.

Where we are going
Robert sometimes says to us when he has to have yet another op: 'What will happen next?' And we have to say to him: 'You're the same as everyone else, no-one knows what will happen in the future.'

We do worry about what will happen after we are gone. Neither of us have any family for the boys to fall back on completely, though Tony's family in the north of England would help them sort themselves out. The boys would probably both manage without us – possibly they would combine forces but they couldn't cope with Corena. We're still trying to find the best way to tie everything up for them in case they get left alone.

Both Claude and Robert will have to overcome more problems in the future. Robert finds it difficult to come to terms with the effect his disability has on his relationship with women. Claude isn't very interested in girls yet but he could get hurt.

Seeing them grow up and become independent, reasonable young people has been a great reward for us. We're proud when we compare them to so called normal people growing up in normal families. It's not the big things that matter most, it's the way they've both overcome so many little things – we say little, but they're big things to them. The way Claude has triumphed over his physical ill health and prognosis; he's going to be a really nice person in his own right. The way Robert bounces back after every one of his operations . . . as long as he can keep on doing it he'll be fine.

Robert

I'm Robert. I'm 26 years old and I'm independent. Whatever my Mum and Dad have said, that's what they feel and that's alright. I like the story they have told – some of it is funny. There are some personal things I don't want to discuss. I don't want to talk about anything to do with my birth parents because that's my personal business. I did go and talk to somebody at PFC about finding them. They wanted me to "practice" speaking to my birth parents. They wanted me to talk down an empty telephone! I wasn't having that. I had to do it when I was ready. I know a lot of people could have got into trouble because I wasn't 18, but I had to do it. It was my private decision.

A while ago I met up with Barbara who was the Matron at the Nursery I lived in. We've always had her number and I rang her up out of the blue. It was nice, it was a one off but I may see her once in a while. She said: 'You've changed,' and she said I was always her favourite. When I was there, I looked on Barbara as a Mum.

I do think PFC do a lot of good things, but I do think they put pressure on people who have been adopted. I stopped going to PFC picnics because it reminded me all the time about being adopted. It's not that I don't like being adopted, but people who have been adopted are like any ordinary person, and when they're 18 they will want to leave home. But because they're adopted, it's a big issue. Then there's pressure on families too, about race and things like that. My Mum did everything to get Claude interested in race; he wasn't interested and she worried about what people would say. I say to her: 'It doesn't matter what other people say.' I know when I left home right after Corena came, people said: 'What's happening? They've taken another disabled child and Robert has gone.' But I always meant to leave home and I did. I've always said to Mum: 'If I fall ill or have an accident or end up in a wheelchair, I don't want to lose my independence.'

I'm much closer to Claude since I've left home. When we were growing up it was hard – it was him giving out all the love and me pushing him away. Now we're friends, we're brothers – we're closer from my side. I don't feel as close to Corena but she is my sister. I can look after her. I was picking her up from her club and we went for a bus to go home and there was this woman staring at Corena like she was an object. And Corena just shouted out: 'Why is that woman looking at me?' I said: 'Because she has nothing better to do.' If any time in the future it's just me and Claude and Corena, whatever decisions are made for Corena, I want Claude and me to have the right to bring her home and to take her out and not be questioned. At the end of the day, we are a family and being adopted doesn't make any difference.

I'm not macho because I was brought up by females when I was little and I like female company now. I go out with my mates but their girl friends find it easier to talk to me. It was difficult for me and Dad at first – he wasn't sure I liked him because he was a man. But Dad was brought up in a Home too, and I could talk to him about that. He was strict and he knew about things. When I was about 13 he said to me: 'You thinking of bunking off school or anything? Because if you are, you've got me to reckon with as well as the teachers.' I didn't like school but I never bunked off. I don't thank the school for doing sums and reading – I thank my Dad for that. He sat me down when I was eight and he made me do it.

My way of coping with Noonan Syndrome is to forget I've got it and get on with it. I think Noonan Syndrome is a pain in the arse. If people stare I joke about it. But everyone has to do their own thing – it's no good them reading this and thinking that's right for them. I think books sometimes put things in your head that confuse you. I'm not saying that books can't help; they can help and they can't. When people say to me: 'You've been through a lot,' I say: 'No, there's people worse off.' I've been brought up to think that. It's not that my parents don't think I've been through a lot, but it was to boost my confidence. When I was 19, I'd had enough of operations and being poked about. Now I'm back with the hospital having my feet straightened. Next I want to put on some weight. It's a bit difficult to fit clothes. I buy my clothes at Gap for Kids and it can be embarrassing go into the changing room with ten-year-olds.

I blame the hospital I was born in for being put in a Home. They said I might not live. Then when I was two, it was like, 'Oh well, perhaps he'll live until puberty.' Then they found out more about Noonan Syndrome and changed it to: 'Robert will need hospital treatment through his growing up,' which was true. They shouldn't say all those things in front of children, because children do know more than adults think they do. Even very little children.

I'm finally getting Disability Living Allowance, which I've been trying to get since I was 18. At the moment I can't work, and when I do work, I get setbacks when I have to go to hospital. They need to make Noonan Syndrome more well known to the Benefits Section.

Now I'm 26 and my Dad says: 'I bet you wish you'd listened to me when you were younger,' but I say: 'No, everyone wants to do things on their own when they're young.' How else do you learn but by your mistakes? I sometimes think I've grown up too fast from the time I was adopted. I didn't like toys and games and I was always on to the next year, looking ahead to growing up and what I was going to do and where I was going to be, but I couldn't have done that without parents.

Chris and Tony have the final say

We think we know what our sons are capable of, but no-one really knows what they are capable of until they are faced with a situation. It was like that for us when we adopted them and it will be like that for them in the future. We'd do it all over again and we hope they would.

3 Place the wheelchair first
Mary, Patrick and Margaret

The story of Mary and Patrick has already been written in *Find Me a Family* (see Further Reading). If Patrick had lived he would now be 26 years old. Mary has asked to have an abbreviated version of that story told here, in the same words, but this time using their own names.

When Mary was ten she was taken into care and placed in an orphanage in Ireland. She stayed there until she was 18. On Sundays the doors were opened to couples in search of a child. Mary watched as the liveliest, most perfect babies were picked up and cooed over, while the dull, disabled and disfigured ones were left behind, together with most of the older children, who were in any case only considered as a source of cheap labour for large families. Mary grew up silent and unresponsive; she related only to the babies and children who were constantly being left behind. Some of the nuns at the orphanage encouraged Mary to train as a nurse for what were then described as "mentally handicapped" people.

Mary qualified in England and worked in hospitals and children's homes. When she heard of PFC she decided that it would be better to adopt one or two children than to give too little to so many. She came to the agency and said: 'I want to adopt the most handicapped child you have.'

Patrick was six years old and suffered from a rare and degenerative fatal disease. Tuberous sclerosis affected his brain and all his organs. He was severely retarded, epileptic, partially sighted, hardly able to walk and never likely to speak. He lived in a world of his own making bizarre sounds and movements and could be violent and uncontrollable. Mary saw Patrick's poster and said he was the child for her.

Doctors gave the opinion that Patrick needed nursing, not parenting. The residential workers at the Children's Home where Patrick lived were suspicious of a single woman who was proposing to share her life with a child they could not contain; even the social workers who had referred him had not really expected that a family would be found for Patrick and now mistrusted the choice.

Mary and Patrick proved everyone wrong. They learned to love life together. Patrick had hardly ever been out of the Children's Home and he was fascinated by the noises of the street, the sounds of rustling leaves and running water and the gurgling of drains. He became obsessed with drains and during her visits to the Children's Home, while Mary was getting to know Patrick, she spent many hours with him sitting by the side of the road listening to drains. She meant to start off from exactly where he was. During the preparation time she began to take Patrick on buses and trains as they would not have a car; she introduced him to her friends and their homes for they would not live in seclusion. Mary also needed to find somewhere to live and to establish her rights to benefits, allowances and services as the single mother-to-be of a disabled child. She needed to mobilise her support network because she knew from the beginning that she would have to have regular help and relief. She needed to line up a sympathetic GP who would know something about Patrick's disease, a co-operative Health Centre which would provide a nappy service and an inventive occupational therapist who would fix aids and adaptations to give Patrick freedom and keep him safe. Mary did it all, but not without causing some consternation and giving some offence.

When Mary was allocated a suitable flat, she achieved something remarkable. The sitting room was the centre. One half of it was a cosy place with armchairs and a sofa and low tables and soft carpet, pictures and books, flowers and music. The other half of the room was a playground: tough lino on the floor, a sand tray in one corner and a paddling pool in the other; mobiles hanging down from the ceiling, bright posters on the walls and a rotating disco light which threw brilliance and shade and colour at the press of a button. A large box contained a carefully chosen assortment of toys: red plastic hammers that rang bells, large cuddly toys and things that rattled and squeaked and shimmered and shone. The grown up part of the room was curiously explored by Patrick but not disrupted. He handed Mary records and cassettes to make music, and music became the greatest pleasure in Patrick's life. On his eighth birthday Mary bought him a small electric organ so that he could make his own music.

No door was closed to Patrick. Whereas in the Children's Home he had been kept in a room with mattresses lining the walls and barred windows, Mary had rails fixed along the passages and stairs and every room was made safe for him: a guard around the cooker, concealed central heating, cupboards within his reach containing all the things he liked best to eat, and a low bed he could safely fall out of but never did. There were bath aids, a raised toilet seat, an electric toothbrush, bubbles in the water and bubbles to blow. After a year, Patrick was out of nappies, climbing into the bath on his own and asking to brush his teeth.

The garden was Patrick's special place. There was a fence with a child-proof gate. He could go in and out of the garden as he chose and Mary could see him wherever he was. He liked to touch the grass and to hear the cars go by. Mary bought him a swing and he delighted in going higher and higher. Mary bought him a bicycle with stabilisers and a crash helmet and walked behind him up and down the path. Patrick, who could hardly walk when he came to her, could run and ride a bike and swing high.

Mary used her intelligence to tune in to Patrick's world. They went to concerts and Patrick sat quite still and listened. They went to the country and Mary shared Patrick's pleasure in the smells and sounds and the red flowers he could see best. Sometimes they just went and stood on Westminster Bridge for an hour or so. One Easter they went to Lourdes and Patrick was equally excited by the aeroplane and the myriads of candles in the holy grotto. They spent one holiday on a barge on the canals.

Patrick went to a special school but Mary could not agree with the teachers that education was of great importance to him. So she kept him at home whenever he was tired or there was something to do together.

Occasionally Mary herself was exhausted and had to rely on her friends to come in and take over. One winter Mary became seriously ill and Patrick had to go and stay with her friends. In spite of all the progress, Patrick remained a sick child and sometimes he was very sick. The frequency and violence of his fits increased and there were more and more consultations with doctors and periods in hospital. When Patrick was nearly ten, Mary knew he would die soon although doctors, amazed by his progress, had diagnosed that he could live until he was fifteen. Patrick had still more fits and he developed a pallor so different from the healthy glow he had acquired on Mary's diet of protein and fruit. He no longer ate the treats he found in the cupboards and he could not manage any steps. The teachers agreed that Patrick should only come to school when he was well enough. Mary got him a wheelchair and they moved to an even more suitable flat. The swing was in the new garden but hardly used now. Patrick became incontinent again; he could no longer do any of the things he had learned to do. Mary railed against his illness. She could not tolerate it, she became frantic in her efforts to save him, she would have shaken him into life if she could.

Mary brought his bed into the sitting room so that Patrick could rest at the centre of things and never feel on the outside. He died at home in his bed during a seizure. Mary was holding him because he was always scared by his fits and she held him whenever she was near enough. And she tried to resuscitate him.

Mary would often say that Patrick was "totally daft" and that she loved him for it not in spite of it. She described how he taught her to listen to what he could not say and how she loved that rich silence.

With hindsight
Sixteen years later, Mary was able to reflect on her life with Patrick.

*　　　*　　　*

Mary
What I have taken away from that situation remains in my heart. Patrick is very much alive for us. Anything I could say now, to add to the story, would seem pointless. It was his simplicity that drew us together. Like at Christmas, when everyone else was going mad and stuffing themselves, he'd just stand under a street light and love it. That made him very special. Of all my children he was the one that was most like me. We were two misfits that fitted together.

*　　　*　　　*

More children
Even if prospective carers are already proven and experienced parents,

it cannot work out every time with every child. Mary wanted to enlarge her family while Patrick was still alive.

*   *   *

Mary

First of all I took a 14-year-old boy I already knew from one of the Children's Homes I'd worked in. I thought it would be right for us all. But I found out I couldn't deal with the passivity of someone with Down's Syndrome on a permanent basis. I might have pushed myself to go on, but there was another family for him which was more of a community and which suited him better than the one-to-one relationship he was getting from me. So I let him go after a few months and he made the move and flourished. He's still there and he's nearly thirty.

Much later, when I already had Margaret, another girl of ten called Tamsin who had been emotionally and mentally disabled by traumatic events in her life, went straight to my heart. But her damage triggered off a reaction to damage in my own childhood and put me back in therapy which caused me to be emotionally dysfunctional for a period in my life. During this time I wasn't able to use the support of social workers and I wasn't totally honest with them. I fouled up and seemed to be playing off one lot of helpers against the other. I look back on it with sadness and regret because I loved this child and we had bonded together. I fouled up on the workers I trusted but I fouled up most on that child. After one year with me and before she was adopted, she was removed. I didn't abuse *her*, but I abused the system that had abused me as a child; she suffered because I was caught up in living the nightmare of the past and couldn't live in the present. She is the loss of my life.

*   *   *

Mary first heard of Margaret through PFC when Patrick was already very ill. A year after he died Margaret was still in the Children's Home because families who came forward retreated again when they understood exactly how disabled she was and how dependent she would always be. Mary felt ready to take on the challenge. She told

Margaret that she chose the one who couldn't walk.

*   *   *

Mary

I took Margaret as a 14-year-old tetraplegic child in a wheelchair with cerebral palsy and learning difficulties. That's what you could see. But what you see isn't what you get. No-one knew the extent of her deep-seated psychological problems. She'd suffered the sudden and unexplained death of her mother when she was ten and her stepfather had sexually abused her. She never told anyone until she told me. Given Margaret's limited understanding it was impossible, in spite of therapy, to help her to feel more at peace and to lead a happier existence. On meeting Margaret, you can get the impression of someone much brighter than she is because she is relatively articulate. She can chatter. But when you probe there's no depth behind her words. She repeats what she has heard.

We had to move house again to accommodate Margaret's range of wheelchairs. One for indoors, one to go out, one to go to school, one she could work herself, one that had to be pushed and one that could be folded. Really, when you place a child who needs to use a wheelchair, you should place the wheelchair first and not place the child until the adopters have settled with the chair. Getting the wheelchair right has been the biggest problem – we haven't got it right yet. They make standard wheelchairs for people who aren't standard. I go on fighting the same battle. And there's so much that can go wrong with the powered wheelchairs – I'm still struggling after 15 years.

In order for me to cope with Margaret I've always needed ramped access, bath aids, an overhead hoist, toilet rails, a commode chair, incontinence aids, cot sides, tail lift transport and mobility accommodation – a bungalow or ground floor flat with wide doors. Nobody has ever queried or refused anything we've needed – they may not have understood but they meant well.

Hard times

As Margaret got older her psychosis became more evident and irreparable. This showed itself in a variety of disturbing, destructive and unacceptable social behaviours. She smeared her bed and walls and carpet when she soiled herself and she regurgitated her food at will. She threw herself from her bed, her wheelchair and the toilet; she picked at clothes to make holes in them; she mutilated herself. She still does most of these things. I bought a new carpet for her room last week, which she chose, and she smeared it with faeces the next day. I took her out to the pub for lunch on her 29th birthday and she waited till we got home and then brought it all back again.

I took Margaret to love her but how could I love someone who rejected all efforts on my part in such an unrelenting way? I realised why she was doing it and understood what was behind it – the hurt and rejection she'd felt – but it didn't make it any easier. I couldn't love her then and I don't now. But the quality and amount of *care* Margaret has always received from me, and will go on receiving, is the very best she could get anywhere. Knowing her as I do, I really believe that. She's 29, she's in perfect health and she's as content as she's ever likely to be.

Even worse than the things Margaret does are the dreadful things she says. When she went to school she'd tell the bus driver that I wouldn't give her breakfast. When she got to school she'd tell the teacher that the bus driver had dropped her and when she got home she'd tell me that her teacher had smacked her – all in one day. She's never stopped doing that and it spoils everything for her. She tells stories about any helpers or teachers she ever has: she says they hurt her, steal her money, don't feed her and ignore her. She's told people that I drink heavily, that I starve her, beat her and lock her up. No-one from social services will come and look after her now because she accuses them all of ill treating her. She's got turned out of every Day Centre I've found for her because she tells lies about all the care assistants. I've used respite care for Margaret when it's been offered in the past, but it always turned out badly after a few times and they wouldn't have her back. It starts with Margaret telling tales and even if I've warned them they get anxious and investigate and then, when they find out they've been had, they won't have her back because she makes real, real trouble. You name it, she's said it.

Margaret first went to a school for the physically disabled because there was no choice for her. I was very pleased with this school because the Headteacher had a positive attitude to disability and adoption. She put up with a lot from Margaret but in the end it was impossible to leave her there because she caused so much havoc with her story telling. They transferred her to a specialist boarding school for children with cerebral palsy. She went to this school for nearly three years from age 16 to 19. It was awful. I felt undermined and redundant as a parent; they were against adoption anyway. They also believed all Margaret's stories and discouraged her from keeping in touch with home. The school social worker recommended that Margaret should go straight from school to independent living and persuaded Margaret that she wanted to do that. So that is what happened. Margaret started to go to the independent living accommodation in our borough for weekends and holidays instead of coming home. All the residents had their own studio flats. There were staff to help care for them but the residents themselves had to make the arrangements for the care and support they thought they needed.

Managing independence

When Margaret moved in permanently to the Independent Living Unit it was a shock for her. I was told it was nothing to do with me so I couldn't help to prepare her. It was a totally unsuitable placement. She was left unsupervised and expected to organise her own care on a points and time system. She didn't have a clue. She had to ask to be taken to shops and to plan her own meals and manage her own money when she couldn't even add up. They put her into a special course for disabled people at the local college – I was never told why she left after two weeks. They encouraged her to drink alcohol as a sign of independence and she'd be allowed to stay out until midnight and to get drunk. She was given freedom of choice when she didn't know how to make a choice.

I discovered Margaret was pregnant in June 1988 when she'd been living "independently" for about a year. I noticed that some of the new clothes in her wardrobe were size 16. When I asked one of the workers about it, he said: 'Of course, Margaret is much happier now and putting on weight.' I felt very hurt by this comment. I asked what she was eating and they said: 'Oh she lives on junk food and she drinks and she smokes.'

I knew there was something wrong. When I took her to the toilet I felt how heavy she was. I called the local authority social worker out because I felt Margaret was definitely pregnant and I needed some back up. She came at once – she was a fantastic social worker. While all this was going on the residential staff were flying around in all directions and not really speaking to me because, of course, Margaret had told them that I was an awful parent and not fit to be a mother. We got an appointment with the GP immediately and he confirmed that Margaret was 24 weeks pregnant. I took one deep breath, Margaret was crying and we went back to the Independence Unit.

I saw the Head of the Home and told her Margaret was pregnant and she said: 'Impossible.' Being Irish I turned round and said to her: 'And it isn't going to be a virgin birth.' I was totally, totally dismayed. As far as I was concerned Margaret had been raped. All the staff were saying: 'What's going to happen? What's going to happen?' and then the Head of the Home said: 'She can't stay here if she's pregnant.' Bearing in mind she was six months pregnant, she'd not been seen at the hospital, she was smoking and drinking, she'd grown out of size eight clothes into size 16 and no-one had noticed or cared, all they were now saying was: 'She can't stay here.'

I reacted as any mother would although Margaret was an adult and had landed me in trouble so many times. I was working then; I had two nursing jobs. I dropped everything and rang them to give in my notice. I asked the Unit to keep Margaret for one more night so that I could go out and buy a bed for her and other things she'd need. Margaret had left home, I'd lost another child and I was building up my own life. I was living in a nice small flat with 20 steps up to the door, so it wasn't going to be easy. I told Margaret: 'You are coming home.' Not: 'Will you come home' or 'Are you coming home?' just 'I am taking you home.'

I was so angry, so very angry, I couldn't conceal what I felt. There was no explanation or apology from anyone. I asked our own GP to come and see her. She was stretched out on a bed in the sitting room so that the foetus could move. She'd been all squashed up in the wheelchair and in her bed. My main concern was to feed the foetus because it had obviously not been cared for. So it was fish and fresh vegetables and milk – trying to get it all into Margaret to build her up. All this was going on but nobody seemed to know who the man was, who the father was. In the end Margaret said it was a man with ginger hair who was working in the

Unit instead of going to prison. He abused her – I use the term lightly because it was more than abuse. Margaret didn't understand what had happened – couldn't have stopped it or run away or shouted. I've gone through many things in my life, but that has to be the worst.

If it had happened in my home, with someone I had brought in, I would have been considered irresponsible and not been given access to my own grandchild. As it happened in social services, no-one was blamed. It all had to do with freedom of choice, they said. But I said to them: 'If she had freedom of choice, then surely contraception should have been on offer.' But that would mean inserting the cap for her or making sure she took the tablets because she can't do that for herself. So where does that leave "freedom of choice"?

Having choice hasn't helped Margaret. When she has a period – ever since she started – she smears the blood everywhere. I've asked for something to stop her periods but she won't consent so they won't give her anything. After the birth I asked for her to be sterilised but they said I had no right and, again, Margaret didn't consent. She doesn't under- stand the questions but they accept her answers. Margaret used to talk about boys she fancied in a childish way but I think these feelings have been deadened by being pregnant and having a child.

I've let Margaret come in and out of living at home as she pleased. I was warned about teenagers coming in and out like it was a revolving door. But no-one warned me that with a young woman as disabled as Margaret, I'd have to let in a pram.

The third generation
Margaret stayed at home until six weeks before the baby was due. Then I asked for her to be admitted to hospital and I went in with her. I didn't have any midwifery experience and I was worried in case something went wrong. She was put on an open ward with the other mothers and she looked no more than a child herself. I slept in a cubicle near her. We had very little money because I'd given up my job and couldn't claim social security, and we only had a one bedroomed flat to go back to. Life looked somewhat grim. There didn't seem to be any financial help from anywhere but friends gave us the essential things for the baby. I looked after Margaret in the hospital. No-one else seemed to know what they

were doing with her. They had never met a tetraplegic with cerebral palsy who was pregnant. People were quite horrified by her. It was perhaps the only time in 15 years I've really felt like her mother.

Katie was born very quickly but the trauma of that birth will stay with me absolutely for ever. I realised Margaret was going into labour and put her into the S position on her side. She had to have an epidural and, because her spine is so twisted and battered, injecting into it proved to be an absolute nightmare. Trying to reassure Margaret and myself was very difficult. When Katie was born I said to the obstetrician: 'Shake her, rattle her and make sure she's all there.' Although she was a four pound baby she didn't need an incubator. I was pleased because she did need to bond immediately.

One has to respect Margaret's wish not even to hold the baby. She couldn't. She was a child herself emotionally and she didn't know what it was all about. Katie was given to me. I was treated like the parent and taught to look after her. I was in my mid-40s, I'd already been through a lot and I knew I had to get it right because I was responsible for this new life. Katie was never left on her own in a cot or a pram. She was always with me – tied to my back or my front while I did the chores and looked after Margaret.

We were offered a good flat with a garden and the three of us stayed together. For Katie's first two years there were several physical difficulties due to the neglect of the foetus in the early months of pregnancy. She overcame all of them. She has a hereditary weakness in both hands and feet – this has got much better through swimming and dancing and learning the keyboard and clarinet. She inherited cardiomyopathy from Margaret and is monitored at the Children's Hospital but she carries on like any healthy child. When Katie was four and a half I adopted her with Margaret's consent.

Multiple family relationships

Katie knows all about our family relationships. She understands them but she won't feel the full impact until she's older and until she realises what it means that her mother – and later her children's grandmother – is helpless, confined to a wheelchair and has severe learning difficulties. Katie loves Margaret; she's been brought up to love and respect her. We talk about Margaret as Katie's first Mum – she knows she grew in Margaret's tummy.

She's also very proud of being adopted. On Mother's Day we were in church for the Brownies' parade and the children had daffs to give to their mothers. Margaret wasn't there and Katie gave hers to me. Then the vicar asked if anyone wanted flowers to take home to their mother. Katie asked for another bunch and gave them to Margaret and said: 'Happy Mother's Day'.

Katie and Margaret play together. Katie has already overtaken Margaret but they still play together. They colour in and play with dolls. Margaret is usually the mother in their games and Katie is the baby, which is interesting. I'm the auntie who's visiting when I come in to give them a drink. That's the only time Margaret pays any attention to Katie – in a fantasy world. In the real world she shows no interest in Katie. She shuts off from her. But then I think: Why shouldn't she? Here's Katie on the one side, exceptionally beautiful and talented in so many ways. At nine years old, she's the best reader in the whole school. She's a champion swimmer, dancer and springboard diver. She's musical and leads a full life. On the other side, there's Margaret, her mother, who can hardly feed or wash herself, has to be taken to the toilet, turned at night and is totally dependent for all her needs. Each hour of the day must seem like a lifetime to Margaret, while there aren't enough hours in the day for Katie. Right in the middle of that situation is the heartbreak: for Margaret, for me and will it be for Katie in the future?

There aren't any words about what I feel for Katie. My emotions are stronger than words. I felt she was a gift. Someone I could protect from the moment she was born so that she would never be hurt or abused. I made up my mind that this child, who was the result of such terrible circumstances, would grow up to be well balanced and normal. She and I would rise above expectations.

When Margaret came to me I wanted to keep in touch with her birth family. We went to see her grandmother but Margaret didn't seem emotionally equipped to either want or understand the contact. Then when Margaret said that she had been sexually abused by her stepfather, I tried to find out the truth from her grandparents – but they clammed up and Margaret never saw them again.

We kept in touch by letter until they died. They knew they were great-grandparents and I took Katie to see them once. I also tried to make contact with Margaret's two brothers, but they were both a dead loss – so was Margaret's natural father – they didn't want to know. Our friends have become our family. We have wonderful friends. We moved to the Midlands in order to stay close to a couple who are Katie's godparents. I have developed heart disease and will soon need an operation. I know the risks and I have made arrangements in case anything happens to me. Katie would go to her godparents and Margaret would stay here in the bungalow with another disabled person and full-time carers from social services.

Past and present help

We had real support from the local authority social worker who was Patrick's worker and from PFC who placed all the disabled children. But it would not have been possible to do any of it without a close group of friends who understood disability. They knew me well and I trusted them absolutely.

We've always had a lot of professional people coming in and out. I object to it – particularly as I've got older – because it invades our privacy. On the other hand, I know I need all these people to keep going. Now we have an optician who comes to the home, a district nurse, an incontinence advisor (since Margaret has elected to be doubly incontinent), a dentist who does extractions on the premises, an occupational therapist, a GP whenever needed, a physiotherapist to check on Margaret's exercise programme, a local authority social worker, and a wheelchair maintenance man and advisor.

'And a sink unblocker,' adds Katie with a giggle.

*   *   *

Katie has come in from school and is having her tea and dividing her time between Margaret and Mary before she goes out again to Brownies. She is not at all thrown by the interview and nods in to listen from time to time.

Katie looks like a whole and healthy eight-year-old version of Margaret, except for an abundance of long, curly, bright auburn hair which is quite unlike Margaret's short, smartly styled blond hair.

*   *   *

Mary

There's nothing we need we haven't got. How many people would be lucky enough to move to a strange area, with a strange social services and a strange housing department and have a two-bedroomed bungalow converted into a three bed with an extra bathroom and shower added on, and with ramped access to the garden at a cost of £20,000 – without even requesting it? There's nothing else you could want.

We have never had a problem about money except when I had to leave work suddenly to look after Margaret and then Katie. I haven't gone outside the home to work since. Sometimes we've had help from organisations like the Rotary Fund for holidays and things like that but on the whole we've managed on allowances and benefits and Income Support. Now that Margaret is an adult she has her own income which I have to manage for her. Margaret has had a Community Care assessment and they fund her for four weeks respite care a year. They used to pay for a carer to help me get her up and bath her daily, but because she needs two carers, to avoid unfair allegations against one of them, social services won't fund them. It's the same with any other provision, like Day Centres. She needs two carers at all times including on the transport and because they can't fund that, she has to stay at home. I have to rely on my friends for help with Margaret. Since we've come here, she really has her own apartment which goes straight out into the garden. She loves the sun. Or she'll sit out in the front and watch the people go by. Everyone knows her and will stop to chat.

Foresight

When Margaret was a child I always believed her behaviour would change. When she was a child her behaviour was a challenge but as an adult it is a crisis or a disaster. A disabled child pulls at the heartstrings; a disabled adult with the same behaviour, or worse, can be repulsive. What one accepts from a child, one does not accept from an adult. Margaret has grown into a woman but she has stayed the same.

Knowing what I do, I would do it again if I was allowed to say: 'I will care for this child because she needs it, but I will never be able to love her and I want to be given an Adoption Order on that basis.' Margaret is cared for as a well loved patient but not in the way a parent loves a child. That has never changed and it never will. Margaret and I talk about this openly now – it is accepted between us. We even have a joke about it. I call her my daughter from hell and Margaret laughs and says she is not from hell, she is from outer space. That's what keeps us together; there is no pretence. If you are under pressure to pretend, that's when things fall apart. I have no guilt about it now but I used to have nightmares about not loving her.

When people find out that Margaret is adopted, they say: 'How wonderful,' but I say to them: 'Come in and live here for a week and then tell me how wonderful it is.' I'm not Mother Theresa, I'm just Mary. I care for Margaret, I care for her deeply, but to say I love her would be stretching it a bit. If anyone hurt a hair on her head I'd be there to defend her – is that what they call love?

*   *   *

Margaret was having a good day when I visited. The sun was shining and some of her favourite television programmes were on. She enjoyed her lunch and her tea. A young neighbour who has adopted Mary as her mother came in and stayed to get Margaret ready for bed. She goes to bed very early.

While Mary collected Katie from school, Margaret chatted and we agreed to write down some of the things she said. She was quite clear what she did and what she did not want written down.

*   *   *

Margaret

I don't feel little any more.

I am Katie's mother but I like Katie to call me Margaret – more like a sister – because when people see it like that it feels better.

I liked it when I first went to Parents for Children and everyone was around me and the other children. It was like a party and this posh Irish lady came in and she was my Mum.

At school they tried to make you more independent. It was alright sometimes but it depends what you had to do. Some of it was hard.

It was a bit bad when I went to live independent. They didn't explain and I didn't know what to do – about my own shopping and money and things. There were people looking after us but I didn't understand the booking to get help.

I have feelings that it is hard to say about but sometimes, by my face, my Mum knows.

When I was in boarding school I went to America. I nearly didn't but I went in the end. In a plane – it took seven hours. We were there a whole month and it was all planned for us. Then the Americans came over to England but that's when I left and I didn't see them.

*   *   *

Margaret talks well and has a sense of humour. She says she has always had one. She told me the story of ordering her new wheelchair – a different model to help her to sit up straight. She said: 'It will take a year,' and then laughed when she saw my face and said: 'It will be ready next month.' She sounded just like Mary.

4   Pray for a house
Eleanor, José, Firas and Emily

Eleanor and José are the parents of two boys and two girls who were born
to them and of two disabled adults, Firas and Emily, who were adopted
as children. They are the carers of two "long time" (José's term) and up
to four short-term foster children and they give respite care to the most
disabled young people in the borough. They offer a haven of warmth and
nurture to a variety of friends and relations; theirs is a "multi-national"
and a multi-ethnic household: Ireland, Mexico, Iraq, Uganda, Spain and
black and white Britain are woven into the family network. Eleanor and
José are still young, strong and full of energy: both of them work full
time in the home and are also active in a number of child-centred
organisations outside the home.

*　　　*　　　*

Eleanor
I was born in Ireland. We came to live in London when I was about seven,
so I've spent most of my life in England. When I was a young person I
was very interested in working with children. I used to find myself
voluntary jobs to do just that. At one time I was baby sitting for 30
children in our area.

When I was 18 I went to live in a small Catholic lay community up in
Manchester with what were then deemed "homeless girls". It was an
inspiring place. The woman who had started it had a vision of what was
needed and those girls got excellent care. They had been written off by
all the other agencies. At that time, girls as young as 16 were coming to
us from prison. You could still be locked up for not attending school! I
worked there for five years. It was a very good grounding experience; I
often think, 'how would they deal?' when I have these troubled teenagers
to look after.

Then I went to college to get a certificate in child care and came to
The St. Joseph's Centre to work in The Little House. It was a Portakabin
where they were offering respite care for disabled children or for disabled

children and their families. It was a very flexible provision. Sometimes they left The Little House to the parents and looked after the disabled child in the Centre itself to give everyone a break. I knew the people because when I was still at school, I had worked with them as a volunteer, taking disabled people on holiday. I stayed there until the Crusade of Rescue decided that this project was very viable; they took it over and moved us to Campion House – larger and more permanent premises up in Enfield. It became a less flexible service but it provided respite for more disabled children and adults and for young people with very challenging behaviour. Firas was one of the children admitted to The Little House who moved with us to Campion House. And one of the volunteers at Campion House was José. I was struck by him immediately – and by his wonderful smile. He helped to look after Firas – he was speaking in very broken English and I had no Spanish – yet we became very close. I'd made up my mind to remain single but by the end of the summer we were talking of marriage.

José

I come from Mexico. I come from quite a big family; I am one of 10. In Mexico, at the age of 12, I left my family and joined a congregation of missionary priests. I became one of the students. I visited my family once a month and when I moved further away I saw them about twice a year. Then I left my family altogether and came to England to finish my studies with the Missionary Society. When I was here working as a volunteer in a Children's Home I met and got to know Eleanor. The thing that impressed me about her was that she was a very busy person. And she was anxious about a boy she was trying to adopt. My first feeling was: 'If they don't want her to adopt that boy, what is the good of fighting? She is trying to do something good and they don't want her to do it. She should look for somebody that would be easier.' I couldn't understand that spirit of fighting. It was her stubborn spirit that made me start talking to her to see what was her point of view – and I was impressed.

Within a few months I decided to leave the congregation where I was studying. I went back to Mexico to think about our situation and to talk to my priests and family. While I was there I decided to leave the congregation altogether. I came back to England on the understanding of Eleanor and myself that we were not sure whether we wanted to live together. Although she paid for my fare and English studies, we were free. After about six months we agreed that we wanted to remain together and we got married.

About Firas
Eleanor

When I first met Firas he was twelve years old. I remember I was asked to get him up and there was this child with snot hanging down from his nose to his mouth and wet up to his ears. He couldn't do anything or understand anything we said to him: one, because he was a severely disabled person who had no speech and two, because he wasn't used to people speaking English around him. He came to us because his mother was in hospital with terminal cancer. Originally he had been admitted to hospital with her because no-one knew what to do with him. He could not use any statutory provision because they were here on visitors' visas from Iraq but his father was able to pay for his care. His mother died while we were still in The Little House and we continued to look after Firas. There were questions about how he would stay in this country but we worked with the Home Office and his father went on paying for him out of a trust fund left for him by his mother.

Firas was miserable. He needed a lot of attention. He couldn't eat ordinary food because he was only used to liquids. So we were giving him food that was very mushed up. We sat him at the table and he could get the food to his mouth but he spat it all out again. We had been told that everything he ate had to be covered in chocolate or curry powder. Breakfast ran into dinner and dinner ran into tea and there wasn't much time for anything else. After two years he could eat everything with a knife and fork. It was the same with getting him toilet trained and dressing himself – that took ages. He was a very under-stimulated person. There is nothing wrong with him except Down's Syndrome. His father said to me that they had never heard of mental handicap in Iraq. He presumed it was something he could take him to England or to Europe for – to get a cure. He told me that. They didn't have a clue. Firas's mother didn't know there was anything wrong with him until he was four. His father had been told the day Firas was born that he was a "mongol" but he didn't share that information with his wife.

When we'd looked after Firas in our community for two years we decided that one of us should adopt him to secure his future. As I was his main carer and I really loved him, I said I wanted to adopt him. In the back of my mind I had this idea that I would have a family of adopted and fostered children. I'd heard about PFC when I was still in Manchester – it must just have opened. I wrote for information. They wrote back and said that they couldn't work with anyone in Manchester because it was outside their area. But I remembered about it for future reference. And also we had a mother with a disabled son who was adopted through PFC coming to Campion House. So we approached PFC and asked if they would take on the project of getting Firas adopted. That was the easy part. We then had to wait another year for Firas' father to turn up again. We couldn't write to him. He was a member of the government in Iraq and no-one there knew that he had a disabled son. When we said that I wanted to adopt Firas he didn't quite understand. I was a single person and he thought I wanted to become his next wife. I had to get it across to him that adoption did not involve marriage. And he gave his agreement. Then we started the legal process and PFC got a very good solicitor who helped me through the High Court procedure. I had to have a home for Firas so he and I moved back to The Little House and I put my name down on the local housing list. Firas was 15 when I adopted him and I was 25.

José

While I was in Mexico, Eleanor went to the High Court and it seems that she managed to convince them that it was alright to be single, that it was alright to be young, that it was alright to adopt a child with disabilities and that it was not going to spoil her life. Even if she was reducing her chances to get married. So when I came back from Mexico, Firas was adopted and they were waiting to be rehoused because they were living in a mobile caravan in the grounds of St. Joseph's. We went on holiday with the children from Campion House and when we came back there was a flat for us.

We didn't have a good start. We started as a couple with one big child already. I remember, on our honeymoon Eleanor was worried about Firas being left behind. Until now, that was the only time we have been away without children. So that wasn't very straightforward from the beginning. When we were married we adopted Firas for a second time jointly. And by this time we were already thinking about Emily.

About Emily
Eleanor
Emily was a child with severe brain damage who had also come to The Little House and then to Campion House for respite care. When I met her she was three years old and all you could see of her was her hair. She was a little girl who wanted to stay curled up in a ball. You had to pick her up to open out her legs and her arms and then she would scream. She didn't want to be made aware of the world. You could walk her if you held her hands and guide her to eat and sit her on the potty, but she didn't do anything for herself. The physiotherapists and people involved with her couldn't understand why. They felt it was a motivational problem and that if we kept on with Emily something would click. By the time we were talking about fostering her, she was five years old and living in a hospital unit out in Herts.

José
I could remember a little girl called Emily from Campion House. I wasn't very happy about it because I couldn't stand her screams. All I could recall about her was her screaming – very high pitched. I thought it would be difficult and I wished that the scream would not be there. It was another stubborn battle from Eleanor. My position was exactly the same again: 'Why don't they want her to do it? What was the point of wasting all her energy?' I was still impressed by her, but I was somehow divided. I thought: 'If Emily comes that is good, but if she does not, that is better because then I don't have to put up with her screams.'

Eleanor
Emily's parents wanted us to foster her. Her mother is black and comes from Uganda; her father is white British. I spoke about the family's request to her social worker, and she was very amenable but the person who took over from her wasn't quite so keen and really stuck her heels

in about doing an assessment on us. She took two years to take us to the Fostering Panel. When she visited us she was very anxious to put forward all the obstacles. No matter what solutions we thought of, she'd think up more obstacles. We were living in an upstairs maisonette with Firas and one of my brothers. She came and said I would never be able to get Emily up the stairs if I was pregnant. Even when I gave her a list of all the people who would help me, she turned round and said: 'But are they insured?' So I carried José up the stairs to show her how strong I was. But she wasn't persuaded. We were turned down by the Panel on her recommendation and it was decided to advertise for other foster carers. There was no response, and after another six months the local authority asked whether PFC would take Emily on to find her a family – otherwise they would put her in institutional care. Emily became a political football: the local authority really felt that disabled children shouldn't be in families if their own parents couldn't cope; they wanted to raise the money to build a Residential Centre for children like Emily. But PFC accepted her and told the social worker that they would first work with us and that possibly we might be the right family for Emily. I remember the last visit from that social worker when she gave us a lot of forms explaining the difference between fostering and adoption, what it would mean in terms of local authority allowances, and wished us luck. She knew then that she had lost the battle but it wasn't her battle any more – somebody else had taken it over and it was no longer her responsibility.

After a short while it was agreed that Emily could be placed with us. In spite of the fact that by this time she was living in a residential nursery and the staff didn't think we would be able to manage such a severely disabled child. Her parents were still having her home every weekend and they were in contact with us. We would have cared for Emily permanently without adoption – she already had parents and fostering seemed to fit the bill. But in the end adoption did too. It made us all more independent.

José

Emily joined us about three years after we first applied. I remember feeling: 'How can we cope with it?' I imagined 20 years ahead as a package. Until I thought: 'It's only today really. And you are not being asked to build a house today, you are being asked to put on one brick.'

In the beginning

José

I somehow considered Firas part of Eleanor; he was there even when we were courting. With Emily it was a gradual build up because she started coming to stay with us. Sometimes I used to go to her own mother's house to feed her and I used to pick her up from the nursery to bring her to us. So when she moved in, it was not a big change. The only thing is, we had to start our mornings early – 5.45 every day. It was touch and go whether we could get Emily to the toilet in time. She only gave half a minute's notice. If we missed it I'd have to wash her and dress her all over again. The taxi to take them both to school would be at the corner at 8.20 and I had to be at work for social services at 8.30. Eleanor would already be at work since seven o'clock. So I could not leave the house until the children were collected. When I was made redundant we decided that it was better for the family if I work at home.

I still didn't like Emily screaming. I didn't know if I would get used to it. As it was, after two or three years she lost the high pitch she used to have and she was pleasant the rest of the time when she wasn't screaming. She was also pleasant to look at: beautiful features, hair and hands. Anyone would desire to have her looks.

Eleanor

By the time Emily came to live with us she was just seven and her limbs had already stiffened and grown in bent positions. She should have had constant exercising but in the residential units they had mostly left her sitting on a bean bag. She has never had any means of communication. It's just the way she looks and smiles and screams. But you do have to know her to understand what's going on.

José

Sometimes when we only had Firas and Emily we would stay in bed longer at the weekend. When we got up there would be Firas by himself downstairs with cereal in a bowl and milk all round the place. It showed he knew where the food was and that he could be independent. You could see he was improving. But with Emily we knew she wouldn't get better – we wanted to stop her getting worse.

As time went on
José

After Emily we added two older "long time" foster children with challenging behaviour to the family. When our birth children came they just joined the family as it was, they didn't know any different. But we did realise that if we were going to remain healthy, then we had to have help. Miriam was born on Boxing Day 1985. She was the first of four. It was obvious we were not going to cope well without help. We didn't know where help would come from but then we had a phone call from a friend in Spain, to say that a young woman wanted to come and learn English and could she stay with us for a couple of days? She came and stayed three years. She was really our first living-in help. She could be an *au pair* because she was European – and for whatever reason she decided to stay with us rather than look for a "proper" family. Then we had another student from Africa and some of Eleanor's brothers started to help. There was no way the two of us could have managed with the demands all the children made. These demands were their right because, after all, we decided to bring them to us, they didn't choose to come. And so I think it was correct that their needs were met properly.

Later my brothers and sisters and nieces from Mexico came to stay with us and to learn English. When one went back another came. It worked out that we always had three or four people from the family with us to help. We have to have people we can trust. It works both ways. We help them with their studies here and pay their fares. Or sometimes we pay for their professional studies in Mexico because it's cheaper there. And friends from our first *au pair* came from Spain. Also my sisters went to college and met other *au pairs* who were not happy in their places so they came to us. They were all good people. We explained to them what it implies, living with us, and that they have to share because we were crowded. We only had a three bedroomed flat – it was already full. Everyone seemed to put up with the living conditions until we were rehoused again.

We didn't have time like a normal couple to go out and enjoy ourselves.

I like travelling; I still miss it. I think if it had not been for Firas and Emily we would have been like any other family but now we have a real extended family. My parents ask all the time for us to send the children, including Firas and Emily. They have both been to Mexico. And we have this network of friends, relations and helpers – and the network grows.

Eleanor

One of the things I notice when I look at photos: to begin with Firas and Emily were the centre of the family – then when our birth children came they weren't the focus any more. They had to accept that other people did some of their care. They are both such creatures of routine that the important thing was to keep it going. I do wonder how they felt – if they could have expressed it. Firas was very much involved with Miriam to begin with. He liked to hold her and to laugh at her. But when Miriam started to climb on him he'd push her off like the cat.

The first time Miriam noticed something different about our family was when we had a disabled foster child. She wanted to know why this child couldn't walk and I had to make the link with Emily for her; she was born into it and didn't realise. She and the others have questioned why our family has to do this, but that's more to do with the short-term foster children than with Emily and Firas. We've got photographs of Emily looking quite interested in the babies but what she made of them is anyone's guess.

Contact with birth families
Eleanor

Both Firas' parents are dead; his father died six years ago. He used to visit every couple of years – whenever he was here on business. I got someone to write in Arabic to his widow, his second wife, but never had an acknowledgment. He left no money to Firas. He was always cross that his mother had left him some; he thought it was a waste. I wish there had been more contact with his father and with the wider family.

*   *   *

Emily's mother and father came to the adoption hearing which surprised the judge. He had his photograph taken with Emily and both sets of

59

parents. At first the adoption hardly changed the arrangements for contact and continuity. Except that now, Eleanor and José were the full time parents and the birth parents offered respite care.

*   *   *

Eleanor

They gave Emily respite the first year and they'd come to parties and family occasions and we went there. When they separated it was her father who kept up the contact. He comes every week at least and also teaches our children history. Her mother has remarried and moved away. She keeps in touch with cards and the occasional phone call. We see Emily's brother and sister when they come to stay with her father. It's difficult to know how much Emily responds but we've always felt that more goes on than she can express.

Religion

Eleanor

Firas' mother was a Christian and requested us to bring Firas up in the Christian religion. She wanted him to go to Lourdes and he has been. His father was a nominal Muslim and did not object. We have had Firas baptised and José was very proud when Firas was confirmed. He was 16 and he was confirmed with all the other youngsters. Emily's birth family is Roman Catholic and she was already baptised when she came to us.

Ethnicity and racism

José

I think there have been more issues about disability than about race. We noticed from the beginning that people stared at Firas and Emily. Teenagers imitate Firas and we would be aware of it; children call them names. In our last house people damaged our fence. We are odd – so it is hard to say how much is racism. There is a high level of racism around. When I came here first and was walking along the road, drivers used to beep and put their fingers up. I did not know English signs and thought they were being friendly so I smiled and did the same. We are a mixed race family. Mexican and Irish is not the same as Ugandan and English or Iraqi. The difference does matter but it is more important for Emily and Firas to have a family than a colour match.

Eleanor

You struggle for the ideal but you don't sacrifice a family for a child for the sake of an ideal. Neither Emily or Firas are aware of the day of the week but we have made an effort to put Firas in touch with his own culture. I think language is more important than skin colour. That often gets forgotten.

Health
Eleanor

Nine years ago Firas had pneumonia and they didn't give us much hope. He took a long time to recover and he's fine now, but the warning was there. His chest is vulnerable.

Emily had to have an operation on her hip when she was ten and has become more physically handicapped since. As she has grown older she has become a very deformed person. She has sclerosis of the spine, "windswept hips" and no muscle tone at all in her legs. Her hands stay in a closed position all the time now and they get very messy because no air can get to them. She has no mobility, she is incontinent and she has a mild, almost constant form of epilepsy. Her hearing seems to be reasonable but her eyesight is limited. After the operation her screaming got worse again because she had to be made to move which caused her great pain – two volunteers helped daily with almost continuous exercises while she was at home. It made her seriously depressed. She couldn't understand why she was in so much pain. Now she is quite a contented adult. She has probably reached her maximum disability level. She enjoys life as best she can.

Education
Eleanor

We started to educate Firas in Campion House; he didn't qualify for free education because of his visitor's status. When he did go to school we were disappointed. He left at 19 and he learned less in five years at school than he did at home in two.

61

José
And that was making sure they both went to a good school with a high ratio of teachers. There was a school nearer that was more crowded.

Eleanor
I always felt we should have had more time with Emily in the family before we sent her off to school. I used to make spot checks to see what was happening in school because we were dissatisfied. I felt the deterioration in Emily's hip was due to how they were handling her at school. It wasn't the school's fault in a sense; she was in a class in which every child needed one-to-one attention and there were only two teachers in the class. After the operation she went back to school on a part-time basis, for physiotherapy only. We had a Welfare Officer on our tail because we wouldn't send her back until we had a re-statement of her educational needs which included a one-to-one worker.

When Emily was 12 and still out of school, I went and queued up at an ordinary convent school as though I were an ordinary parent and filled out forms and put her name down. Then I managed to see the Headmistress and explained that we wanted Emily to go to an ordinary school part-time and how good that would be for the other pupils as well. Emily had never been asked to another child's home or had anything to do with non-disabled children of her own age. The Headmistress agreed to have Emily one day every half-term. She went with a helper and after that, for the first time, other girls would come up to us in the street or the church and say 'hello' to her. But after a while the invitations from the school just stopped – and so did the contact with the local girls. We asked that she should go to an ordinary school for part of the time when she was re-assessed. They wrote it down but never managed it. But they did provide a one-to-one worker.

*　　　*　　　*

Experience of their own and Firas' and Emily's education led Eleanor and José to explore Education Otherwise, an organisation which derives its name from a description in the Education Act of full-time education outside the school system. Their four birth children are consequently being educated at home. One of the teachers is Emily's father who, like the others, is thanked in various ways including wholesale food supplies.

*   *   *

Supports and services
Eleanor
I was used to communal support from Campion House and when we had our own home many of those people became part of our new network. So we've always had support.

José
Then my family joined us – we never had to go outside for much. It was always better not to disrupt Emily and Firas. We had respite care built in. If anything happened to Eleanor and me all our children would get cared for by our extended family. We trust them enough to work out what should be done.

We are lucky with the friends we have. We belong to a marriage support group. Four or five couples from our church meet once a month in each others' houses to share experiences and offer practical help. They are very accepting; we are always welcome in any of their homes with whosoever we bring.

Eleanor
We knew PFC was there if we wanted anything – like help with getting our first home through the council and buying our van which we still have twelve years later. PFC raised half the money for it and got Emily's local authority to lend us the other half interest free. And we used to go to all the PFC study days and picnics. We've stayed in contact with several of the other families we met there.

We had wonderful help from Emily's local authority with all the equipment and clothing when she was first placed. Anything we antici-pated they provided. Now we have all the aids and adaptations we need and Emily's wheelchairs are specially made to fit her shape. We've found our local social services more supportive since Firas and Emily have been adults.

José

The experts we needed were all there but Eleanor always had to find them. She was like a directory; everyone else came to her for information. She found out about activities, centres, specialists. Social workers would come and ask her advice.

*   *   *

Housing

As the family grew, and Emily's need for wheelchair space and access became more pressing, the council provided a five bedroomed house. Soon even this was overcrowded and the family looked around for alternatives.

*   *   *

Eleanor

Emily was in a plaster cast and we had to hoist her upstairs. We had to find something else but we didn't know how. We did everything the council suggested to us. We looked at exchange lists and I wrote to every housing association and religious organisation in the South East. We had many blessings sent by post but nothing tangible. When the council housing officer asked how far we'd got, I told her: 'We've set up a prayer group.' Then we went to a "Faith and Light" event for disabled people at a shrine in Walsingham. I was sitting with someone from the St. Joseph's Centre who said: 'Everything I've ever prayed for here has come true.' I said: 'Pray for a house for us then.' A few weeks later she asked me whether I had written to the Servite Housing Association and I said that I had. It seems they wanted to rehouse 50 people with special needs for their 50th birthday. So then she wrote to them as well and after another few weeks she rang me and said: 'I've just had the founder of the Servite Housing Association here to give me the plans of your new house.' They practically built the house for us. They adapted an existing house in the area and extended it. Now we have nine bedrooms and a room and bath for Emily on the ground floor.

José

We take short-term foster children from one local authority and do respite care for another. We will also be taking adults with disabilities because other people seem to want the children but not the adults. They have built on another extra room and bathroom downstairs so that we can take people with profound disabilities in a wheelchair – and they can make noise without disturbing the rest of the household.

Money matters
José
On one side we have an enormous amount of money coming in with all the allowances and benefits but on the other side there is an even greater amount going out every week. We do get everything we are entitled to. And we are lucky because we get a triple adoption allowance for Emily which will go on until she is 21. The trust fund we had for Firas was not so good because it prevented him getting other benefits. Now it is used up and he can get the benefits. Eleanor stopped working when we had our first baby and I was made redundant soon after, so we qualified for more allowances. It's a matter of juggling – somehow we manage to give everyone their share.

Eleanor
The Independent Living Fund (ILF) pays for carers to look after adults in their own home if the local authority is contributing £200 worth of services a week. So that takes care of Firas. I'd like to have some kind of guarantee of financial support when Emily's adoption allowance finishes in order to pay for her carers. Even if we can get ILF help in the end, there's likely to be a gap which we won't be able to afford.

José
We are vegetarians, we do our shopping wholesale and we have good friends.

Attachment and separation
José
With Firas, the attachment to him was there before he came to us. With Emily, it grew very much with the things that made us cross with her as well as with the things that made us happy. Like having to get her more mobile and aware of her surroundings. Emily was more of a struggle than

Firas. The least thing took a lot of work – but it makes you feel you are fighting alongside her because you don't want her to lose what she has gained. It would have been easy to leave Emily sitting all day on a bean bag; we were fighting with other people who were wanting her to do that.

Eleanor
I think Emily gets used to the people doing the hands-on care of her. If they go away and come back she starts laughing as if she's showing pleasure. And she seems to know when someone different is trying to feed her. I'm not sure how much she notices José and me now that we're not doing the physical caring. Firas is different. Again, you can't communicate verbally, but if we've been away and come back, he gets terribly excited. And he shows affection and can respond in physical games.

José
Now that we have an adult son and daughter, we are like any parents with grown up children. You don't stop worrying about them and when they're disabled you have even greater responsibility.

Eleanor
If all the carers upped and left, it would be down to José and me again.

José
From the beginning we always expected them to be as independent as possible. We have trained Firas to dress and wash himself and make a simple meal – his own breakfast. He doesn't always do it but all our efforts went into making him do it.

Eleanor
It wasn't possible to train Emily. But we could train ourselves to acknowledge that she was becoming an adult. Like not saying "girl" but "woman" when we talked about her.

José
The same with Firas. He should be treated as an adult and he has a right to an independent household.

Eleanor

Separation was achieved gradually. When Firas got his own flat he used to come with us to decorate it during the day and come back here with us to sleep. Then he spent one night there at a time and it was built up. He has always come back here, some of most days, so it wasn't a great jump for him. The same was true for us – it was gradual and we saw him every day.

José

We were aware that Emily's independence would be very limited. We have slowly let other people take over her care so that she is more separate. In years to come, perhaps she should be in her own flat with her own helpers – but how would we ensure that she would not be abused?

Degrees of independence

Eleanor

When Emily left school I was worried about her going to a social services day care provision for adults because no police checks are made on the staff. The reason we found out was because we knew a friend of a friend who was in all sorts of criminal activities and was employed in adult care. So it's a very easy way for abuse to happen. Whereas all the health authority staff are police checked; I know it's not fool-proof but it must put potential abusers off. The danger of sexual abuse is a chronic problem for Firas as well. Neither of them can speak out or defend themselves and there are so many opportunities to abuse adults like them. Firas is a short, sexually inactive man of 30 who still looks like a boy. Emily is very small and slim. She has developed physically and has irregular periods but she wouldn't even notice the blood and she is dependent for all her intimate needs.

*   *   *

All people with disabilities have a right to be assessed for care in the community. Eleanor and José have fought for the community care assessments to take account of all Firas' and Emily's needs. Now they both have packages of adult care to suit their individual requirements.

*   *   *

Eleanor

Firas has his own council flat. He shares the tenancy with an ex-foster daughter. Nobody ever heard of someone with serious learning difficulties applying for a flat. But we put his name on the housing list and after six years he was offered a flat. They said he would have to be able to manage his own tenancy. I said it would be managed as the rest of his life was managed. So he signed the tenancy form with me holding his hand. Lola, José's sister and Xavier, her husband, live in the flat and look after Firas in the mornings and evenings. Other helpers come in at the weekends.

Firas goes to a Day Centre twice a week. I wasn't happy with him being there full-time because he has a tendency just to stand and flick his fingers. The trouble with him is that he falls between two barrels. He often lands up with the very profoundly disabled who are in wheelchairs as well. Because the staff have to see more to the others' personal needs and because Firas' behaviour is not demanding, he gets left. So we've worked out a programme which includes a music and movement session. Then for the rest of the week José's brother, Andreas, takes him to the sauna, out to the pub, the Barbican Centre, shopping, to his own house and into cafés and such like.

José

Emily has her own room which was specially adapted to take her needs into consideration. Now Eleanor and I don't look after any of her physical care – only in an emergency. There are carers who take it in turn to look after her when she is at home. They are all members of our family. This gives her independence and recognises her as an adult. All the carers are near her own age. They play the same awful music and stuff which she seems to like. We think it is very important for her to be with people of her own age.

Eleanor

She is the first young disabled person in the borough to have a package of day care built around her. This is partly due to the social services Day Centres being full for wheelchair users.

José

And to the stubbornness of her mother.

Eleanor

They have provided two agency social workers for 35 hours per week. They take her to hydrotherapy three times a week, which she needs more than anything else. I said: 'I'm not prepared to agree anything until the hydrotherapy is sorted out. That has to be the main part and we can fit everything else around it.' Then they take her to a Day Centre which is a health authority provision and they stay with her one-to-one all the time. She joins in activities that are suitable for her such as trampolining. And they have a white tower room. It's all these lovely, moving lights and white bean bags and soft cushions and dreamy music. Then there is tactile cooking, which is tasting and feeling the food. And using computers. This keeps her busy five days a week.

Looking back and looking forward

Eleanor

If we hadn't kept Firas, an institution in Eastern Europe was the next option as far as I remember.

José

I dread to think what would have happened to him without a family.

Eleanor

Emily's local authority would have preferred a residential unit. I think she might have been drugged to stop the screaming.

José

And she wouldn't have had the one-to-one we have always given her.

Eleanor

But she would always have had her father. He would never have abandoned her. I think it's a bit more difficult now in terms of financial support than when we started out. People don't realise what it costs to take care of these children. You should never expect to do it by yourself and help costs money. Most people don't have large families to take a share of the care.

José

You have to think beyond childhood. We now have two very profoundly disabled adults who will need continuing care and the cost of that does not diminish.

I would do the same again but not precisely in the same way. We all learn to adapt and to change.

Eleanor

We are thinking of doing it again. Now that our youngest birth child is four, we are wanting one younger, with disabilities. We have been looking around. PFC don't usually have children as young as that and other agencies throw up their hands in horror when they hear about our family. They say: 'So many children!' I can't get them to see that there is individual care for all of them.

José and Eleanor

We will keep on looking.

*   *   *

Eleanor and José went on looking until they felt that too much time was being wasted. They have now had their fifth child by birth, a daughter called Thirza which means "pleasantness" in Hebrew.

5   I did it for him, not the money
Norah and Gary

Bite off more than you can chew, then chew it
Set yourself more than you can do, then do it
Hitch your wagon to a star,
Keep your seat – and there you are

This was one of Norah's mother's sayings; it is one of many Norah remembers and quotes to help her through the hard times.

The beginning
Norah was already in her 60s, a widow and a pensioner, when she heard about Gary who was then nearly 14 years old. Gary had cystic fibrosis, a short life expectancy, learning difficulties, poor sight and serious behavioural problems. He had spent almost his entire life in hospitals and Children's Homes. Yet Norah's interest in children in need was not awakened by Gary. When she was five years old a neighbour asked her what she wanted to be when she grew up.

'I'm going to be a mother with lots of children,' said Norah.

'And how many children will you have?'

'As many as I've got dollies.'

'How many dollies have you got?'

'Twenty-seven,' said Norah without hesitation.

She has been filling her life with children ever since and the children she has cared for in one way or another greatly outnumber the dolls.

*   *   *

Norah
I was an only child and I pestered my mother to foster as I always wanted a brother or sister. So first we took Annie, aged nine. We already knew her because her foster mother, who died of cancer, was a friend of my mother's. Annie stayed with us until she left home.

71

We moved to this house in 1939 and my dad died six weeks after. My mother was a widow early like me. We decided to apply to the London County Council to foster and were given two brothers and two sisters, all under six. We had another brother and sister at the same time, aged 10 and 12. We had them for quite a few years and would have liked to keep them permanently but it wasn't possible. Over the following years, my mother and I fostered more children: some short term and some longer. Overall, I've looked after 50–60 children.

I never bothered with boyfriends; I was too busy with helping to run the Brownies, learning first aid at the Red Cross and working at the brush factory from eight in the morning to eight at night. Didn't get married till I was 38 – to the chap next door. All I wanted was children but I had one miscarriage and then a still birth when I was 41. I was very depressed after that.

*   *   *

Norah and her husband adopted a boy of two who had suffered early disruption and then they took another young boy who was considered too disturbed and mentally disabled to be placed with a family. After her husband died at the age of 59, when the boys were teenagers, Norah and her mother went on being a family with unusual child care arrangements: child minding resulted in a long-term private fostering placement, foster children's children were given a home and no child in need was ever turned away.

However, troubled children rarely become trouble-free as they grow up. Norah has had her share of disappointments and worry, but her instinctive understanding of children who have been hurt has enabled her to stick with them no matter what they did.

*   *   *

Norah

I don't always approve of what they do, I don't encourage it, but I can't condemn it.

I heard about Gary six months after my mother died in 1978. I was in a low state. Both of my boys had left home and I only had Jane, my private foster daughter, who was then aged nine. My social worker said to me one day: 'Have you read the local paper Mrs L? There's an article in it you'll find interesting.'

'I know what you mean,' I said. 'I've read it about the fostering. There's going to be a meeting.'

'Will you come if I pick you up?' she said.

'No I won't,' I said. 'I'd stick out like a sore thumb – they'd all be young people looking for a child and me in my 60s.'

*   *   *

Nevertheless Norah was persuaded to go to the PFC Open Meeting. There were posters with photographs and descriptions of disabled children needing families, pinned all round the walls.

*   *   *

Norah

No-one else seemed to be taking any notice of Gary's poster, so I kept on and on coming back to it. In the end I asked: 'Could I be his social aunt?' It took six months to be accepted. I was introduced to Gary in June. It was in the Children's Home. He didn't want to talk to me. Didn't want to come in the room even. He was very unsociable. They said: 'This lady has come to see you, she wants to be your friend.' 'She can bugger off,' was all he said. I took one or two things that might interest him but he threw them on the floor. I tried several approaches but we didn't get anywhere. They looked on it as a disaster but I didn't. I mean, these things take time. Next thing I knew they rang up and said: 'Gary wants to know when you're coming to see him again.'

*   *   *

Norah went on visiting. Then Gary came to stay with her for a weekend. During the summer holidays, and again for the October half-term, she took him to her caravan on the south coast.

*   *   *

Norah

Between October and Christmas I sent cards and letters and phoned – sometimes he'd come to the phone and sometimes he wouldn't. His local authority social worker came just before Christmas and asked if I'd lost interest because I didn't want him for Christmas. She said: 'It's like they say, I'm not surprised you can't cope Mrs L.' I said to her: 'Will you let me say my piece. Let me tell you why I won't have him for Christmas. He's done nothing but talk about what he's going to do at Christmas in the Home – all I hear is how he's made the decorations and the pudding and everything. Then you want me to take him away and make him feel cheated. That's the trouble with you social workers, you only look at it from your side not the child's side. I'll have him after Christmas,' I said.

Then she asked if I'd foster him. I said: 'You were blooming well not even sure about me being his social aunt.' But she said: 'The committee knows you now and as long as you outlive Gary, that's all we're concerned about.' I said I couldn't guarantee it but I'd do my best. They offered me £40 a week but I said: 'You'll give me what I ask for or I won't have him. I want £25 a week.' I wanted him to know that I was doing it for him not the money. Money was never a problem. When Gary was 18 he got adult benefits and we always managed. He was one of the family and no amount of money could have made him better. When Gary moved in I told him: 'If we need more money, we'll take a lodger.'

Gary's parents were both slow learners. All the mother wanted was to be married and have children. Gary was the fourth child they had – all with cystic fibrosis. The first three died in childhood. When the parents were told Gary was affected, and perhaps a bit worse than the others, his mother said: 'I've never had Gary and I don't want to have him to lose him.' He had to stay in the hospital for a year to have operations on his pancreas and stomach. Then he was moved from one Children's Home to another – no-one wanted to keep him because of his behaviour, I suppose. They tried fostering when he was eight or nine but that didn't work either.

When I first had Gary, he was uncouth, ill-mannered, on the defensive, thinking everyone was against him. It took a long time to get through to him. I didn't take to him straight away, I wondered what I'd taken on but I've always welcomed a challenge and you don't start a thing you don't finish. They'd prepared me for him but most of them didn't live with Gary. It's living with someone teaches you what to do. You have to take it day by day and you learn by your mistakes.

I'd never heard of cystic fibrosis before Gary. It affected his lungs and his breathing. He had to have six different sorts of medication every day and he was on a strict diet. He couldn't eat anything with pips in it or any fats and he had to have powdered milk. I was given diet sheets but in the end it was just common sense. The disability made him very small and barrel-shaped. He was only the height of a ten-year-old when he was 14, but all his clothes had to be bought big and cut down to fit his stomach.

He could write his own name but he couldn't do anything else at reading and writing although he improved later. He was good at colouring. He'd get very frustrated when he couldn't have something or do something and then he'd be violent. Once he threw my iron out of the kitchen window and he had terrible temper tantrums. The least little thing would start him off. I tried to avoid arguments and to give him confidence. He was old enough to have a right to choose for himself about things like his bed time. I gave him his own house door key which made him feel grown up even if he hardly ever used it.

If Gary was shown how to do something, he could manage, like washing up. But mostly he had no idea when he came. Once he said he'd make a cup of tea for me and he put the electric kettle on the gas and the bottom dropped out. I blame the Home for that; if they can teach him to make Christmas decorations they can teach him how to put the electric kettle on.

Our worst battle was over the medication. Gary would refuse to take his tablets and that would make him ill. I made him believe that I would be ill if I didn't take my tablets – then I'd refuse to take them unless he took his. He got quite worried about me getting ill and so we both took our tablets. It was the first time I realised he was getting fond of me.

Another problem was that Gary only liked doctors and dentists and people like that if they had the same name as himself – Green. Luckily his specialist had that name and we found others in the telephone book. There was never any question about Gary changing his name to mine. He was a teenager and he was bright enough to know his own name. Adoption never came up; if he'd wanted to be adopted I would have but even then he could have kept his own name. He called me "auntie" – I always like to give the children the choice. When my own mother fostered the four brothers and sisters, three of them called her "mummy" but the oldest boy never would. One day, as were tucking them up for the night, she said to him: 'What would you like to call me? If you don't like mummy, how about auntie or gran?' He thought for a bit and then he said: 'I don't know any grans and aunties, but I want to call you matron, because matrons are nicer than mummies.' In the end he called her "mummy matron"; I've never forgotten that. I know that Gary used to say I was his mother at school and I asked him about that. He said it was nice to have a mum sometimes even if you call her "auntie".

Gary got on with Jane who was much younger but she was a bit impatient with him. The older boys didn't have much to do with him because they weren't at home. One of them didn't like me having Gary, but the other one has learning difficulties himself and was more like an older brother to Gary when he did see him, which was not often. Some people stopped coming to the house because they didn't like Gary but others, who knew how to talk to him, got to know him better and then he was alright with them.

I didn't want any respite care for Gary at the beginning. I didn't want him to feel rejected. Then later on, when I did want some help, they said no-one would have him because he was too difficult – but if he'd been an easier child he wouldn't have needed respite care. They more or less said that as I was fostering him I had to get on with it. That's what I did – you mustn't look for improvements all the time, it might take 20 years for something to show. You have to dwell on the little things that work – like learning about electric kettles and taking the tablets.

I didn't join in any groups but I took the cystic fibrosis newsletter; that was quite interesting. And there was another woman nearby who had two sons with cystic fibrosis. We used to speak on the phone. I made more time to give Gary individual attention and as time went by he grew in understanding. He learnt by talking to me not by schooling.

The middle
Gary went to a special school and they were patient with him. They kept him an extra year till he was 17. They did things like give the children driving lessons and Gary asked me to stand at the front door

and watch him drive past. He wasn't really doing the driving, and it didn't last long because the driving instructor left, but it gave him confidence.

As Gary grew older he became weaker in his legs and so did I. I used to have one of those invalid tricycles which Gary could ride. He had a bike of his own too and he was very good on that. He had a new bike which got stolen but I bought him another, second hand, because the bike was part of his life. I taught him to go on errands for me to the local shops. It took a long while before he would go but then he really liked it. He couldn't read but I used to draw him a map with arrows and all the buildings on it. He wouldn't go without it. Once or twice he brought me back a present that I knew nothing about.

If Gary learnt to do something he could do it pretty well. But only if he wanted to do it – you couldn't make him. He got good at gardening and any housework. When he washed up he cleaned the whole kitchen. But as he got older he became more frustrated at all the things he couldn't do and his violence got worse – but he was never violent towards me and he could be very kind.

When Gary was 15 we took in Jimmy for two years because his mother was ill and depressed after losing a baby. Jimmy was only three – the son of a girl I'd looked after from the West Indies. I'm still his nanna. It did Gary the world of good to have Jimmy. He really cared about him and Jimmy looked up to him as a big brother. Jimmy left the same time as Gary started at the Day Centre. Then we took in a man with a nervous breakdown who only had one leg. He stayed for a month and I had to help him strap on his artificial leg. Gary said to me: 'He needs a man to do that.' So he helped him from then on. It was Gary's idea and it brought out the best in him.

The cystic fibrosis was stable. We had regular visits to the specialist. He told me that if Gary went on with his medication and if I went on coping the way I was, Gary would live to be 30 or more. But it was a disability that would never get any better. The specialist was very understanding: when Gary left school he wanted to have fish and chips once a week like Jane and I used to have in town. He knew he wasn't allowed fried food. We stopped having it so that Gary wouldn't feel left out but he was so upset he complained to the doctor. And the doctor said he could have fish and chips once a month – that made Gary more co-operative about the rest of his diet.

Gary never had any contact with his own family. Sometimes he said he'd like to see what his Mum and Dad looked like and where his brothers and sister were buried, but then he'd say they were horrible and he wanted nothing to do with them. It was just his retaliation for the rejection. I used to talk about it with him if he gave me an opening, but you can't force it on a child. I asked the parents to visit through the social worker but they wouldn't admit to Gary's existence. I brought it up from time to time with social services – they didn't want to take it up because they were afraid it would end in a row. But as I said to them: 'Would that matter? Otherwise you can only tell Gary what you've been told or what you want him to know.'

Sex was never an issue with Gary, he just wasn't very interested. But I never would leave Jane and Gary in the house on their own. Jane was developing and Gary wouldn't have known about those sorts of feelings. I thought the school would teach him but I don't think they did because when he met a girl he liked at the Day Centre, he said to me: 'The other boys say I've got to have sex if I take her out again. I've heard about sex but I don't know how to do it.'

I told him not to bother about it and just to enjoy the friendship. The girl was deaf and dumb and Gary tried to learn sign language which I encouraged. No one ever advised me about Gary and sex. You'd think they would with there being no man around.

Before they put him in the Day Centre they tried Gary with Youth Training Schemes. He had a job in a garage but he couldn't do it. Then he worked on the greyhound track clearing up the dog mess which he didn't like – he squirted the manager with the hose-pipe, so he had to go. His last job was with a builder, picking up junk and putting it in a skip, but they found Gary asleep in the skip and sacked him for being too dangerous. He wasn't over-keen on the Day Centre either but he put up with it.

The end
Around the time Gary was 19 or 20, I was finding it extra hard work to look after him. Not that he was particularly naughty but he got more and

more easily frustrated and violent. I couldn't help him because I was pretty worn out. I didn't want a break from him – I didn't want him sent away – I was afraid of losing him. I wasn't only thinking of myself but of Gary feeling rejected which I think in the end he did. I just wanted more help in the day time, more Day Centres; he could have worked in a charity shop, there were plenty around at the time, and he liked sorting things. If he was handled right he could be very helpful and capable within his limitations. He could have been paid a bit of pocket money to make him think he was grown up and earning. But they didn't give us the choice. They said: 'He's a man now and should be left to get on by himself in the community.' They said they'd supervise him a bit and he'd come home to visit me.

At first they promised Gary a flat to live in with other disabled young people but he wanted to have a flat near me and he couldn't cope where they put him which was a long way from home. Then they tried a residential place not too far away but they wouldn't keep him – I suppose the staff couldn't cope with Gary. I should have been told when arrangements broke down, or why, but I was treated like I had no interest because I was only the foster mother and he was only coming to visit me.

Once when he was visiting I missed £10 from my purse. I knew it had to be him. He rang me when he got back in the Home and said he was worried about me losing that money because I hadn't got much. He said he hadn't taken it but he'd send me £10 when he drew his benefit. And he did. He said he was sending me a clean note which was better than the dirty one I'd lost. He was handicapped enough to give himself away but he was doing his best.

Then they found this special residential place miles away where they take people permanently. It was too far for me to visit and Gary could only come home in the holidays. I wrote to him and phoned him every week. I think it was a nice enough place in its way and you've got to let them grow up. They looked after him alright but they didn't insist he take his medication. They thought it was up to him to take his tablets but considering his condition they should have found ways of getting him to have them – they should have taken a firmer line because it was so important. He'd been there nearly a year and I was expecting him home for Easter. They rang me two weeks before and said he wouldn't be coming to visit at Easter because he'd just died. A week before his 23rd birthday.

It was just as though it was nothing to do with me. He wasn't my boy. They didn't say so in as many words but that was behind it. Like Gary was only a lodger. They hadn't even let me know he'd gone to hospital. I would have moved heaven and earth to get to see him in the hospital. As it was, I didn't know he was more ill than usual until they rang me to say he was dead. I was too upset to go to the funeral. I sent money for a wreath but it was too late to help Gary.

I still feel Gary might have lived longer if he'd stayed at home. I would have liked more support to help him to become independent without going away. Someone once asked me: 'Out of all the children you've had, about which one would you say, if you could have your time over again, I wouldn't have that one?' And I said: 'I'd have them all again, and I'd be that much wiser and make a better job of each one of them.'

Gary was one of my children. It wasn't love at first sight, the opposite if anything, but you mustn't judge by first impressions. I expected the worst but hoped for the best. You have to get through the bad bits before you can come to the good. I think I was the only person Gary was ever fond of – from little things he said – he never said it directly. If he'd lived we'd probably both have ended up in wheelchairs and we'd have been able to look after each other.

*　　　*　　　*

Norah is in her 80s now and can only leave the house in a wheelchair. Her home is like a centre for the neighbourhood's children and anyone else who wants a sympathetic ear. She says: 'I may be disabled but I can still talk.'

She can do more than talk. She collects and sorts clothes and toys for the Salvation Army and fills large cardboard boxes for orphanages in Romania. For good measure she puts in some of the beautiful things she is constantly knitting with wool people give her. Occasionally she manages to collect money as well and she has persuaded a manufacturer to sell her enough sweets to last the children from one Christmas to the next and all the birthdays in between. Over the years, she has got to know about some of the children in the orphanage and has "adopted" ten of them. They each get individual parcels to meet their special needs. This year, she has added to her list the nuns who look after the children. And every Christmas she rings the good sisters to have a chat.

Norah thinks Gary would have liked to help with the parcels. He liked presents and sending things. Among Norah's treasures are a wooden painted engine Gary made for her at the Day Centre and a letter he sent her a few days before his last illness.

6 Twins are not alone
Gill, Michael and Martin

Gill and her adopted twin sons, now aged 21, live in a roomy, rambling house on the edge of a small village in Mid Wales. Gill tells the story.

*   *   *

Gill

In 1984 I was a teacher for the deaf in a Midland city. My own two children had left home; I was divorced and enjoying my freedom. I was into gardening and having a good time. One day in the staff room they were talking yet again about Torvill and Dean. I was fed up and picked up a magazine and saw an item about black, deaf, seven-year-old twins with very few communication skills, who lived in a Residential Nursery and went to a well-known boarding school for the deaf. PFC was looking for two families for them. I was so angry at the idea of splitting these twins that I rang up the agency and started telling them about other means of communication than signs and words and I said that they shouldn't be split up. They told me that it had been really thought about and the advice from experts was that the boys didn't communicate with each other at all, and that any family would have a hard enough task looking after one let alone two of them. At the end of the conversation I said that I'd got a big house and if they couldn't find anyone else to have them both, I'd have them myself. I felt pretty safe because I was 45 and single and I thought I'd be ruled out for adoption. I was invited up to the office at PFC and, as it happened to be half-term and my two friends were going to London anyway, I just went along with them.

I saw a video of the twins, Michael and Martin. It was awful to see them rocking. They were very much like children in an institution, yet at the same time they had a spark about them. The financial side was worrying me but, as soon as I was told about the probability of an adoption allowance in the future, it made it all seem possible. I discussed it with family and friends very early on and somehow I found that I was going ahead. When I learnt that the twins could be mentally disabled as well as deaf, there was a hiccup. I felt that I could never cope with autism, for instance. I decided that I couldn't go on without seeing the twins. They were said to be unaware of people, so I arranged to go down and meet them in their Residential Nursery. I went with a senior colleague from school who was an expert in communication skills. I needed to know at that point whether Michael and Martin could come into my home and attend my school because that was what I would plan to do. We spent the day with one twin wrapped around each of us, monkey fashion. I can only put it down to the fact that we went in signing, because the residential staff had warned me that the boys would pay no attention to us. I couldn't turn them down after that.

The school and the Nursery would still have preferred two families for the twins and they certainly would not have chosen a single mother. They kept on saying that Michael and Martin didn't relate to each other and didn't need each other. One of the residential workers just thought it was funny when Martin went away on holiday and Michael didn't understand and kept on looking for him.

After Easter, arrangements were made to see the boys at their boarding school. I think the Head accepted that perhaps I was really going to have both boys because he told me that if they were going to change their home environment, they shouldn't have to change their school environment at the same time: it would be too upsetting for them to move up to the Midlands and to go to a new school. The only way around that was for me to move down to the South coast for a year because it wouldn't have worked to have them for the holidays only. I discussed this with my own Headmaster – no, I didn't discuss it – I *told* him that I wanted maternity leave for a year. Education Head Office said I definitely could not have maternity leave to adopt what were, by then, eight-year-old twins, although I could have had it to adopt a baby. I wrote a letter protesting and they wrote back that I could have 12 months unpaid leave, which was fine.

Then, in a bit of a panic, I drove down to the coast and went into an estate office and got the choice of two houses to rent. I couldn't get to see one because the people were still in it, so I went to see the other and it was perfect. It was in a lovely residential district, with a large lawn at the back, all fenced in well with a strong gate. It was a mile from the school and a short walk from the sea, and it was only £35 a week. I couldn't believe it. So I went straight back to the agents and told them I'd take it. They said we'd have to clear out for the school holidays when the family from London wanted it, but that suited us fine because I intended to take the boys to my own home in the holidays.

PFC planned to introduce me gradually to the children – come down at weekends to get to know them and that sort of thing. But I couldn't see that it would make much sense to Michael and Martin for me to keep appearing and going away. I just wanted to appear and be their rock and never more leave. I didn't want them to think that I was one of those who flitted in and out like the residential staff seemed to do. I did go down and stay for one weekend because everyone wanted me to.

Then I had a lot of sorting out to do at home to get ready for the move, so I left it until the last three weeks of the summer holiday, which I spent with the twins in their Residential Nursery. I didn't enjoy it; I was as upset as the children with the staff going on and off duty. I'd be sitting on the bed, having a nice conversation with one of them, when she'd look at her watch and say: 'Whoops, I'm off now,' and she'd be gone. It was quite an eye opener really. I got to know the twins pretty well in those three weeks; we were inseparable. First they had mumps and we were in isolation together for a week. After that we had a wonderful time going out to the village every day. Only Martin would hold your hand but he was still inclined to dash into the road – he had two near misses while I was there. Michael was given to quick rages – he would swipe everything off the table in a cafe or throw himself against a plate glass window. At the end of the three weeks we loaded all their belongings into a mini bus and Michael's key worker drove us to our rented house.

Moving in
Everyone definitely wanted me to have paid live-in help when I took the boys and that was quite traumatic. I had to advertise and interview and arrange for people to meet the twins and every one of them fell through. In the end I had to wait until we'd moved in and then I found a mother's help locally. I didn't have to pay her very much and I don't remember any financial problems at all. The boarding out allowance, which I got until I formally adopted the boys, was probably more than my salary. I

wanted to adopt Michael and Martin from the beginning; I'm quite possessive really. I felt that what I was wanting to do for the twins was the right thing and I didn't want anyone else interfering. I had to wait because it took such a long time to sort out the adoption allowance and in the meantime I had to foster because I couldn't do without financial support.

I always felt like I'd kidnapped the twins. They didn't have enough signs or language of any kind to understand what had happened. They were just living somewhere else. It was me being with them all the time, that constant presence rather than carers coming and going, which was different. The school staff "vetted" the property. They didn't want the twins to have the lovely double room I'd got ready for them – they said they'd leave the taps running in the basin. I'm sure they wouldn't have done really, but to please the school I put them into a small room with bunk beds. Michael didn't sleep in a bed anyway. He used to sit on the floor, legs outstretched, bent double and bang his head between his legs until he dozed off. He had a lump on his forehead and people thought he would have it for the rest of his life. In the winter he had a chesty cough from getting so cold on the floor. Both boys were still wet at night. Martin was over-active most of the time and constantly with me. Michael would sit sometimes and line up his cars. They didn't play together but they watched each other and were jealous of each other. Michael was the boss and would hit Martin if he annoyed him; they didn't fight because Martin didn't hit back. They looked pretty well alike then. They were quite tall for their age and slim – Michael was the heavier of the two. Martin was so wild that I had to have him on reins to take him out and the Mothercare toddler size still went round him. He didn't walk, he just bounced, with arms and legs going all over the place. They both needed constant attention. I couldn't even leave them to go to the toilet. Basically, the mother's help and I had one each all the time they were home. We used to walk them the mile to school and pick them up again – that was excellent – they'd hardly ever been out of the Nursery or the school except in a minibus. They were institutionalised in some positive ways too. They ate everything that was put in front of them and they had good table manners. So they could go into restaurants. Only Michael screamed if he could see anyone getting served before him. The routine they followed was very strict; in the early days I thought they were just sticking to what they'd known in institutions.

The impact

I used to be bruised all over because Martin didn't cuddle – he clenched and clutched and wriggled and pressed as if he was trying to get inside you. Michael was softer and could relax to have a proper cuddle. But then he had the most awful temper tantrums and had to be restrained because he'd bang his head against a concrete wall and scream and scream and scream. I was frequently tired all day from trying to train Michael to sleep at night. I'd put him in a bed next to mine and try to keep him there and stop him rocking. It took six months before he slept in a bed and stayed dry. He still woke and rocked but he didn't get out and sit on the floor. Martin took a year longer to be dry at night.

The Head at the boy's school was very kind and would have offered me a job but I was too exhausted to go out to work. Actually I enjoyed being a full-time parent again because I could see the improvement. I did miss my own children who still lived in the Midlands; for me the worst thing was being cut off from my family and friends. People came and stayed but not all of them could take the twins. Every holiday we came up to my home city so that the boys slowly got used to it. We travelled by train. The worst bit of the journey was crossing London from Victoria to Euston; sometimes we got a taxi but if there were queues we had to go by underground – the boys wouldn't stand in a queue.

The very first train journey we ever made together was on the first Saturday of the new term. As my mother's help and I went through the barrier at our local seaside station, we met the Head of the Special Needs Department from the twins' school coming out. I will never forget the look of incredulity on her face when I said we were going to London for the day. It was actually my first PFC picnic, an annual tradition. That journey was hard work. The twins were so active – Martin dashed off and grabbed a magazine from a lady passenger and both of them enjoyed swinging on the old-fashioned luggage racks, the sort with nets that looked like hammocks.

We went back and forth to my home town by train every school holiday and, by the end of the year, the twins were well into the routine of train travel and much better behaved than some ordinary children. We have since made many journeys by train, plane and ferry boat as well as car. They enjoy the movement and change of scenery.

After the end of the academic year we planned to move into my own house and I expected to go back to teaching and expected that the twins would come to my school.

Unexpected hurdles

During my year away, the local education system for the deaf had been reorganised. The Head of the primary school for deaf children from back home visited the twins at their current school. He turned them down because of their other disabilities. I had two choices: to live at home and sort out the schools or to move permanently down South so that the boys could remain at their present school. I decided we should return home. The school I was offered, I didn't like. I wanted them to be at a school for the deaf so that they could be in a signing environment.

They were offered places in a large school in the middle of the city which teachers think of as a dumping ground. It took lots and lots of children with different severe disabilities. I tried to keep an open mind and went to see the Head and was gaily told that one of the twins could go into a class of twelve with a nursery nurse who knew some Makaton, and the other one could join a class with a teacher who knew a bit of sign language so that she could translate. I said that the boys had been in classes of three or four where everyone signed and that it wasn't a question of translating but of using signing as the teaching method. I wrote and asked to meet with the Director of Education, as was my right. It wasn't a good interview. The officer responsible for placement and statementing was also present. He wouldn't let me say what I wanted and he was trying to tie me in knots about the difference between Makaton and BSL (British Sign Language). But the point was that this was an oral school not suitable for deaf children because neither Makaton nor BSL was the universal language of the school. So I said: 'Alright, I'll teach them at home.'

I taught Michael and Martin at home for two terms. The authorities hassled me a bit, and my own Head wasn't pleased about my taking more time off, but they did pay me for giving home tuition and, although they said the boys only qualified for twelve hours a week, it helped. I had to find another mother's help so that we could each concentrate on one child at a time. We fitted out one of the bedrooms as a classroom and we had two very nice terms. We used auditory aids, borrowed from my school, and we had a full school day. We time-tabled all the activities like shopping, cooking, swimming, walking and learning life skills. I taught the helper to sign and the boys learned in a signing environment. They really got settled in during this time because they knew where they were.

We finally sorted out the schooling when the education authority found they had six non-communicating children, all about the twins' age, who needed to learn by signing. So they managed to form a special class and a signing teacher for the deaf was brought in to run it. I still didn't like the school but I couldn't turn it down – they provided everything I asked for. Michael and Martin stayed there for just over four years, until they were 14.

Connections with the past

The twins' mother was very young; she hadn't long ago come to this country from Jamaica and she had a violent boyfriend and four children under four in a high-rise flat. Clearly the twins must always have been difficult and, after an episode of domestic violence, they were found locked in a room to protect them from the boyfriend. They were dirty, hungry and neglected and taken into care. At the time I put down a lot of their problems to the disruption in their formative years. I thought I'd be able to make it up to them and heal them by offering stability and consistency. Their mother wrote them a letter explaining her difficulties and sadness at giving them up. She said there would always be a place for them when they were 16.

I thought about her when the boys got to be 16 and, when they were 17, I asked PFC if they could trace her. They did and I sent photos and wrote about how they were and said we would be willing to meet her if that's what she wanted. To be honest I wasn't risking much, because the twins wouldn't have understood anything about it. But I should like to have met her – she has always felt very close to me. She hasn't made contact – perhaps it's too painful for her. If she really thought of them as being able to knock on her door one day, it would be very hard for her to see them now. We have a photograph of her but, on the whole, the boys are only interested in photos of themselves.

Michael, however, is also interested in photographs of staff from his nursery days. He has learned the finger spelling initials of their names – he needed to know their names. Martin has never shown interest in that.

A few years ago we revisited London and the twins' old school on the coast; we met up with as many people from the past as we could muster. I thought it might help Michael to lay a few ghosts. They certainly recognised the staff; Michael showed great pleasure in meeting those he used to like. I think he may have recognised some of the children who, of course, were young adults by then.

Ethnicity

When Michael and Martin were placed with me there was a strong move towards same-race placements. The twins' local authority had a high proportion of black staff and councillors to reflect the local population – they were against transracial adoption. They had greater concern about my being white than what particular qualities I had for the job. PFC had a more flexible policy at the time and we had, in fact, discussed the twins' racial identity. I felt that the twins were deaf first and black second. The deaf have their own culture and mother tongue, which is sign language, and the boys would grow up with that, which is more important for them. I also knew that the deaf club in the city was multiracial. But the classification in deaf culture is to do with the mode of communication rather than colour. The twins didn't understand that they were boys, what mothers and fathers are, anything about identity, let alone about race. They still haven't changed much in that respect. Sometimes I've seen them look at photographs of black men more intently than at others, but I think they're only looking to see if it is one of them. In the end, with the PFC worker representing me, the local authority agreed to the adoption; they knew a lot about race but they didn't know much about disability and they didn't know Michael and Martin. It was all done on paper. If you've got no experience of disability, words don't mean much, do they?

Special problems and special solutions

The boys had always been frightened of dogs and that became more of a problem in the city. They'd jump on you for protection – arms round your neck and legs wrapped round your waist and you had to hold them and stand still until the dog had gone by. In the city you couldn't go down to the shops without passing one or two dogs. Also the boys were getting bigger. I knew the fear came from Michael – Martin didn't bother when he was on his own. When they got too big to jump on you, Michael would run away – he'd jump on a wall or over a fence. Martin would panic and dash across roads, rivers, and railway lines; it was necessary to grab him and hang on, but when restrained like this, he would beat me over the head with his fists. On more than one occasion people thought I was being attacked and approached with their dog to help! I went to a psychologist to ask for advice. They worked with us until we left the Midlands. They tried behaviour therapy and acclimatisation, but you can't control the appearance of dogs and it didn't work. That was a good part of the reason for moving to Wales which was an area we already knew. We started coming for weekends to a cottage in the wilds and we moved to the village when the boys were 14 and I took early retirement. I was quite prepared to teach them at home again but I didn't tell the authorities that.

All the children here are integrated into mainstream schools or placed out of county, which is the more expensive alternative. They suggested we try the local comprehensive with me in attendance. I stayed with them for seven weeks and we proved that they could be safely placed there. It was ironic that they could fit into a large comprehensive in Wales but hadn't been accepted into a city school for the deaf in the Midlands. They stayed on until they were 19 and I couldn't fault the school. They employed an excellent signing teacher for the deaf and she had just the two of them, with a signing assistant, for the whole five years. They mixed with the other children at break times and they'd go out with the special needs class. They came on tremendously, particularly Martin, and Michael was a lot happier.

Diagnosis

Many of the tendencies you can attribute to autism, you can also attribute to Rubella damage. I didn't want it to be autism because I wanted to be

90

able to do something about it, and I knew I couldn't do anything about autism. There was a high incidence of Rubella among African-Caribbean immigrants – they didn't have natural immunity – and as both boys were the same, it was feasible that they were damaged at the same time during the mother's pregnancy.

When we came to Wales, their teacher said that the dog phobia was ruining their lives. We wrote to the director of a day clinic specialising in psychiatric disorders for the deaf. We just referred Michael, but both twins had to come with us, and he saw them both and very quickly said: 'Hasn't anyone ever told you what's wrong with these boys? They're autistic.' He did offer me a month's residential placement for a full assessment and we thought that would be useful for long-term planning. So I spent a month with the twins in a nice family flat attached to a deaf psychiatric unit in a North of England hospital. There was no help whatsoever on the dog issue but they did clear up another mystery. From the beginning Michael had what I first termed nightmares and then, when he had them in the day, I called them "funny turns". They were diagnosed as temporal lobe epilepsy or partial seizures which are now well controlled with drugs, so it was worth it for that outcome alone. For the rest, they confirmed that the twins were autistic and we had to get on with it. I've only recently accepted the diagnosis and that I must learn something about it. There's a lot of work being done on autism now.

Twinship
There's been a kind of opinion that Michael and Martin, like other twins, do better when educated separately. I suppose it's to stop unnecessary competition or one depending on the other or sometimes because they don't make friends if they're together. But really, Michael and Martin have been educated together since they left their first school and Michael has learned a lot by watching Martin learn. Since they've been 16, they've each had their own family aide from social services to develop individual leisure activities. For the first year at the Social Activities Centre, they were put into strictly separate groups – I thought they were doing it just for the sake of it and not to suit the twins. It could turn out that Martin got no swimming at all that way, while Michael had three sessions a week. Now they do some things together and it works fine.

They've had their own rooms since we came here, but they don't always stay in them. They still come to find me if they wake up early in the morning.

As young men, they've developed more individual tastes and habits. Martin's got a sweet tooth and Michael prefers savoury things. Michael likes comfortable clothes, baggy trousers and rugby shirts; Martin has his own ideas of smartness. Neither of them watches television – they don't connect with it. Martin is heavily into complicated jigsaws but Michael spends his time bending and arranging cutlery. That's his main obsession at the moment – I'm waiting for it to wear off.

From time to time I've got a little depressed – having doubts about what I decide for them. For instance, would they be just as happy if they'd stayed at their boarding school for the deaf? However, I have never doubted that the right thing was keeping them together. It would have been tragic if, as well as losing their mother and half brothers and sisters, they had lost each other. They seem to know what each other is thinking and they know each other's moods very well. I'm comforted in the knowledge that they will always have each other, whatever happens to people around them to whom they form some attachment. They are not alone.

Training for independence

The twins have been taught things like cooking since they were eight but they still need someone with them all the time they're doing it. They have no sense of time or motivation; it's like cooking with your four-year-old – they might enjoy it but you wouldn't send them off to the kitchen to bake a cake. They can clean windows, vacuum, wipe down the kitchen tops and do the washing up. But again, unless you were there guiding and encouraging and pushing them, it wouldn't be done. At the weekend when they get up and wash and dress by themselves, it can take three hours. When we came here, I trained them to go 25 yards to the garage for ice cream – that took some doing but I still can't build on it because of the dog problem. Martin can recognise about 60 written words, which means he can read a shopping list. They both use very basic sign language and they have no understanding of oral speech.

When Michael and Martin left school at 19, I applied to the

Independent Living Foundation (ILF) to fund a communication support worker for each of them to enable them to access the Day Care Services. This allows them complete flexibility – they don't have to stay in the Centres and can have programmes tailored to their needs. Their communication workers stay with them seven hours a day, five days a week. They are interviewed and employed by me as the twin's agent, with the funding direct from the ILF.

Apart from the communication workers and the family aides who give them each two evenings out a week, I've had a Community Service Volunteer (CSV) since they were 18. He lives in and provides an extra pair of hands. When we're out it means that there's another person in the car with us – the twins don't understand that I can't sign while I'm driving. Martin constantly demands: 'Kiss me,' as I approach a particularly bendy piece of road. It also means that they can go with him to the men's toilets. That's a problem when I'm on my own with them. I can send them in and then I have to stand and wait, and I can see by the looks of the men coming out that there's some kind of a difficulty. I'm also aware of the risk of sexual abuse because they are so vulnerable. The CSV comes on holiday with us and we often go away for weekends; or he can take them on an organised holiday for young disabled people to give me a break. That's the only break I've had so far, but I'm working my way round to sending them to a local respite care home with the CSV as their support worker. Most of the volunteers stay about six months; they learn to sign by watching and they go to formal classes at the college. Social services pays under their adult Care in the Community scheme. I really needed this service when the twins were 16 but it wasn't available to children. It's very hard when there isn't another carer around. I'd only been up here a year when I had to go into hospital at two days notice. It was the Easter holidays. My daughter had to leave her work and take my place for a week; there was no-one else who could take the boys. Now at least I've got this network of carers who can help out in an emergency.

I was a bit sad when autism was named, but I also feel I can accept Michael and Martin as they are and some of the striving to make them more capable and independent has gone. Now I know that they are going to need support throughout their adult life, and I can work to that end.

Choices and opportunities

The choices and opportunities the twins have had so far have been my choices for them, and I suppose that will carry on while I'm the responsible person. I chose to leave them at school until they were 19 because their schooling was covered by the Statements of Educational Needs. Had they transferred to college, there would have been no legal requirement to provide a teacher for the deaf. Then the choice was between the College of Further Education and the Social Activity Centre for People with Learning Difficulties. There wasn't a course at the college they could have followed. Martin does yoga, cookery, athletics, horse riding and dance through the Social Activity Centre. He's got very good at horse riding: he can steer, trot and canter but he can't stop. Michael does silk screen printing – his bed spread will be on display later this year – cookery, athletics, he's in the crack team for swimming and he makes bird tables and fencing in wood work. They do all these things with their communication workers.

Martin did work experience at the local Co-op while he was at school and he still works there on Friday mornings stacking the shelves. He enjoys it but they don't pay him. It wouldn't mean anything to him if they did. Both Michael and Martin are members of the local leisure centre and go twice a week for the fitness machines, the jaccuzzi, the steam room and the sauna. Michael likes the steam room best and he comes home with boiled eye balls. Then they also do the social things like going on the beach and out to cafés. Again it's my choice that they don't drink or smoke – I'd have to teach them to do it – and I'd rather teach them to blow their noses – I've not yet succeeded in doing that.

Adult relationships

My relationship with the twins now is still very much what it has always been, except there are less cuddles with Michael and Martin isn't as physically demanding as he was and he doesn't follow me around. I tell them that they are now young men. They are aware of each other and they are certainly used to being together. They look after each other. When they pour drinks or lay the table for instance, they might leave me out or one of the carers but never each other. Martin is getting more sociable but neither of them really has friends, though recently they have begun to take notice of a couple of the other young people at the Centre. So they are still developing their social skills.

Martin is seen as the friendlier of the two; his face is so expressive when in an outgoing mood – you can see what he is thinking. When visiting, which he enjoys, he soon discovers who is in charge of the kitchen and will charm his way into their good books. He gets on better with the women – he's regarded as cute. Martin is a bit more wary of men. He's been very friendly with the last two CSVs, but they both suspect that their long hair has confused him. Michael is much more thoughtful and moody. He needs time to get to know people and has difficulty in expressing his emotions.

My own son is also called Martin and is also deaf. He uses hearing aids and has good speech and is an audiological technician in a school for the deaf so he is also fluent in sign language. He lived with us for a time and the twins especially enjoyed physical play with him. When he is coming to visit, they can get quite excited, but once he's arrived, they might not pay him any attention. For five years we took a boating holiday with Martin as Captain/Engineer and with various friends as crew. We've boated in France, Ireland and Scotland with the twins as well as in England and Wales.

My daughter can stand in for me – they know her very well – but in a way they just accept her as they do me, as the provider. Both of them have some relationship with their communication workers and family aides and CSVs, but they don't miss them when they're absent. As long as they have their needs met, they'd probably be alright with anybody. I don't feel indispensable except in the sense that I've got the knowledge about what they need.

I was worried about how they would cope with sex, but on the whole, really they seem to cope with it well enough on their own. Because they don't make relationships, they don't bother anyone else or each other.

Michael and Martin do know who people are. We have kept in touch with one of their previous key workers from the Residential Nursery. We stay with her when we go up to London and she's been here for holidays. Then there's Paul, a teacher at the boys' first school, who meant something to Martin. He's always keen to see Paul although nothing much happens when we go. Paul probably thinks I'm making it up, but

Martin really does sign his name and is quite insistent about it. Perhaps he just wants to check that Paul is still around and once he's seen him, that's enough. I think these links are very important.

I've missed having a partner sometimes. It would have been nice to have someone to discuss the twins with. On the other hand, I've really appreciated being in charge, not having to argue about anything and being able to do what I thought was right for them. But that responsibility, at times, is heavy for one person, especially when there's a conflict with authority. I've been made to feel that I'm "only a woman" and probably they thought a dotty one at that!

Remaining needs

I've decided that I want Michael and Martin to move to a home in the community, near me, with signing staff, before they are 25. Basically I want to be able to make sure that it's set up in the way they need and that all the current activity arrangements can continue. We have worked so hard and long to keep them in the community, it would be silly to let them go to an institution now. It would be like saying there was no point to anything I'd done. I'm talking about it to people and I'm looking at how it's been done in other areas. It's the obvious next step – for the twins it's a natural progression to leave me and home. If they stayed with me another ten years, they wouldn't become more independent and the move has got to be made because I won't always be here. The sooner it's made the better; it will mean I can be around longer to visit and for them to visit me. There are some suitable schemes but in the end it will be a question of funding, possibly fighting for it. It's got to be a signing household; it would be no good trying to slot them into an existing household and it would be no good fitting in other young people who didn't sign. It's not just a matter of a vacancy somewhere and, if I left it too late, that's what it might amount to. There's an annual review of the twins' community care needs and every year I firm up on my plan. I'm on good terms with all the workers here. They've taken on board that I'm the authority on the twins and I never feel intimidated about saying anything.

Afterthoughts

It's been an interesting adventure rising to the challenge. It's almost too big to put into words. I've met a lot of people I wouldn't have met otherwise and I do think Michael and Martin have had a good and happy life. I had a great deal of joy bringing up my own family. I thought it was over and I loved teaching. If you'd said: 'You've got to give up teaching to bring up the twins,' I'd have said: 'Well, no.' I thought I could do both, and I did for a time, but in the end being a parent is more satisfying than being a teacher. It's longer term, you can see things through and you can build on the foundations you've laid.

*   *   *

Martin and Michael

Gill said that the twins would not be able to make any kind of comment about their story or add anything to it. She thought that their behaviour and appearance would speak for themselves. Michael and Martin were brought home by one of their communication supporters in the middle of the afternoon. They are tall, slim young men, not as alike as they were when they were children. They went straight upstairs to take off their shoes; a habit they have retained from their days in residential care. Martin came into the sitting room and with some encouragement signed 'Hello'. He made straight for the table piled high with jigsaws and went on with a thousand piece puzzle as though his life depended on it. Michael had to be persuaded to exchange the cutlery in the kitchen for a plate of biscuits and a drink in the sitting room; he also signed 'Hello' and disappeared again into the kitchen the moment he finished the biscuits. When I left, Martin was still intent on his puzzle and Michael was equally intent on an arrangement of bent cutlery on the kitchen table. They both signed 'Good-bye' when Gill reminded them.

After Gill had read the first draft of this story, she suggested some additions which have been included and she wrote in an accompanying letter: 'I'm still a bit concerned I haven't been able to bring out the energy of the boys; the smiling fun of Martin's disposition, even his enjoyment of sending you frantic with his nagging; or the feeling I have for Michael's deep need and my not being able to fill it.'

7 Baby girls like us
Pam, Helly and Sarah

Pam and Les adopted three girls with Down's Syndrome in quick succession, starting with Helen, called Helly, twenty years ago. Helly is now 23, Sarah who followed is 20, and Emma, known as Em, and the only one who came as a baby, is 14. Em is too young to be included as one of the 20 children whose tales are told in this book, but she is as important a member of her family as Helly and Sarah. Pam is the storyteller for all the family.

*   *   *

Pam's story
I am just an ordinary person that was brought up in care. There were nine of us and we were all split up. I traced my brother, Chris, and two sisters, Rosie and Gloria, when we grew up. After care, I went into nursing. I was nursing disabled children and I always thought it would be nice to be able to adopt children with Down's Syndrome. I couldn't see why they had to be institutionalised – I thought they would benefit from being in a family environment.

When I met Les, he was a guard on the railway. He stopped the train for me. I was going to work at the hospital and, being my normal self, it was last minute, and he stopped the train. That's how we met. He had three grown up sons – one adopted – and he was a widower. He'd nursed his wife for ten years before she died of senile dementia. I used to see Les on the station every time I went off duty to the local town. He always seemed to be the guard on the train. We started going out together. He knew where I was nursing and he picked me up from the hospital and I took him to the ward I was on. He saw the severely disabled children – he was in his element playing with them. We decided then that we would like to adopt children with Down's Syndrome; Les wanted to have a daughter. But at the time, in the early 70s, that wasn't possible; adoption was for ordinary children not children with disabilities.

We got married and we did try for a child of our own but I lost it. We applied to our local authority for fostering, at first, and we were told we could only foster an older teenager. They wouldn't contemplate putting children with disabilities in families – they were put in institutions. We couldn't have a young child because of the age gap between Les and I. There was a large gap – 28 years – and the local authority had an age limit for fostering and adopting and Les was over that limit.

Then one day, Les came home all excited off the train, off the very late shift at about twenty to one in the morning and he said: 'Look what I've got.' I said: 'Well, that's *Woman's Own*, what about it?' Inside there was an article about PFC placing children with severe learning difficulties. We wrote to PFC and we were on our way! That's how we came to have Helly and then Sarah and later Em.

We had some aggravation with social services because Helly was the first child with severe disabilities placed for adoption in the county; they didn't have a clue. They didn't really know how to take us. PFC managed to sort it all out and eventually we got to the court and Helly was adopted and then Sarah and then Em.

*   *   *

The adoption hearings were important events in this family's history. Helly would not sit still or be quiet while the judge talked to her parents and finally she began to screech. The judge, hoping to pacify her, gave her his large bunch of keys, and Helly, with unerring aim, threw them back in his face. Pam and Les were not amused, but the judge made the order.

*   *   *

Pam

With Sarah, the social services recommended an interim order because the social worker from the local authority thought we were taking on too much. She didn't know the difference between mental handicap and mental illness. She said to me: 'What about when they get older? What if one of them gets out of bed at night and tries to strangle you?' It was just ignorance. I sent her to the school to see what older children with Down's Syndrome were like but she was adamant. Luckily the judge listened to us and the guardian *ad litem* and PFC. When it came to Em, the judge said: 'What do you want me to do, where do you want me to sign and are you coming back for a fourth?' I said: 'More than likely but don't hold your breath.'

Les's family didn't like the idea of us adopting disabled children in the beginning. They didn't understand what handicap was about. The oldest, adopted son came round soon enough and his children mixed in with ours quite well. The youngest son got used to the idea in the end, but the middle son could never understand that our daughters weren't mentally ill. My brother Chris and my two sisters who were in contact all supported us. Les got Chris a job on the railway and he became a live-in member of the family for several years. When Helly was ill he used to be left to look after Sarah and they got on really well. My sister Rosie was always visiting and buying clothes for the children. Uncle Chris and Auntie Rosie are their favourites.

All our doctors and medical teams were very good once I sorted them out. They're with us all the way. My GP says: 'I'm not behind you, I'm by your side!' But we fall between the medical services of two cities. If we lived down the road, we could have had incontinence pads – as it was, I had to fight for them. Everyone said it wasn't their department but I insisted – I even took it to the local press. Now everyone in the area gets the incontinence service if they need it.

The Headmistress from the school and the class teacher, who has taught all three of our children, have always backed us up. We could rely on them and we knew that PFC was always there. We only had to pick up the phone.

Contact with birth families wasn't much talked about in those days. We had information about them; it was never suggested we should meet. I was determined to adopt, rather than foster, because I could never have parted with them, but I wouldn't have minded contact. Les would have objected though. He was older and very protective. It wouldn't bother me if any of them wanted to get in touch now, only we've never heard. I talk to the girls about being adopted and being chosen but it doesn't mean anything to them. They have no idea of a birth family and adoption is just a word they've heard fom me.

I never forget the day I was in Tesco's; I had Helly and Sarah with me. Helly was being a bit vocal and this woman turned round and said to me:

'Why didn't you have them put down?' I'm not a violent person, I didn't hit her but there was pandemonium in the shop. I was shouting: 'How dare you, they're my daughters. They're the most vulnerable people in the world and it's up to all of us, including you, to look after them.' She said: 'They should be locked away.' And I said: 'Well, actually I've adopted them.' She was flabbergasted. If people think these things, they'd better keep their mouths shut and not say them about my daughters.

Adoption allowances weren't in when we had Helly and Sarah but anyway we would have wanted to manage without. It was very difficult at first even with the attendance allowances and child benefit because it costs a lot more to bring up disabled children. Les used to work overtime and at night to earn the extra money. When Helly was five we got the mobility allowance as well which made it easier.

Les retired before he was 65. He did everything for the children; he worshipped them and they worshipped him. We took them out everywhere with us. We went to restaurants with them and we took them on holidays to our caravan. When Les retired, he was on voluntary work for the ambulance service. He died suddenly in September 1989 aged 68. He'd taken a patient to the hospital for dialysis, he came home and said he felt ill. He wanted something to eat. I'd made him semolina, his favourite, but he insisted on having a piece of toast and a cup of tea. He said: 'You just sit here with me and have a cup of tea. I feel really awful and I'm going to lie down after.' He went upstairs. The girls were in bed. I heard him vomit, so I was up there and he started to be unconscious and he vomited again. Unfortunately Sarah and Em were at the bathroom door by this time and were crying and screaming. I left a friend who happened to be visiting to look after them. The ambulance took Les to his favourite hospital and I went too. The men did everything for him, they said: 'He's one of us,' but he was dead.

When I got back hours later, Sarah and Em were still awake and very distressed. I'd told my friend to lock the door, meaning the bathroom door, because of the mess on the floor, but she misunderstood and locked Sarah and Em into their bedroom which upset them more. Helly has always had a room of her own and for once she slept through. She kept on asking for her daddy but never understood what happened. Sarah and Em know that he's in heaven. They think it's a good place where you can have what you want. So they say: 'Daddy has a red car and a dog and two cats.' It's had the most lasting effect on Sarah: whenever Helly has a fit Sarah thinks she's going to die and she associates vomiting with dying.

One of the things both PFC and the judge at one of the adoptions asked was: 'How do you think you would cope if you were left on your own?' And I've managed just as well. I did break down for three months with clinical depression – that was triggered by the suddenness of his death together with the experiences of myself in care. Chris kept in very close contact with the children – it was the first time they went into respite care. Chris told them Mummy was poorly and was getting better. Once I got myself sorted out and I had them back home, they recovered quickly but they're still inclined to be more clinging than they were. Social services and the doctors say they don't know how I coped with three disabled children – I can't get it across to them that it's no more difficult than looking after three children without disabilities on your own. Les taught me to drive, so I can cope with any emergency. My GP says I have a special talent for communicating with children who have learning difficulties but it's just normal to me.

While Les was still alive, I started some voluntary work for Age Concern and I met up with an old chap from down the road. He ended up as part of our family. He became a grandfather, if you like, to our three daughters. He died a year after Les. I'd been giving him a lot of care and I was made his next of kin. I took on most of the responsibility but he had an elderly cousin and this cousin had a friend and that friend was Ivan. Ivan came and took over some of the responsibility for clearing up and arranging the funeral. He knew my daughters from the start. We became good friends. My children took to him immediately. That was the main criteria for anyone coming into my life: my children had to accept him as well as him accepting the children. And it went on from there. A year later we started to live together as a family. Ivan has a profound hearing loss. He went to a special school for deaf children and learnt to speak perfect, so he's very sympathetic to disability.

It must be that you're both committed. It can't be one wanting it and the other tolerating it. Les and me never hesitated about adopting our daughters. Having disabled children has made relationships with my partners more close. Les was the father by choice, but you also have to be a very special kind of person to take on a family like ours, which Ivan has done. Les was the girls' "daddy" and Ivan is their "dad". We make allowances for disabilities but we've always treated them like children first and now like young adults. Adoption makes them extra precious.

*   *   *

Helly's story

Helly was three and a half years old when we first heard about her. She had Down's Syndrome and we were told that she was also very backward. No-one else seemed to be interested in her. We were given all the information there was. She was living in a Residential Nursery where they trained children's nurses and she was in a room with all the babies. Her backside was raw when we had her because she'd been left in her cot all day. No-one could warn us about her heart condition because no-one knew. The doctor at the Nursery had only seen her once when she had chicken pox and it wasn't picked up at the routine adoption medical. After we found out about Helly, PFC got all the children referred to them to see a cardiologist if there was any suspicion of heart problem. And that's most children with Down's Syndrome. But it wouldn't have made any difference to us – we would have carried on with Helly even if we had known about her heart.

Introductions were arranged with us staying in a hotel near the Nursery. It wasn't convenient, but PFC was very adaptable. They went out of their way to make it easier for us. We stayed until she was used to us.

When we met Helly, her physical condition was worse than we had expected. She could hardly sit up. She was rocking all the time and banging her head. She didn't know how to use her arms and hands. We still have a photo of her with her arms out, sitting at the table, being fed. She was dribbling with mucous running all down her face and her chin was raw. We still fell in love with her. They were all things a little tender loving care would put right. She was our daughter.

With a child who has a very low intellect, I don't think it's necessary to have long introductions. It's enough just to get to know them. You work at bonding when you have the child regardless of age and ability. When they try your patience it's part of the bonding. You're either going to make it together or you're not – but you go in with making it in mind. When we felt ready to take Helly home after three days, the care staff wanted to postpone the placement. PFC supported us. They came out to the Nursery on a Sunday – and we took Helly home with us.

Helly settled down lovely with us. It was hard at first. You had to come off the level you were on and come down really low to reach where she was. She was a self-contained little person and she still is, but she also became very affectionate. She didn't sleep much at night. I was amazed. Someone who could go so many nights without sleep. The doctor said: 'She will go to sleep when she's tired,' and I said: 'Oh yes, when will that be?' I was just napping when Les or Chris were home. She still doesn't need a lot of sleep. Medication seems to work the opposite way on her or not at all. We're still having to be aware of her all night. We have an intercom to our bedroom and closed circuit TV with a remote controlled light behind her bed because she has fits and needs watching.

We soon discovered that Helly had *petit mal* a lot of the time. Then we noticed that she had difficulty breathing when we did exercises with her to tone up her muscles. 'Why is she going purple?' I asked myself. I mentioned it to the paediatrician and nagged him to death until he got her an appointment with a cardiologist. We found out that Helly had a severe heart condition which was fatal and inoperable. He said she wouldn't make five. She was precious to us as it was, and when we realised we were only going to keep her for a short time, it intensified our feelings for her. We put in straight away for Sarah. We didn't want to wait because we didn't want to replace Helly. We prepared ourselves for devastation, to see it through as a family.

Helly wasn't jealous of Sarah. She looked on her more like a dolly. They had different personalities when they were young. Helly was always inclined to feel: 'That's mine and as long as you don't touch it that's alright.' Whereas Sarah would share.

You had to spend hours and hours teaching Helly the simplest things – taking the spoon to her mouth had to be broken down into stages – but when she did something, it was immensely satisfying. She went to school when she was four and education has always been excellent but mostly I've worked it out by myself from intuition. It's like how you'd teach a baby to do things. It's a lot of repetition. The attention span is so short that it has to be little and often. The biggest thing Helly did was proving the doctors wrong. They said she'd never walk, never talk, never be continent. Everything the doctors said, Helly seemed determined to defy them. Alright, she didn't walk until she was eight but she did it. They said her mental age was that of an 18-months-old baby but she learnt Makaton very quickly to supplement her speech. We got her out of nappies in the day by the time she was walking.

Helly survived against the odds. Every year they said she wouldn't and she did. We had to learn to cope on automatic pilot because of lack of sleep. Even when you're ill yourself you have to go on looking after them. Then when Helly was 12, they diagnosed sclerosis, which means that all her organs are being squashed up because her spine is curving to the right and she's losing flexibility and motability all the time. We had to fight for the adaptations we needed, like a stair lift, the pavement dropped for access, and patio doors to the garden so that we could get Helly in and out and up the stairs. But we knew what we were entitled to have and we got it for her.

After Les died, the children went on going into respite care one weekend a month. I asked for family link care but they couldn't find a family that would take Helly, so she went to a residential place for children with disabilities. I kept putting in complaints about the way she was coming home. She would come back with a wringing wet nappy when she wasn't even supposed to be in nappies during the day. And she would constantly screech, so I withdrew her.

Helly left school when she was 18. She wasn't happy, she was in a class with one boy who frightened her. At that time they were still saying this is her last year, and I thought we'd make the most of it with quality time at home. This went on until she was 21 and I took her for her annual checkup. The doctors were amazed. They said that the fatal pressure on her heart had completely disappeared and that there was no medical reason for it. The specialist asked me if I believed in God. She's still checked every year, but the danger from the heart has gone. They would even be prepared to operate on her back now but we've decided that it wouldn't be right to put her through any more pain she can't understand. She's had enough.

Social services kept saying to me: 'She needs respite care, she needs respite care,' so our social worker looked through everything available and we were stuck with one place: a respite centre at a local hospital. She went for an initial visit and then for one weekend a month starting in May '93 while Sarah went to her link family and Em stayed with us, so that we could do more for her. Em is the most able of the three and she needed one-to-one attention to bring her on. For the first few months everything was fine. Ivan and I decided we'd have a proper holiday and take Em with us. We flew to Spain – neither of the others were allowed to fly because of their heart conditions. Helly was in that place then for 17 days. When we came back she was irritable and high as a kite. I queried her bowel motions because they were very loose. They said it was the change in diet. She went for another weekend the following month. When she came back she had self-mutilated her neck and I took her straight to the doctor. The day after she performed oral sex with a toy dog that had a very erect tail. We were gob smacked. I rang social services straight away and got the social worker up here immediately. She contacted the Community Care team and they promised to have an investigation. They gave us an assurance that Helly couldn't have seen anything and nothing like that could have happened to her.

August came and she went for respite again. She was high again when she came home and self-mutilating. I took her to the doctor again. This time he queried abuse and I explained that they had investigated and assured us that nothing like that could happen. He said try once more. So we did because we'd booked a weekend away with Sarah and Em in September. When she came back she was perfectly alright. So I went to the doctor and said: 'Look, there's nothing wrong.' He said it must have been a coincidence – keep your eye on her but let her go back because you need the break.

We sent her again in October; this time when we collected her she was wild and uncontrollable. Her main carer had rung me and said they'd had a bit of trouble with Helly. She'd been found at night wandering without any clothes on. On the way home she was constantly punching herself and we had a job keeping her strapped in the car. She was like a wild animal. We called the doctor out to calm her down because I feared for her sanity. She was throwing herself about and bruised from where she hit herself. She got worse. Over Christmas she was punching herself, screaming day and night and didn't want anyone to come near her. She wouldn't go to the toilet or in the bath and she was smearing excrement all over the place.

By the beginning of January she was playing out more sexual acts. I called social services and the GP came and informed the police. The police didn't believe it. They couldn't see how anyone could want to do that with someone as disabled as Helly. I said to them: 'Every time he took her to the toilet he must have given her one.' They asked me if I would consent to a medical examination and I said yes but it would have to be done under a general anaesthetic. So that involved finding a doctor and a hospital who would do it. We took her into the gynaecological ward of our nearest teaching hospital and the police surgeon performed the examination. We were with Helly when she came out of the anaesthetic in the recovery room and the surgeon said to me: 'In all my years as a police surgeon I have never seen anything so horrendous as the damage that's been done to Helly's back passage. All the muscles are completely destroyed.' He also established rape. Then the coppers had to believe me.

So they had a full enquiry. They had three male workers in that place and they said there wasn't enough evidence against any one of them. No-one was even suspended. The health authority accused the police of saying that there hadn't been an opportunity for the abuse to happen – the police denied it and asked the health authority to retract their statement. They didn't but wrote us a letter saying: 'We are sorry you have been upset.' We all know who did it because Helly said his name clear as a bell during her psychosis. She can't go in the witness box and he still works there and social services still use the establishment. The only thing that's changed is that male carers are only allowed to look after the personal needs of male clients. Everyone knows what happened but they'd like me to keep quiet about it. I've even been warned of libel. But I say this to them: 'I'd like to see the judge that would put me in prison for libel and leave my three daughters for someone else to look after.'

During all this time, Helly was in a psychotic state. In six weeks she slept twelve hours. The doctors from the practice were coming daily and nightly. My own GP sat down with me one day and said: 'She is never, ever, going to recover from this. She doesn't have the intellect to get over it, but unfortunately there is nothing wrong with her memory.' There were three courses open to us. One was we could go on as we were, which was an impossibility. Helly was ripping carpets, stripping walls, tearing down curtains. It was bedlam – it was hell really. The second choice was to put her on strong anti-psychotic drugs. The third choice was to have her certified and placed in a long-term psychiatric ward. So I said: 'No way are you taking my baby,' and we started her off on the drugs. She'll have to be on them all her life; they may have to be increased or changed if they stop being effective. She's on an even keel now and I'm trying to reduce the dose but the psychosis flares up without warning. If she misses one tablet or brings one back, she's off.

When a child is abused there are psychological effects on other members of the family. It's hard to enjoy sex when it's been so damaging to your child. And I have to live with my guilt: I let her go. You find it so incredible yourself to believe what happened that you can understand other people doubting it. But I've found out since that Helly isn't the first or the only disabled person to suffer sexual abuse. And there's nothing for these young people, at least not in our area. We'd have to come to London to see a therapist who knows anything at all about the needs of disabled young people who have been abused.

Now we've put in for compensation from the Criminal Injuries Board. Helly had a legal aid certificate and her own solicitor. Because we turned down their first offer, on the advice of our doctor, legal aid has been withdrawn and we have to deal with it all ourselves. They wanted more information. We have to prove that it wasn't only stress caused by abuse at the time but also the long-term physical and mental damage. Helly had *petit mal* when she was little – it cleared up as she got bigger but it came back after the abuse. Now she has *grand mal* as well.

Helly was the most special child and that has always remained. Waiting for her to die – and she doesn't, she defies them – that's made her that extra bit special. She had a bad start to her life and it looks as though she's going to have a hard finish to her life. But at least we can say that while she's been with us at home, and we've had her for twenty years, she's had a happy life. That's the main thing for us: keeping Helly happy and out of pain.

Sarah's story

Sarah came 14 months after Helly on 24 January 1979. She was nearly two. We'd seen her photo in the PPIAS newsletter even before we had the photosheet from PFC. There were two Sarahs with Down's Syndrome. We went after the one nobody else wanted.

Sarah had just been moved to short-term foster carers from a Children's Home. This time we both went up to meet her, and to see the cardiologist with her, but then I did the introductions on my own because one of us had to stay home to look after Helly.

When Sarah joined the family everything was in an upheaval. We moved almost as soon as she arrived; we'd been living in a railway house and they were selling off their property. Because of Helly's condition we had a council house within a week.

With Sarah we did know all there was to know about her health from the beginning. At least we thought we did. The specialist said she had a hole in the heart, which is common with Down's Syndrome, but it was nothing to worry about. It was all they could have found out then. As she got bigger, I kept saying there was something wrong with her – she would pass out for no reason. But the doctors were saying I was neurotic because of Helly. We had a medical at school when Sarah was five and I said: 'Unless you refer her to a cardiologist, I'll take her straight to the hospital and wait until she's seen.' In the end they diagnosed Ebstein's Anomaly of the tricuspidipid valve. Sarah is unique: she's the only person with Down's Syndrome who's ever been diagnosed as having it. She has to be careful with physical exercise. She has to have regular check-ups and stress tests. She has to stay on medication for life and because of this medication she has to drink a lot.

Sarah is unique in another way too. As we got used to her ways, we realised that she doesn't show any symptoms when she is ill or in pain. She doesn't notice when she hurts herself and she had pneumonia without us knowing because she didn't even run a temperature. So she has to be watched all the time as well.

To be honest, I didn't attach as quickly to Sarah as I did to Helly. I was frightened to love her in case I found out something devastating about her. But loving her just grew; you couldn't hold back from her. She tries so hard and will go out of her way to help. She was a very rewarding child. She was never jealous of Helly or of Em. She took Helly in her stride and she thought Em was her baby.

I've kept Sarah and Em a bit away from Helly because we always thought she was going to die and we didn't want them to become too attached. Now Sarah and Em are very close but they are also very caring about Helly. They don't understand about Helly's mental illness and they have no idea what abuse is. I try to explain by relating it to her bent back. This is a physical sign they can see and I say: 'Helly's back is making her ill or irritable or whatever.' They can see that Helly's back is different from their own.

After Les died, Sarah started going to a family for respite care. She liked going and Anne, the mother, became a friend to all of us. Sarah is still always happy to go and stay with her. She's very amenable as long as she has a reasonable family routine. Now Anne is Helly's daily part-time carer as well and she comes and lives in to look after all three of them occasionally so that I can get away.

Sarah didn't start off as bright as Em but she made slow steady progress until she was eight years old and caught up – then she reached a plateau before she started going down again. We tried her in a special class in a mainstream school but that didn't work out. She was overwhelmed by the number of children. So we put her back in the special school and she took some time to settle down again. She continued to make slower progress until she was 16. By that time she could put three or four words together to make sentences. Then she went to a smaller unit for eight young people with learning difficulties but her level of intelligence is deteriorating. They suspect that Sarah is carrying the Alzheimer's gene; they don't want to do the tests because it wouldn't help her. She forgets everyday things though she can remember further back. She doesn't manage her own periods like she used to; she can only copywrite her name now when she could do it on her own before. But she's a happy girl. She likes to be out and about, she likes animals and she loves babies. She stands back and watches. The only thing that upsets her is vomiting – she still associates it with her father dying.

Sarah had a test done at 16, because of her heart disease, which is usually done on older people. It showed that her heart was like someone's in their late 40s. So Sarah has three ages: her chronological age, her mental age and her physiological age.

The continuing story

Helly and Sarah are young adults now but they certainly won't be leaving home. I wouldn't want them to live on their own if it meant being looked after by carers. I would never have wanted it and I couldn't think of it after what happened to Helly. I don't know yet about Em. You can't even take Helly out of doors; it triggers her psychosis. If we need a doctor he comes to the house. We've tried to break her in slowly but it hasn't worked.

Social services keep saying to me, 'They have a choice,' but I say to them, 'Yes, they have a choice, but if they don't have the intellect to make a choice, someone has to do it for them, and that's going to be me and not you'. I feel the authorities are a bit in awe of us since the abuse. I've told them exactly what we need and we more or less get it. Both Helly and Sarah have had an assessment under the Community Care Act. We have the Self Operative Care Scheme: social services and health pay me a lump sum every month directly to my bank account. I can use it as I want; I use it mainly to pay Anne to share the care of Helly and to provide respite for all three. I have to keep some back for emergency payments in case Helly has to go to hospital.

Sarah left school at 19 and goes to a college of further education daily but only part-time. Special arrangements are made for her so that she has transport when the others walk or go on the bus. When they go swimming she has a one-to-one attendant. It's called a foundation course for young people with learning disabilities – it's supposed to prepare them for independence. It won't do much that way for Sarah but it means she's mixing with her peers and it reinforces what she has learnt by rote. She can stay there until she is 25 and she enjoys it which is the main factor.

Ivan tries to take Sarah and Em out as much as possible to ordinary things like discos and what have you at the Working Men's Club. They have a thoroughly good time. We used to take all three of them out for Sunday lunch but now we can't go with Helly. She thinks she can see someone who looks like the abuser and she's off. It makes her petrified to go out.

I didn't find it hard to let Helly and Sarah become more separate as they got older. I'm very protective but not possessive of them. Only since the abuse I'm inclined to mistrust more and that makes it harder to let go. I'd be happy if Helly could have more independence in her own home – that would mean having more carers and we haven't been able to get social services to pay for that. Or I would like something that could be guaranteed safe where both Helly and Sarah could get used to more independence so that they would be able to manage better when I've gone. Society wants disabled young people to attain independence but doesn't provide the safe environment they need to be independent. It's very hard for them. They see kissing and such on TV and they don't know what's appropriate. Sarah will touch the boys in college and you have to teach her: 'Yes, that's what teenagers do, but you can't because you don't see where it's leading.' Social services are pushing to give Sarah choice and independence but they don't realise that Sarah will say yes to anything. The principle is alright but the Children Act doesn't deal with individuals.

It's awful to think of what will happen when we've gone – we're all of an age, Ivan, Chris and me. We could all go together. I'd want them to stay in their own home with a carer to look after them.

*   *   *

'What would you do if you had a magic wand?' I asked Pam. 'What would we do?' asked Pam, looking at her daughters. 'We'd like to have my dream come true, wouldn't we girls? Anne and I would like to have a large house and fill it with disabled children for short-term and respite care and run it as I think it should be run – as a family unit. I've tried to get social services interested in my dream but they don't want to know. They'd put in the equipment and send the children but they haven't got a house to give us. It all boils down to finance.'

Ivan came back from work in time to join us for the end of the interview. He and Pam would like to adopt another disabled child together. The agencies they have approached have not altogether welcomed their interest. Pam feels that little has changed since she and Les were first turned down 20 years ago. Then the objections were to the age gap between them, to Les's age and to Pam's history in care. Now that Pam has proved herself as an exceptionally capable carer, the only objection is to her exceptional children.

While Pam talked for most of the day, Helly was at home as usual and Em was home because it was half term. Sarah went to college and came back while we were still talking. The carer, Anne, was around to help out in the morning. In the afternoon the three young people with Down's Syndrome played, drew, did puzzles, looked at books and watched *The Sound of Music* on video. They chose their own video and worked the machine themselves. Sarah and Em looked after Helly when she became restless. Pam stayed in the background, fully aware and in charge of all that was going on. Helly had a cocktail of medication mashed up in fromage frais three times during the day, everyone had lunch including Ivan who came home briefly, coffee was in constant supply and Pam managed to have several cigarettes in the garden room while she went on talking. Smoking is not allowed in the rest of the house. The atmosphere was busy and contented. Photos of Helly and Sarah and Em are proudly displayed all over the sitting room walls. Some of the photos show Les and some show Ivan. I wanted to know whether Pam's daughters were aware of their shared disability. Do they know that they are different, that they have Down's syndrome?

*   *   *

Pam

They wouldn't understand the words "Down's Syndrome" or "disabled". They think of themselves as ordinary young people in an ordinary family and that's what they are.

*   *   *

Pam explained to her daughters that the lady who had brought them to Mummy and Daddy was coming to visit and was writing their story. Later, she asked them whether there was anything they wanted to tell. Sarah and Em said they would like the baby lady to bring a baby for each of them. 'Twins?' suggested Pam. 'No, baby girls like us.'

8 It's got to be what he wants
Pat and Mark

Mark was four when he was referred to PFC for adoption. He lived in a Special Unit for children with severe disabilities. All the very young children in the Unit moved around on "tummy trolleys". This was a flat padded surface on small wheels which the children could steer by lying on their tummies and pushing themselves along with their hands, rather like surfers. Mark had spina bifida: he was unable to walk, had poor control of all the muscles below his waist and had a shunt in his head to drain excess fluid from the brain. He was a beautiful child with big china blue eyes and straight blonde hair. He also had learning difficulties.

Within a few months a family was found for him; Pat and Dave who lived in the West Country with their seven-year-old daughter Haley.

Dave and Pat separated when Mark was 11 and Dave died six years later of a heart attack. Pat met her new partner, Ben, when Mark was 12. He too died suddenly in 1995. Now Pat lives on her own and Mark lives in a Special Unit for wheelchair users. He is 24 years old.

*   *   *

Pat

After Haley was born we were told that we definitely couldn't have any more children. We quickly decided that we would like to adopt but we never thought about a handicapped child until Dave said that's what we wanted; someone he could help. One day I was reading *Woman's Own* and there was an article in it about a little girl from PFC. So we went up to London to their offices, but when we enquired about the little girl we were told that her mother wouldn't sign the papers for her to be adopted. We were told about Mark and we saw his picture. Anyway we decided to go to all their sessions on preparation for adoption and they told us about how to cope with handicapped children and about any child that was going to be adopted. I thought it was really great because we were all in a group so you didn't feel under the spotlight. I still think about the other parents there and wonder how their adoptions went.

We never thought of fostering because neither of us could bear the thought of letting the child go. I can't do it with animals and I certainly couldn't do it with children. When we went for Mark all our friends thought we were mad. Absolutely crazy! They could not understand why, if we'd got one child, we wanted another, especially a handicapped child.

I'll always remember the first day I met Mark. We'd gone up to London to visit the Home and before he'd been told who we were or anything he just introduced himself. He came up the passage on his tummy trolley, full of life and said: 'Hello Mummy and Daddy'. And his friend Martin came up as well and said: 'Don't take him, take me!' And I just said: 'Well, I'm not going to take anybody today!' I also remember being told that Mark might not cry when we left him because he couldn't show his feelings, and I took all that in, but when the time came for us to go it was me that was crying my eyes out!

We went back, of course, and that time it was to meet his key worker and ask her about how to look after him. We went up several times and then we all stayed there for a week in a flat they had on the site where the Home was. We learnt such a lot that week because it was a hands on experience. When we finally went home with him the key worker very kindly came down with us to settle him in and stayed with us for two or three days. She was a big help to us – absolutely great. She used to say: 'I'm not very orthodox, I do things my way.' And they were really good ways – all sorts of little tricks she had. I built up a real trust with her; she was so easy to get on with.

During the introductions we were given an appointment to see Mark's consultant who explained everything about his spina bifida to us, although I must say we didn't take it all in. You get carried away with doing all the things you have to do for him, the joy of having him and you just forget what you've been told. But I'm sure nobody said to us at the beginning what his life expectancy was. It was a social worker we had down here who said to us rather abruptly one day: 'You do know he could die at seven.' That was one of the biggest shocks I've ever had, because nobody had ever told us that. I could have imagined that he could have died at seven because he had so many medical problems. One of them was that his legs and feet were facing the wrong way and he had to have several operations. I've sat for hours in hospitals waiting for him to come round, on my own hour after hour. But I promised Mark that I would never leave him or go away and I've stuck to it, even through the bad times.

Early days

When we first had Mark I completely fell in love with him. He looked just like Haley: same blond hair, same blue eyes, they looked like sister and brother.

I can remember Haley and I taking him for walks in his pushchair and we'd meet friends who used to talk over Mark's head. They'd ask me how he was doing today and I'd say: 'Well, ask him!' They seemed to think that because he couldn't walk his brain didn't work either. In fact, when he first came his speech wasn't very good but he could say a few words. He often didn't understand what we said to him and he used to echo the last word we'd said all the time. He didn't come out very plain but in time he learned. We used to sit down with him for hours talking to him and reading to him. It took him a long time to call me Mum but when he did he used to say: 'Cuddle me Mum.'

(The tears come into Pat's eyes at the memory. She wipes them away and continues.)

So I'd say: 'Alright, a two-minute cuddle,' and he'd say: 'No, a four-minute cuddle,' and I'd say: 'Oh alright then! A four-minute cuddle.'

When he first came he could only eat with a spoon. He was four and a half and I thought I just couldn't allow him to continue like that. We gave him a knife and fork and just insisted that he keep trying. He'd had a lot of things done for him at the Home and he was a bit babyish.

In those early days he screamed a lot and it seemed as if he screamed at anything and everything and we never knew what he was screaming for. For example, every time we gave him a piece of meat or a bit of fish he would have a tantrum. One day, when David and I were talking things over, we realised that he'd probably never seen a whole piece of meat or fish before. So we minced everything up like he had been used to and explained to him that it was exactly the same.

I started to explain everything to him very carefully and if I could show him I'd show him. The first three months were great – he was an angel! But then we actually had a few problems: he found a lot of things frightening because he'd been rather sheltered and we suddenly introduced him to all sorts of new things without realising it. He was terrified of men drilling in the road, for example.

I think he missed the Home – there were so many people in it – and then coming to a two parent one child family in a three-bedroomed house. At first he used to sleep in Haley's room because he hated having a room to himself.

If I just left his side for a minute, even to go to the toilet, he'd say: 'Aren't you coming back?' So I wondered if someone he'd been close to had ever walked out on him. I rang the key worker at the Home and asked her. She told me a member of staff had left and no explanation had been given to him. It made me realise that no matter how young children are, and even if you think they can't understand, it's really important to explain things to them because some of it registers.

Of course that worry of his made things much more difficult every time he had to go into hospital for an operation. From about five he had a series of operations on his foot and he'd always ask if I'd be there when he woke up. It must have been about three years before he lost that insecurity. He wouldn't go out and play with the other kids because he was petrified I wouldn't be there when he came back.

Normally after he'd gone to bed I'd go upstairs to check how he was and usually he'd gone straight to sleep. But sometimes he'd be lying there wide awake and when I asked him why he couldn't sleep he'd say: 'Because I don't want you to go away.' At times in the beginning he was quite obsessed with the idea that we were going to leave him.

Adoption

As he got older, I used to talk to him about his parents. I didn't want him to grow up thinking that they hadn't really loved him so I tried to explain to him the circumstances of why they couldn't keep him. We had all the information in a long letter from PFC. I told him that he had sisters and all about his family, but he never asked about them without me bringing up the subject. Not once.

I always believed that adopted children should be told the truth about their adoption. I think if you tell one lie you have to tell another to cover it up and the lie gets bigger. When it does eventually come out you've made it all much worse. So I told him right from the beginning that he was adopted and that we loved him. I often used to talk to him about it, using the same phrases over and over again so that he would get the idea. I'd say: 'You've got to think yourself really lucky,' and he'd say: 'Why?' And I'd say: 'Because out of all the kids there was, who did I pick? – YOU!' And he'd say: 'Yeah! you didn't want anyone else?' And I'd say: 'No, do you remember Martin (a friend of his from the Children's Home)? He asked us if we would adopt him and we said no, we've chosen you!' Mark used to love that story.

Some adjustments and difficulties

Things happened that Haley didn't understand, for example, why her favourite aunt would give her £5 at Christmas and give Mark £10. As she would say: 'I'm her real niece and Mark isn't.' So I rang her up and asked her not to do it but she did it again. So then I confronted her in front of the children and said: 'You cannot do this, it's not fair. I had it done to me as a kid and it really hurt and there's no way I'm going to let anyone do that to my children. You either take all the money back or let me split it between them.' She was a bit cross about it but I think in her way she understood what I was on about. I told Haley that Auntie didn't love Mark more than her, it was only that she felt sorry for him because he couldn't walk. It was just as if her Aunt was punishing Haley for Mark not walking.

All the same I didn't really have any big problems with Haley when Mark came. She had a few tantrums like any child would and it was usually if she thought Mark had got away with something that she'd been told off for. But I explained to her that I did smack Mark for some things. In fact, one of the very worst things that happened was when a young woman from the hospital school used to come and see me about Mark. She was horrified when I told her I smacked Mark. She told me straight away that I couldn't do it. I said: 'Well look, you either let me bring Mark up my way or you take him.' She thought I was joking but I wasn't. Actually, to tell you the truth, I would never have let them take him but I was so mad that I went upstairs crying, flung some of his clothes into two carrier bags and said to her: 'You take him. If you're not going to let me bring him up the way I want to do it, I don't want to know. He's got to learn right from wrong.' I know they say you shouldn't smack children but sometimes when they're so naughty, and there's no other way to get through to them, it's the best way. I'd never beat a kid, I think that's terrible, but an ordinary smack on the hand which tells them they've stepped out of line and you've got to behave yourself, then yes, a smack is the best thing.

Sometimes Mark used to sit on the floor and just scream for no reason – there must have been a reason but there was nothing I could see that I'd done wrong. I think it was a safety valve; he just had to scream sometimes. But in those days I couldn't cope with it because I didn't understand it. As I've got older I understand it better. All the same, the constant screaming got on my nerves something terrible and I used to take the dog for a walk and go to the top of the hill near us, where it's quite isolated, and scream to myself at the top of my lungs until I felt better. I just had to let it out somewhere.

Mark's disability
When Mark was first with us the staff at the Home told us we must do everything we could to get him to practice walking in his callipers and we did. Every day we would all clap and cheer as he walked the length of the living room which he did occasionally manage. Dave put a lot of time and effort into it and it was him that finally got him to his feet using tripods that the hospital gave us.

Our hospital doctor told us that the more we got him to walk the better would be his chances of not getting kidney trouble. You get that if you sit humped up in a chair all day. But you see at school they didn't persevere, they just said he wouldn't walk and would scream, so they never insisted. They asked us not to send his tripods to school with him anymore.

It was also unfortunate that the school had two physiotherapists and neither of them could see that you had to be a bit tough with Mark. So he never learned to walk. In fact, the physiotherapists now say that if he had exercised more when he was younger, he could be walking more, but it's too late now.

Schools, education and after

When Mark lived at the Home he went to a little playschool on the premises but when he came here nobody would accept him; they had no facilities for disabled children under five. I think he really suffered from not being able to mix with other children and he was left on his own with me. I think he suffered an injustice because of that and his screaming fits were probably caused by frustration.

When he did get to five I found a local primary school for ordinary children; they said they'd be really happy to have Mark. I was so pleased because I felt it was important for him to be with normal children as much as possible. But to my disappointment the local education authority wouldn't allow it. They said it would be too much for the teaching staff to handle him. In the end we had to agree to him going to the hospital-based special school where we thought the standard of education was really poor. We didn't think they pushed the children to do all they were capable of.

There was another problem with the Hospital School as well and that was the Head herself. I found her attitude to Mark very difficult to take; to her he was a sweet natured beautiful boy who could do no wrong. She gushed all over him. That wasn't good for Mark because they didn't insist that he stick at things until he learned them and I felt that it was terribly important that he learn to do as much as possible for himself.

The relationship between us and the school fell to an all time low over some bruising on his face. Mark couldn't tell me what he'd done so the next day I rang the school to find out because by then not only was his face badly bruised but he'd got bleeding from his ear. They just said they didn't know anything about it. A fortnight later when all the bruising had gone, I was summoned to the Hospital School to see the Head, a doctor and nursing sister. They were very hostile and accused us point blank of beating Mark up ourselves. Three hours I was in there! I came out, put Mark in his pushchair and with tears streaming down my face, I pushed him all the way home. I met a friend on the way, a mother of another child at the same school and she couldn't believe what I'd been accused of – she knew I'd never beat Mark and I'd never hit him across the face.

Soon after that I had a local authority social worker start to visit on a regular basis and she said she was just checking up on Mark. A few months later she was actually there when the school bus brought him home and there he was with his face all bruised again. She got me to ring the school straightaway and, when I insisted, they eventually said Mark must have fallen off his callipers and hit his face on the handle of his tripod walking frame. Of course I immediately said: 'Don't you think that's what happened last time you accused me of beating him!' The Head denied it completely and accused me of causing trouble. I told her I had the social worker with me and she could see the state of Mark's face for herself. In fact, the social worker looked into it at the school and they confirmed that he had fallen down that day and hit his head on the tripod. David promptly wrote to the Head of the education department and we got a written apology for the accusation. But of course, although I tried to stay on good terms with them for Mark's sake, I never hit it off with the teaching staff.

I used to get him up extra early in the morning before school to give me time to teach him to dress himself. I had to really insist that he had to do it all himself and that included buckling on his callipers which had heavy leather straps and buckles. They were really bitchy things to get on but I felt he just had to do it. Gradually he learned how to do it all, but some mornings he would simply refuse to do any of it, or get half way and just stop. I felt it was no good if he just relied on me to do it all for him because I wouldn't always be around.

I was always getting told off by the escort who took Mark to school because he wasn't ready. Some mornings they had to wait till he was dressed, but one morning I felt as though I'd had enough and I told him he'd have to go to school exactly as he was – with his underpants and vest on. I put his coat on, put his clothes in a bag and just handed it to him to take to school. I got told off by the Headmistress who said I wasn't allowed to send him like that. So I said: 'Well, either he comes to school like that because he won't get dressed or he won't come to school at all!' If she had been a more understanding person she'd have realised what I was trying to do. If the school had been better at communicating with the parents it would have been a lot easier.

However, when the time came for him to start at Secondary School, I had an interview with the Head who asked me what Mark could do for himself. When I told him that he could dress himself completely and put on those heavy, fiddly callipers and wash himself, he was quite amazed and wondered how on earth he had achieved it. I told him it was sheer perseverance. He said that half the children who came to his school (for children with severe physical disabilities) couldn't do anything for themselves.

I had to apply for Mark to go into residential school when Dave left us. Before that I used to run a market stall on Saturdays but when he left I had to work full time to make ends meet and I knew I couldn't manage Mark as well. The trouble was I never had any respite arrangements, it was hard to find anyone who would take him. No-one came forward to help me and I had him 24 hours a day.

I have met children whose parents were sending them away because they really didn't want them. But Mark didn't ever think that because he knew I loved him. Actually Mark liked being there very much, perhaps he felt it was a bit like going back to the Home because he really liked being with all the other children. He used to come home every week-end so he didn't mind being at school in the week. The education wasn't too bad but he was always about three years behind. They were very good to him and really tried to bring his work on. He can read and write a bit but he's not too good even now.

Life with David

David and Mark didn't get on together really, I think it was a lack of communication. I'm afraid today that I think David's reasons for wanting Mark were all wrong. He was a show piece for him. I know it's a cruel thing to say but Mark made publicity for David. David ran his own taxi firm and there was a lot of local interest in Mark. Dave used to take Mark with him on taxi runs – he would sit in the front seat and he absolutely loved riding around in cars all day. Of course David was very kind to him and did a lot of things for him but Mark brought fame to David and he sort of used him. When we first had Mark the local paper did a big article about him, took his photograph and all that. At PFC they made a film about us and David loved being in the limelight. When all that stopped and nobody made a fuss anymore, he couldn't cope.

We all went through hell when David took up with another woman. I told David that if he saw her again he wasn't coming back in this house

– but he did come in and he started hitting me around and believe it or not Mark got between us in his wheelchair – he ran his wheelchair into David and he yelled: 'You leave my Mum alone!' I think it really frightened David and he left the house.

I never regret adopting Mark although I used to wonder if David did. I used to get the feeling that he was a bit jealous of all the time I had to give to Mark, he did take up such a lot of my time. Sometimes I had to change his bed twice a night because he got frightened about something.

Life without David

When David and I separated, the three of us got very close and I think it was only then that Mark stopped worrying that he wouldn't always be with us. We made a pact between us – me, Haley and Mark – that we would get on for ourselves without David and enjoy our lives together. I said it was all for one and one for all. We'd been through such really terrible times when my marriage to Dave was breaking up, I even got to the point of thinking stupid things like I couldn't carry on. But what kept me going was the thought that I had to be there for my children. I just couldn't bear the thought that they might have to go to a Home.

I was terribly conscious that the children didn't like to be seen at things like Pantomimes without a Dad. I used to feel it too, but very slowly we all felt much better off without him. Whereas when he was around he used to grumble at them so much that they just used to go up to their bedrooms to get out of his way, when there was just the three of us we used to laugh and joke in a much more relaxed way. We'd have pillow fights; Haley would give Mark a piggy back up the stairs. We used to do a lot of cooking together making cakes and biscuits and that sort of thing. We all used to really talk to each other – yes, we all got very close.

I used to take them to a local club on a Saturday night. I'd save the money all week so I could buy them a jacket potato, ice cream and a drink. Mark used to love it! He'd look forward to it so much and he'd keep asking me if we were going. He would chat to everyone and was much more outgoing than when David was around with his constant criticisms. I don't think David meant to be like that, it was as if he liked the idea of adopting Mark but he couldn't cope with the reality of him being there.

When Mark got bigger and heavier and David wasn't there to carry him upstairs all the time, we asked social services to come and fit us with a lift. We had to knock down a bit of the wall and it just dropped straight down from his bedroom to the kitchen. Anyway, soon after it was installed a terrible thing happened. Poor Mark got stuck in the lift between floors and it wouldn't go up or down. Mark started to panic and couldn't understand what I was trying to tell him. So I had Mark screaming in the lift and Haley crying! I told Mark that I could climb down to him from the top and get him out, so I kept saying: 'I'm coming to you Mark!' I climbed down, got hold of him and handed him up to Haley and he was all right. But it took me ages to calm him down and then even longer to make him go in the lift again.

Life with Ben

When I met Ben, Mark got a new lease of life. Mark was still incontinent then, because he wouldn't even try. The way we finally got him to co-operate was to ask him to keep clean for Ben. He and Ben got on ever so well and Ben was lovely with him so he would often do things for Ben which he wouldn't do for me; but that was fine and I was very pleased. After all, he was 12 by then and I worried that he might go on being incontinent for the rest of his life.

It was so different with Ben – he used to play with Mark – there was such a difference in the atmosphere. Ben was strict but helpful. If Mark wanted to know anything he wouldn't ask me, he'd ask Ben. Ben taught him all sorts of things and he really loved Mark. Mark cried something terrible when Ben died two years ago. He was such a lovely man, everyone loved him and there were 150 people at his funeral. He was someone you meet once in a lifetime and I'll never see his like again.

When Ben died, I asked someone from the staff in the place Mark lives now to be with Mark when I rang him up. I couldn't bear the thought of him being totally on his own in the corridor, where the phone was, and hearing such terrible news. He took the news quite calmly when David died, but Ben was everything to him and I know how upset and distressed he was, especially on the day of the funeral.

(Pat's eyes fill with tears again as she tells me how, when Ben died and she was sobbing, Mark came and put his arms around her and said: 'Don't worry mum, I'll look after you.')

It was just after Ben died that Mark asked for the first time how he could get in touch with his mother. It was a real bombshell coming at the time of Ben's death when I was unable to cope with things. All during his childhood I'd told him about his family and he'd never asked anything. I must admit it did hurt a bit but I don't think he did it to hurt me. I think that he was worrying that if he had lost Ben what would happen to him if I die? So he needed to feel there could be somebody else there for him. I told him I'd help him to find her. It's going to take a while, but it's obviously important to him and I will do it. I'm sure he's worried about being alone. That's why I want him and Haley to be close. Even though they fall out over things I'm sure she wouldn't see him in need and not respond. Mark doesn't do it deliberately but he can be a bit thoughtless and selfish and I think he just doesn't understand the effect that he has on people. Haley's actually done a lot for Mark – like when Ben died she took over the responsibility for Mark's finances. Unfortunately you can't get insurance for people like Mark so the only provision for him is what you provide yourself. But that's what I think families are for. You've got to help one another and I don't think it's too much to ask for Haley just to keep an eye on him.

Mark on his own
Mark lives full time in a Unit 40 miles away and he doesn't come home much. When the time came for him to leave school at 16, he was taken to see this Unit and he chose to go there and live because all his friends are there and there is more for them to do. It's purpose built and very comfortable. My only complaint is that I'd like him to come home more often but he always makes an excuse about the cost of the taxi. I miss him terribly and it was particularly bad when Ben died, and then my dad eight months later, and I felt so alone. My dad came to live with us a few years before he died and I had to nurse him and there I was, suddenly with nobody at all.

Apart from the three visits to hospital for the operations on his leg and a gallstones operation, Mark's health has been very good – better than we'd expected. His legs were much improved by the operations – all straightened out – but he has to use the wheelchair all the time. He's proud of the fact that he goes to college now although when he rings me up he always says he finds it very tiring. They don't do academic subjects, it's more independence skills.

I don't think he'll ever get any kind of job and I expect he'll be in the Unit for the rest of his life. He is happy there and says all his friends are there and he doesn't want to leave them. It's a comfortable modern building and there's staff to see that they're all right and plenty of activities and outings. Although he's as independent as possible, there's still a lot of things he can't do for himself and if he's not reminded he'll forget, so he's always going to need guidance. I think that having other disabled young people round him gives him a lot of support and they'll understand when he's feeling down, what he's going through. He's got a girlfriend now and I think he really is very happy. She lives in the same Unit and is in a wheelchair. Before that he had a girlfriend whose parents didn't want to know because Mark's disabled. It was sad but he seems to be over it now.

I think the facilities and everything where he is are lovely and I'm happy with it for him. I'm just finding it hard to accept that he's not going to live at home – but it's not what *I* want, it's got to be what *he* wants.

Mind you, I feel strongly that people with disabilities like Mark need a family. When I was forced to send him to boarding school we inevitably lost some closeness, but he always knew that I was there for him in the background. I might not be the centre of his life anymore but he knows if he's got any problems we are all there for him. Like recently he was mugged after he'd been to the pub one evening and it was me he rang up and asked for help. That's the only sort of thing I can do for him now. I really wish he lived nearer and I wish parents were encouraged more to visit. He seems to be getting over Ben's death a bit now and so he rings up more often. For a long time I couldn't get much out of him and, of course, I was mourning Ben myself.

When Mark was in the Home his keyworker was a big asset in his life. She's the one person he remembers from those days and he still mentions her from time to time. In fact quite recently he asked me if I'd got her 'phone number. I have got it but I'm not sure if she's still on that number. I'll have to ring her for him because he'd get very confused if it wasn't her who answers that 'phone. I'll take him to see her if we find her.

*   *   *

I went to see Mark. It was nearly an hour's drive across country. He has grown into a handsome and charming young man.

He had got out his old photograph album to show me and he still has a set of photographs taken of him for the publicity to find him a family. He has a good memory of most of the events in his life and seems cheerful and settled. 'I've got a good Mum,' he said.

Haley is married now with two very young boys. She sees her mother every day and, until recently, always helped at Pat's market stall on Saturdays.

Pat sold the business a few weeks ago as she could no longer manage. She has a lot of pain in her knees and has to decide whether to wait for a hospital bed on the NHS or pay for an operation privately.

9 Lynne chose us
Mona, Dick and Lynne

Although Lynne is one of three adopted young people with disabilities in this family, she is the only one who is aged over 20, who was placed more than 12 years ago and therefore meets the criteria for inclusion in this book. Vicky and Zoe have become Lynne's sisters and figure in her story as sisters do. Mona and Dick are the adoptive parents and they do most of the talking. Chris is their youngest son by birth; he lives at home and works locally. Because birthdays are not marked by this family, there is a general vagueness about everyone's age. We finally agree that Lynne is 25 and Chris is one year older. Vicky, who came first, will soon be 19 and Zoe, who was adopted last, is 23.

The family and disability
Mona
Of course I knew there were handicapped people but I'd never thought about how it happened. The ones I knew were all in Homes and I didn't think about their parents or anything like that.

I was a one-parent child – my mother and father were divorced. It was a female household with my grandma – no grand-dad, he was killed in the first world war – my mother, my sister and me. We were brought up very strictly as Methodists. No cars, nothing like that. I'm not saying it was bad, it was fine. We lived in the country in Yorkshire and it was a good country life. Occasionally I was allowed to go to a school dance because the other girls in my class all went and that's how I got to know Dick. We kept on meeting at local "dos" but I had to be in at nine, or at ten if it was special. We met when I was 16 and got married when I was 19.

Dick
I was the second of seven children and the oldest boy. I lived with my parents until I left school at 14 and went to work with my grandfather on

a smallholding. I stayed there until we were married. Then we came out of the Dales to a small market town. The farm I worked on after we were married sold up, so we looked for work further afield.

*   *   *

From this point on, Mona and Dick have shared memories; their accounts of the last 43 years mostly intermingle. When they do not, the speaker is identified. Chris listens and makes helpful comments.

*   *   *

Mona and Dick

We moved down South – it wasn't popular mind, our leaving – and we didn't plan to stay for ever. Still, in our minds, Yorkshire is home. We had five children by birth. The three older girls left home when they married, so we were left with Richard and Christopher, who is the youngest by ten years. Then Ryan was born; our daughter Jane's first child. We'd never thought about disability until Ryan was born – never. He was born on Christmas Day. He was very small and they put him in special care. He wasn't feeding or breathing very well. When we saw him first, I went to Jane and said: 'Poor little thing, he looks like a mongol.' But of course I didn't mean it like that. It didn't occur to us that anything was wrong with him. It was only that he was little and looked odd. The second day at the hospital, they asked us to wait in the office. We thought the baby had died. Then the sister came in and told us he was Down's Syndrome. That was the most traumatic thing. I think I said: 'Oh God, It would have been better if he'd died.' Now I can't believe I said it. We didn't know anybody who'd had children like that.

When they told Jane she locked herself in the toilet and thought if she could just leave him she would. If she'd been able to get out of that hospital, there would have been no way she would ever have come back. But she had to stay – she had no clothes and no transport – and so she started thinking about the baby, about how he was feeling and what he needed. We used to stay awake at night thinking about the terrible thing that had happened to us all. They give counselling to the parents when they've had a disabled child but there was nothing for the grandparents and it strikes them just as hard.

Jane's mother-in-law wouldn't look at the baby, wouldn't touch him – she still won't have much to do with him now. So we made a conscious decision to give as much support as we could. It's been ongoing ever since. He was a cute baby once he got off his drips and things. It took a while but, when we got over the shock and lost our nervousness, we loved him.

*   *   *

Mona was then working part-time for a taxi service; Christopher had only recently started school and she could fit her hours in with his school days and holidays. But she felt she could not justify being at home so much without taking on further commitments.

*   *   *

Mona and Dick
We definitely didn't want to have any more children of our own. So we began to think about fostering another baby like Ryan. Vicky was born six months after Ryan. The local authority social worker who was doing the assessment put a tag on her for us before we were even approved. We had her when she was nine weeks old. We didn't think of any other disability except Down's Syndrome. At that point we were taken over by Ryan, not by disability as such. When we had Vicky, they said: 'Don't get too attached to her,' because we were fostering, but that was impossible. Then we adopted Lynne, a 12-year-old with Down's Syndrome, who had been brought up in an institution. In the end we found Down's Syndrome so easy that we thought we'd take on a challenge: Zoe. There's no name for her disability; she's an adult now and looks like a child of six and has the mental age of a baby.

The family and religion
When we came to live down South on the farm, there wasn't a Methodist Church nearby, so we used to go to the Congregational. After Ryan was born we went to our church and the deacon said: 'Oh dear, how sad.' We were most disgruntled. It wasn't much help for the church to tell us how

we were feeling. We wanted to understand more about it.

*   *   *

Then Mona met a woman she had worked with who was a Jehovah's Witness. Mona told her about Ryan and the woman invited her to her house to look at an article in a magazine about Down's Syndrome.

*   *   *

Mona and Dick

She gave us the magazine and it had a story about two Witnesses who had a baby with Down's Syndrome and how it had affected their lives. We also used to go to a garden centre to buy our fruit and vegetables. We knew the owners were Witnesses and we asked them if they had any more magazines. They gave us some but they had nothing about Down's Syndrome in them. Next thing was they came to our house and gave us a free Bible study. We discovered why there is imperfection and what the real future holds for all of us – because we are all imperfect. That was how we became Witnesses. It gave us the understanding so that we could adopt children with disabilities. Jehovah will intervene within our present life span so we're not worried about what will happen to the children in the future. We might go out today and get killed like anybody else, but because of our beliefs and their upbringing it would go well with them when Armageddon (Judgement Day) comes, even though they are not able to be fully aware of God's requirements. They would be counted as children because of their disabilities, they would be like the original Israelites – God's chosen people – they would be classed as spiritual Israelites.

Chris

If we were left without Mum and Dad I would still be a Jehovah's Witness caring for Lynne and Vicky and responsible for Zoe, although I couldn't look after her. I was brought up as a Witness from the age of eight.

It wasn't a family tradition, but then, no-one is a Witness traditionally because at some time each person has to make up their own mind. For me it was rather late – I was a complacent sort of fellow traveller and didn't make my decision until I was in my early 20s. I would hate to think of the sort of person I would be now if I weren't a Witness. I'd probably not even have stopped at home without it and I wouldn't have had the same relationship with my three younger sisters.

*   *   *

Both of Mona and Dick's sons have become Jehovah's Witnesses. Their three older daughters have not. They describe their lives as governed by the principle of divine love, named Agape by the ancient Greeks, which includes love of the unknown and of the enemy but need not include fondness or affection. They enjoy a comfortable life style. They are an open, relaxed family with many friends; they are rigid only in the sense that the Bible says: 'Narrow is the gate leading to life.'

*   *   *

The family and adoption
Mona and Dick
Because we fell in love with Vicky we decided to have another. We wanted to make it permanent so we tried to adopt. We applied to lots of agencies but when they found out we were Jehovah's Witnesses they weren't interested. If we were upfront, it was a 'no, no' straight away, and if we kept it back until they got to know us, it didn't work either. All they talked of was our views of medical treatments, they didn't care to hear about anything else. They seem to believe we refuse medical attention altogether. They're blinded about our faith. One social worker came to the house and when we said we were Witnesses, she threw her pencil down on the table and that was the end of that.

Then one day, when we took Vicky to the occupational therapist, we met a woman who had a baby with spina bifida. She told us about adopting her through PFC. She said they weren't prejudiced and they judged you on your merits as parents. She gave us the 'phone number and that was the start of it. We saw Lynne's photosheet and we went ahead. We didn't have much choice really, Lynne chose us the first time we met her. When we went to the Home to see her, she didn't know who we were but she came up to us and said: 'Hello, Lynne's Mummy! Hello, Lynne's Daddy!' which surprised everybody because she wouldn't talk about families. I can see her now, walking across the room, all bent and curled up. She still does that when she's excited.

Lynne had lived in a Home for disabled children all her life. She was 12 and she wasn't used to families. She didn't talk much and she was hard to understand. If there were two syllables in a word, she'd only say the last one. The staff didn't want her to go, they were used to her. Two of them kept in touch for a while but one went abroad and we lost contact with the other one when she changed jobs. Lynne doesn't ask after them but she still recognises them in old photos. We never met Lynne's parents. They sent a message to us through PFC after we adopted her to thank us. We've heard nothing since. Lynne remembers her first family name but she never knew her parents. They told her brother and sister and the rest of their family that the baby had died. Lynne has no understanding of birth families or adoption. Her life was the Children's Home and then us. If her birth parents wanted to see how she'd developed, we wouldn't mind. It would be for them to see what they'd missed but they wouldn't get her back – no way, she's ours.

Chris
I must admit I have an abysmal memory – part and parcel of my dyslexia. I do remember I was besotted with Vicky and I was looking forward to Lynne but I had no real understanding of how adoption would affect us. It was something novel and exciting to look forward to.

Lynne in the family
Lynne became part of our life quite quickly. You get used to things – except for the wind-ups. She found out that I hate it when she calls me 'boy' in a certain way – she's laughing and I'm losing my cool. The worst thing is that Dad does it as well, to tease – I think it's sad he has to do that.

Mona: Still, she loves Chris a lot.

Chris: Yes she does and I love her – my reaction to "boy" is completely illogical.

Mona: I say to Chris, 'I know what her excuse is, but what's yours?'

Chris: And what's yours, Dad?

Mona and Dick

Lynne would always have a go. She was very outgoing. She'd only been with us a few weeks when she went up on stage to sing in the pantomime. She became family orientated and she took to us – to *all* of us. She immediately adored Vicky, who was only two, but we had to watch her. She'd take off all her clothes and wash her and change her nappy all the time. She loved the farm and the family just went on as before.

Lynne fits in. They say children with Down's Syndrome need routine – but living with us they don't have it. Lynne has never been confused by a lack of routine. She goes along with everything; she sees life as an adventure. She will rule you if you don't watch out, she'll take you over, demand your attention all the time. On the other hand, once she knows she can't do it, she'll fit in without any trouble. If we go for a walk she'll come with us. If we go to a restaurant she'll come; she's always come on holidays with us – she fits in. Once we were at a camp site and found a river and we said we'd go back to the caravan to get our bathing things. Lynne was off like a streak; we'd never seen her move as fast and she was back without a stitch on, waving her swimsuit above her head. It was embarrassing at the time because she was a developing teenager, but her face was beaming, it was beautiful. Yet she's afraid of water; we've never been able to teach her to swim or to go in above her knees. We've gone back to the same site every year and Lynne remembers each caravan we've stayed in.

Lynne used to hoard things and still does. If you buy her new clothes, she puts them away and that's the last you see of them. In the early days she was taking things that didn't belong to her. She grew out of it as she settled, but it did worry us because none of our other children had done it. And we didn't like to investigate too much because we wanted to respect her privacy. She kept everything precious in her school bag then. Now it's in her green plastic box. She takes it up to her room at night and brings it down again in the morning. It's her stuff – we don't go in it. She has phases of what she likes. When she came it was a toy telephone.

She'd take it everywhere and spend hours pretending to talk and listen or go upstairs with it to do "office work". Lynne couldn't ask for anything in the beginning; she wanted us to make choices for her. She had to learn to ask for things. Now she comes with her purse open when she needs money.

Lynne is strict about religion. She knows that we don't celebrate festivals or birthdays and she doesn't like to see people smoking. If she sees them she says in a loud voice: 'Look, dirty!' It's good because she can get away with it. She goes 'No' and puts up her hand if anyone tries to say 'Happy Birthday' or 'Happy Christmas' to her. She tries to explain but of course she can't. She just says 'No' and puts her hand up.

Once she was in the family, Lynne learned to talk and walk better. Now she doesn't walk as well as she did but neither do we any more. She's really healthy apart from normal colds. She has acne on her face and the only thing that keeps it at bay is antibiotics; it's a choice between spots and antibiotics. We prefer the spots.

Mona

Lynne is "mummy's girl". If I've got a cough she's got a cough, if I've got a pain she's got a pain. In the evening we sit on that settee together and she massages my feet. I think Dick is sometimes mean with her. He talks to her about things she's done wrong in a way that expects her to have more understanding than she has. What hurts me about it is that when he criticises her she mutters and gets upset.

Dick and Chris

She's a great mutterer!

Mona and Dick

We've accepted Lynne into the family and we wouldn't be without her but she hasn't affected our way of life. We had our first baby a year after we were married and that set the pattern of our life and it's remained like that ever since. We'd be lost without any one of them.

Lynne outside the family

Lynne used to go to people indiscriminately, so it's important she's never in a situation where anyone can abuse her. One of our main worries has been over respite care. When we saw a male carer hugging and kissing her, we stopped her going. There was probably nothing wrong and you feel bad that you think things like that. You feel you're the one with a dirty mind, but you'd never forgive yourself if you let it happen. It's hard because she likes to be loved. Sexuality does not seem to be a problem in her life. Her affection is child-like. She has developed normally physically but she's besotted by wedding dresses not by boys. A Brother in our Congregation thought Lynne was in love with him and didn't know how to cope with it. When he got married, Lynne was equally in love with his wife. Now they've got a baby and that's wonderful. It's just that she loves people.

The school was alright. There were battles about religion and on the whole they didn't do much for her. She stayed till she was 19. They said she couldn't have any further education because it wouldn't benefit her. Lynne is willing but she lacks the ability, whereas Vicky could get going if she wanted to but won't. They're so different, the two of them, although they both have Down's Syndrome.

At the first Day Centre Lynne went to, they trained them to wash their own hair and go shopping and make their own dinner. They'd have a meeting in the morning to discuss what they were going to do and how they would spend their money. And there was a café run by the disabled people. Lynne worked there three times a week and liked it. When we moved they said she couldn't stay on. She needs something like that. It would help her; she would enjoy it.

When we moved here, Lynne went to a Day Centre where they left them to wander off across the main road. Whenever we visited they didn't know where she was. We had to take her away. Now she's at a Day Centre two days a week. It's a good one but it's mostly pottery and drama and music. They do organise her to make cups of tea for the other clients which she likes. She gets up early on the mornings she goes because she's keen, but it can take her an hour from getting up to getting herself downstairs.

Just near us there's a McIntyre Foundation House – a Residential

Home for disabled people. They have a bakery and a garden centre and a café. We asked about Lynne going there – just for the training, not to live – but they put us off and said there wasn't any funding. It's always funding. The social workers come and ask if they can help you and then when you say what you want, they haven't got the funding. We'd like her to go to the Day Centre more often, but again it's lack of funding.

We did hope Lynne would be capable of some kind of employment; that she could go to work like other people. It's natural to have high hopes for your child, but if you adopt children with disabilities you've gone into it with your eyes open, you know what you've taken on and you're not disappointed. That doesn't mean you don't want the best for them, but you're more or less satisfied with what you get.

Because Lynne has less day care than the other two, she gets more family treats and outings. She's good company. We like to do things with her. She loves shopping and she'll always come home with a handful of leaflets from the supermarket; she'll study them and then put them in her green box. We'll go out to lunch and it won't make any difference to her whether it's the caff at Tesco's or a good restaurant. She enjoys one just as much as the other. That's what is so nice about people with Down's Syndrome: they don't mind if you're beautiful or ugly, rich or poor.

We go on holiday, we go abroad, we go camping, we go to our caravan, we go out and about together like a normal family. But that's not how other people always view us. We've often caused a bit of a stir. We were in Majorca and an older lady became friends with us and she told us some of the comments guests in the hotel were making: 'Was it because Dick was so old (he is nine years older than Mona) or because of our sexual activities?' We didn't like to ask her what they meant! We disclosed to her that the girls were adopted but she promised not to tell.

Lynne will always need supervision for day-to-day living and personal care. You have to remind yourself she's an adult. But to be honest, we think of her as neither a child nor an adult, she's just Lynne. We don't ever see her leaving home. We're a bit different from other families in that way. Jehovah's Witnesses don't expect their children to leave home unless they get married or go abroad as missionaries. Chistopher is still at home and anyway, Lynne would never manage on her own.

137

The family and change

When Lynne was 19, the adoption allowance stopped. We were the first people in the county to have it. Then she had the disability allowance and the lower motability rate. She also gets income support now, but we didn't find out she qualified until she was 23. Altogether it comes to less than the adoption allowance but we manage. It's not hard when you live as a family – it all gets pooled together. We've never in our life had any disputes or big worries about money. Sometimes it meant doing a lot of overtime to make ends meet but we always got by.

Dick

I took early retirement at 63. I was off sick with Menier's a lot. When I was working it wasn't fair on me or on the people I was working for. Then we had more time for the children and Mona said: 'If you're retired we'll have another one.'

So we decided to have Zoe. We had to move from the farm into a brand new council house in the town. Then we needed more space and we exchanged for this house in a new development. It's a project for disabled and able people to live in the community together. Only the services aren't as good as they were in the previous place. The moves didn't upset Lynne, she thought they were good fun. When we go back and see the other house, she says: 'Oh, the old house, poor thing.'

When we had Zoe, Lynne was quite taken up with her. She could treat her like a baby. She still enjoys mothering or smothering her. She feeds her and she shares a room with her. When Zoe goes to respite on a Friday night, Lynne will say: 'Zoe has run away.' She likes a joke.

Lynne didn't notice much when Richard left home to get married because he was always out and now he still visits a lot. He has had three children over the last three years and Lynne loves to go and help. She goes for weekends. Once when she went, she marched into the kitchen and helped herself to a cup of brandy. She probably thought it was beer – the girls like a glass of beer or shandy.

*   *   *

At this point Lynne, who had been sitting calmly and drawing in the adjoining room, taking things in and out of her green box and watching us, grinned broadly and said loudly: 'Beer!'

*　　　　*　　　　*

Mona

When you start off you're fit, but as you get older you get all kinds of aches and pains. I've got arthritis in my shoulder and my knees. I kept having to go to the GP with little things. He asked if I was depressed. I said no. I thought people who are depressed have bad lives and bad things happening to them. What have I got to be depressed about? Then two years ago I got really low and the doctor said: 'No wonder, with what you've got to do.' He persuaded me to try anti-depressants. I was on them for over a year. It changed my life; now it really is just aches and pains. Lynne is a great help to me, I must admit, and a joy to have. She will wash up and wipe the kitchen tops and sweep the floor. We have a cleaner now – paid for by the Disabled Living Foundation – and Lynette, that's her name, will work along with Lynne; she encourages her. And Lynne really likes cooking. We buy her cookery books and she'll sit and look at them for hours; we get her packets of cake mix so she can bake. I look after Lynne and also Vicky mostly, but Dick copes much better than me with Zoe.

Mona and Dick

Last year Ryan was very sick. He was in hospital for seven months. He was paralysed; we thought we were going to lose him before he recovered. Lynne was upset when we went to see him. She couldn't understand what was wrong but she was upset. She would kiss him and rub his forehead and show her concern. She gives lots of affection, she'd overwhelm you with affection if you let her. With Vicky it's on her terms, but with Lynne it's no holds barred. She's easy to love in return. When any of us have been away she will say: 'I've missed you.' It's hard to imagine life without her and the others. It's all led on – like having one long family. It's only in the last couple of years that the thought of having another one has gone out of our minds.

Really and truly we need someone to help us sort out the needs of all three girls now they're adults. If it hadn't been for PFC we wouldn't have got half of what we did get for them when they were younger. Now we don't know what they're entitled to. We haven't even had a proper assessment for them. We've only just found out that they have a right to have their needs assessed. We're hoping we might have a change for the better with the new unitary boundaries. Lynne might have an opportunity for work yet. Even if she could go part time, or on a job share, something like that. We do need advice; we have support from the Brothers and Sisters of our Congregation, but the day-to-day responsibility is ours.

*   *   *

Mona and Dick asked Lynne if there was anything at all she wanted to say. Lynne couldn't think of anything but she smiled and seemed pleased to be asked. She has no perception of her special needs. She does not find it hard to amuse herself and she is happy if she can help. She won't watch TV unless it is cookery programmes and there are only two videos she likes: *Mary Poppins* and *Beauty and the Beast.*

*   *   *

Chris

All things being considered, being equal, if my parents had ten more years of youth on their side, there'd be no problem at all. There's very little problem now, but all the physical care gets a bit much for them sometimes. That's where I feel I can come in and be useful. But I don't think any of us would have it any different. It's just what we are.

10 There's more to it than you think
Pip and Martin

'How d'you fancy a lad of 16 who might not live very long?' Pip asked her husband as she came home in her car and he was just leaving in his.

'Oh lord, when is he coming?' was all Mike had time for before he drove off.

'We did talk about it in more depth,' Pip insists, 'before we went any further.'

Pip

We first saw a description of Martin in the PPIAS newsletter and when we followed it up we got more information from PFC. We knew that he was living in a Children's Home, that he had been in a boarding school and that his parents had not felt able to take him back to Nigeria with them four years earlier. He was 12 then; he had just been diagnosed as having a serious kidney disease due to Alports Syndrome. His parents feared he would not be able to have the necessary treatment in Nigeria. We were also told that Martin suffered badly from asthma and that his hearing and eyesight would be affected. The prognosis was poor and he needed a family to see him through.

We were prepared to consider whether we could look after him for a few years, but we were not ready to make a commitment to have another son.

Martin

I really wanted to have a family again. I hated the idea of finishing up on my own. In the Home they were always saying, 'You can't stay here for ever.'

I'd always lived in a group – first in boarding school and then in the Children's Home – and I wanted a big family of my own.

Pip

We always used to say: 'If we abandon Martin, it would have to be on Victoria Station because he feels happiest in crowds.'

*   *   *

Pip and Martin were not interviewed together; they each said what they had to say independently. It is a measure of their close, affectionate and considerate relationship that they often seem to be responding to each other's comments.

*   *   *

Martin

They came to see me in the Home and they said they'd like to foster me and I said that was OK and 'When are you expecting me?' And they said: 'Whenever you're ready.' And I said: 'Next week.' I fell in love with the whole family straight away. Paul was only little and he said: 'Why can't he come now?' I knew I'd blend in. I go out of my way to blend in.

Pip

In our minds we – all the family – went to see this boy just to find out if we could get on but we didn't anticipate his need. He came out to us and said to all the other children and staff gathered around: 'Look, this is my new Mum and Dad. I'm going to make you a cup of tea so that when I come and live with you, you'll know I can do it.' When we got back to the car, Mike and I couldn't speak for five minutes, and that was very unusual for us. Martin moved in two weeks later. I don't think it could have been managed any other way. Perhaps no-one knew how much hope Martin had pinned on us.

*   *   *

By the time Martin came, Pip and Mike already had five children aged between three and 15. They had also begun to foster when their first child was two and have kept count of 54 foster children, including some with disabilities. In addition, Pip was a registered childminder.

*   *   *

Pip

I was always crazy about children. There was never any doubt about what I would do. I was going to be a nursery nurse, get married and have lots of children. We both wanted a large family but it was Mike's idea to adopt. We'd given birth to two and there were so many children in the world already who needed families.

We found it was quicker, in the 1970s, to adopt a child from a minority ethnic group and that just seemed perfectly alright. So we adopted three infants in a row. I don't feel any strangeness about it. I am not a wildly possessive parent, so I would never have tried to pass adopted children off as born to me. We've always talked together of their origins. When we lived briefly in a very white area, the children had to deal with some racism at school. We never went in battling about it but we helped them to deal with it as well as we could. I'm sure I can't manage it as well as a black mother would because I don't know how it feels – I can only feel it for them. Martin is Nigerian from the Yoruba tribe. He has a kidney disease. He was 16 when he came to us and now he's 30. He is just Martin; he is who he is. But I think he was glad to join a family with other black brothers and sisters.

Martin

I asked for a white family and it's never bothered me being black with white parents. I felt comfortable with white people. After my birth parents went back to Nigeria, I used to go for holidays to a white friend's home – until his Mum and Dad split up. I don't think I could cope if the world was suddenly divided with white people having to go one way and black people the other. Now I've got a lot of black friends but also white friends and I love having black and white brothers and sisters.

Pip

We were as green as grass, we hadn't got a clue about kidney disease. We were invited to St. Thomas's Hospital to learn and we were introduced to a model patient on dialysis. We thought: 'Oh yes, you go on the machine and then you go home and do the decorating.' Every hospital has a model patient and this one was theirs. We didn't see the others who were ill. It was all unreal to us anyway. Martin wasn't even on dialysis yet. It wouldn't have mattered what they'd told us, we couldn't have take it in.

Martin

I didn't know there was anything really wrong with me. I used to go for regular check ups but I thought it was for asthma because I'd nearly snuffed it when I was twelve. I had a bad attack just when my parents were going back to Nigeria so they had to leave me in hospital. My father came back for me four weeks later but I had another attack and then they left me for good. They had all my things packed and everything. No-one explained about my kidneys until I came to live with Mum and Dad.

Pip

Shortly after Martin came to us, it was clear that he was more ill than we thought. In spite of drugs, diets and fluid restrictions, his health was deteriorating. He felt sick most of the time, he lost weight, he became anaemic and breathless and suffered from an intolerable skin irritation. It was decided that he should dialyse as soon as possible. It took a very long time and many consultations and admissions to hospital before dialysis could be established.

And in the meantime, Martin's condition worsened. Even when we settled down to dialysis three times a week, it meant leaving the house at 6.30 am and not getting back until six o'clock in the evening. And it always made him feel worse straight afterwards. It was like going into hospital for an operation and ending up feeling worse than when you went in.

After six months of hospital dialysis, the health authorities installed a machine at home and taught me how to use it. But the emotional side of dialysis is as hard as the physical one, especially for teenagers. The fact that you've got to do this every other day or whatever, no matter what else is going on or you may want to do. And he had to be on the machine for six or seven hours and sometimes it would take three hours before he could get on because it wasn't always straightforward. And you have to monitor all the time for fluid balance.

He could pass out or vomit and the machine would have to be adjusted. He's always hated dialysis and it wasn't easy to make him do it at home. There were lots of arguments. Then there were all the diet restrictions – he came with diet requirements as long as your arm.

Martin

At meal times every plate used to have more on it than mine, I didn't like that. And at first I couldn't believe I was here for good. I used to ask Mum: 'When will I have to go?' and she'd say: 'You can stay as long as you like, for the rest of your life if you want.'

Pip

In the beginning, Martin had no awareness of how things worked in a family. It took ages to get him to look after his things and value them as his own. He only came with a few clothes and one model electric set. He didn't know about not walking on flower beds in the garden or about leaving enough fruit in the bowl for other people. On the other hand, we didn't know about bringing up boys of that age because Martin was now the oldest. And he was our first long-term institutionalised child. We realised we'd have to help him to alter his behaviour. We had rows like everyone else, but we weren't secure enough to know if we'd get over them.

Martin

I remember the worst row about three months after I came. Because I'd ruined some new trousers. I kept shouting: 'I hate you, I hate you!' and Mum started crying because I was saying it and that was a shock to me. But my Dad came in and calmed me down and I apologised and it was alright from then on. I'm the peacekeeper in the family now.

Pip

The disability was an aid to bonding. It's difficult to know what comes first: you have to like someone a lot to give intimate care and giving it makes you feel close to that person. We took on a huge responsibility to look after Martin and really we weren't expecting to love him or for him to love us. But we did, we got to love him very quickly and just as much as our other children. Within weeks he was using our name. We wanted to adopt him and he wanted us to but we were so wrapped up in keeping him alive, that by the time we got around to it, it was too late to get an

Adoption Order through before his 18th birthday. So we changed his name by deed poll instead but he became one of our children in every other way and he is included in our wills.

Martin: The best thing I remember in that first year was the holiday in Spain.

Pip: When we went to Spain, Martin grumbled every day about how hot it was!

Martin: It was hot, but I'd never been away before.

Pip

Before Martin was 18 he got his first kidney transplant. We were overjoyed when the phone call came. We thought all his troubles would be solved. We had met transplant patients whose lives were transformed – they left hospital after 10 days and never looked back. Martin was in hospital for 11 weeks. The transplant never took off. He had rejection and one problem after another. Even when he was out of hospital we had to take him back daily for the first month, then on alternate days. When we got down to twice weekly it was wonderful. This went on for a year and a half but then it all went out of the window and he had to go back on dialysis. His doctors tried a new kind of dialysis this time. Four times a day, Martin had to pour dialysate from a bag into his stomach through a tube, leave it there for a while and then drain it out into another bag. For some people this works very well, but not for Martin! He had several episodes of peritonitis (infection of the stomach lining) and was only saved each time by antibiotics. Then the treatment gradually crept up from four to seven bag changes a day. At the end there were only two hours between sessions; everything had to be kept sterile and the bag with the dialysate had to be held up above Martin. All the children became inventive and ingenious whenever family outings and celebrations had to be interrupted for this routine. But Martin got sick and very weak, he needed blood transfusions, his blood pressure was unstable and they had to give up and put him back on the hospital machine.

Caring for Martin became a full-time occupation for me. It had an enormous effect on the other children. We thought taking on Martin would be like dropping a pebble into the family stream but it was like chucking in a rock. The shock waves were never ending. I was always there before – it was a terrible shock for them not to have me around. The worry of all those hours spent away from my other children haunts me still. Every time we went to the hospital I had to get a childminder for the youngest or drag him with us the whole day.

Our eldest daughter, who is a year younger than Martin but was much more mature, had to take on household responsibilities. Somehow we had expected that Martin would slot in but he usurped their positions. Luckily, he was such a lovely person! He's always been open and friendly. He forgives absolutely everybody. If I suddenly grew two heads, he'd be the only one who'd walk with me and not ask me to put a paper bag over one of them. He's so understanding of people's fallibilities. Yet he can also be maddening when he is in one of his vague moods. You could spend three hours sorting out what you think the problem is, and then another three sorting out what it really is.

It's just what we call 'Martin with knobs on'.

*   *   *

During these early years with Martin, Pip and Mike stopped fostering. Pip felt she needed to do something outside the home and took on part-time work with social services. She worked in the community helping older people to remain in their own homes, and later she assisted in special schools. All this was fitted in around the family, in spite of a seven year history of arthritis and trouble with disks in her back. Pip still works with older people and jokes that she has merely exchanged pushchairs for wheelchairs. Pip's self-demanding level of achievement was more than matched by Mike.

*   *   *

Pip

We had a stressful period with a move to a place we didn't settle in; it was a predominantly white area which was difficult with our multiracial family. Then we moved again to a town with a better cultural mix. In 1986, when Martin was 20 and comparatively well, Mike and I separated and then divorced. This wasn't the way we'd expected things to go and none of us were prepared for the upheaval. Worse still, it had happened to Martin before in a foster home. We had told him it wouldn't happen again but it did.

Martin
I've got a block about it. I can't remember it, but I know I wasn't happy.

Pip
We moved again to a smaller house in the same area. Martin's education has been more disrupted by his disability than by our moves. He had left school before he came to us. Since then he's done a catering training course. He has to keep warm and working in a kitchen suits him.

Martin
I tried a lot of jobs, but I always got ill and couldn't keep it up. The hospital takes up my time.

Pip
Martin left home when he was 22. He needed and wanted to have some independence. He was still on the local authority books because when my marriage collapsed, PFC had helped to get us an adult foster care allowance from Martin's old social services department. The local authority social workers we had were always very good. They found Martin his first flat in London. But he couldn't cope with the distance from home; not only because of his disability, but he couldn't organise practical things like food, money and bills. So, with medical backing, he got a transfer back to our town.

Martin
I was scared to begin with, but I'm glad I made the effort. When I was in London, I was too far away, but I reckon I could cope better now.

Pip
Martin has been more difficult to separate from than the others. He has a hotline to home. We're on the 'phone to each other every day. When

he's having a bad spell it could be three times a day or more. Sometimes, depending on how he was, I'd be running two households. Although he became independent, he couldn't be independent all the time.

When he was 23, Martin was offered a second transplant. That worked brilliantly – for three years it was really good. He held down a job in a kitchen and his self-esteem went up a hundred notches. Then gradually the tissue rejection started again and at the end of five years he was back on dialysis.

Martin

I wanted to keep my job in the kitchen but I was made redundant just before my two years were up. Which meant they didn't have to pay me anything. There was racism at work: some of them made racist jokes and the Head Chef didn't stop them, he made racist jokes himself. He got on at me in an unfair way – perhaps it was him that got me made redundant. But I couldn't have kept on anyway, because I had to go back on dialysis.

Pip

Now that Martin has moved out of the home, I feel that he shouldn't have to come back here for dialysis although the hospital asked me to do it. I didn't want to create that kind of dependence again. I didn't feel I could give my whole life up to it as I did when he was 17. Then Martin tried to do it in his own flat and it was alright for about nine weeks. But I'd be worried and he hated doing it. Half the time I'd have to make mercy dashes across the town because he wasn't really well enough to do it on his own. It became too dangerous for him and since then he's gone to St. Thomas's three times a week.

Pip

(Martin has lost touch with his birth family.)

His father wrote for some time. Then it became awkward because they turned into begging letters – wanting us to send money and to put them up if they came. There was a man Martin called 'uncle' though he wasn't. He came over about five times but he tried to make demands on Martin when he was too ill to cope with it. In the end it was left that Martin would write. While he was living at home I did encourage him to write letters and he did. But he's not a good correspondent and he's let it lapse.

Martin

I've got some old photos of each of my parents and of my brother and sister. My Mum has a letter with all the stuff about them; we've read it together and she's keeping it for me. As I've got older I feel more bitter. It's a bit like they've died. I've never lived with them and they're not my real parents.

Pip

Two years ago, Martin got engaged to a lovely girl and she semi moved in with him. But the transplant was failing and she couldn't take it. She said: 'I can't stay and I don't want to leave.' I felt so sorry for them both. Martin loves children. He's a favourite uncle and godfather to one of his nieces. The break up confirmed his worst fears that no-one can cope with his medical condition. He does do a lot for himself now and I've pushed him into things to increase his independence. He goes up to St. Thomas's on his own three times a week. If he's too ill to manage, they'll send an ambulance or a taxi for him.

Only sometimes it isn't fair to the driver if he's going to vomit in the taxi – then I take him if I can. Martin still turns to me automatically.

Martin

I can talk to my Mum about everything. I find it a bit harder to open up my feelings to a man. Dad was always busy when he was at home and now when I talk to him on the 'phone, I don't tell him everything.

(Both Pip and Mike have remarried; Mike now lives in America.)

Pip

In spite of the separation and the distance, he (Mike) is still the children's father. He is such a strong personality, that they've never needed or wanted another, but they have grown to appreciate their stepfather who is very supportive. I would like it if the hospital were more supportive. Since the merger of St. Thomas's with Guys Hospital there's been nothing but doom and gloom – less staff and no doctor on the renal unit except for one day a week at the clinic.

Stuff is forever getting lost between the two hospitals. And I've been disappointed in the support for carers available from the Kidney Patients Association in the hospital. Our GP is very good. He always comes out when I call him but he's not really clued up about kidney disease. GPs are not supposed to be specialists. He will examine Martin and then say to me: 'Well, what do you think? You're the expert.'

All young people need huge amounts of support and someone like Martin will always need even more. He has great anxieties which the rest of us don't have to deal with. He would not have been able to get the support if he had remained in the Children's Home and certainly not as a care leaver. Even now that he is independent, he has to rely on some financial support from us. He would prefer to get by without it but his heating alone is £20 a week in the winter, which his benefits don't really cover.

Martin

If they hadn't taken me on, I wouldn't be alive today.

Pip

It's just a question of going on fighting and it's remarkable that he does. I don't think he would have been able to do that without us. There isn't a good way out but everyone lives until they die and he has no intention of giving up yet. I shall be devastated if anything happens to him. No matter what you know, you're never prepared for it. I know he pushes himself now for me.

Martin

She wouldn't let me give up if I wanted to.

Pip

He still makes a great fuss about the dialysis. I tell him: 'You dialyse to live, not live to dialyse.' He's never been able to separate the two.

Martin

I have a good social life. I have a lot of good friends – I've kept in touch with a couple from the Children's Home. We went up to London to a big Afro-Caribbean party before Christmas. Only I got sick and they had to bring me home. I'm a Londoner. I still miss London. If Mum moves to the seaside, I'll go back to London. I'm worried about the pollution with my asthma but there's more going on in London for people of my age.

Pip

Martin used to be very good at roller skating and he was a great dancer but he can't do it now. His illness takes up more and more time and he's not fit enough. He's just had a dreadful year. He's hardly been without some operation for six weeks at a time. He's had to have two operations on his eyes alone.

Martin

I'm a bionic man now – with two artificial lenses.

Pip

He hadn't realised how poor his eyesight had got. Because Martin's fluid level is difficult to control, his eyes would become very dry. He started to wake up in the morning with the cornea stuck to his eyelids and when he opened his eyes it would tear strips off the cornea and he would be in agony. These operations have been such a success, which makes a welcome change for Martin. He rang me up a fortnight after and said: 'Did you know there's a pattern on my wallpaper?'

Martin

Now I want to get my health right; health comes first. Then I want to get another job. Then I want to find the right woman and have children. You've got to have some goals.

Pip

If anyone wanted advice about fostering or adopting a young person like Martin, I'd tell them there was more to it than you think. I wouldn't do it again if I was married – I would do it as a single parent. But there's a lot of things I'd do differently in retrospect. I feel I've failed my other children rather, despite my best efforts. I loved them so much and I tried so hard – but they do forgive me and I am incredibly lucky to have them all. You're wiser with a bit of hindsight. It's been the best of times and the worst of times. I wouldn't have it any different.

*   *   *

Mike and all the members of Martin's family were asked to read this narrative and to make their own observations. Mike has sent the following from the USA:

Mike

Martin was, and is, one of the kindest, most thoughtful people you will ever meet. Knowing Martin's history (both emotional and physical) one expects bitterness and resentment. What you get is a level of tolerance which surprises and humbles you. In addition, Martin's attitude to race is an example to us all. Since I have been in the States and seen the disasters that arise from perpetual two-way bigotry, I have come to understand how valuable people like Martin are. The intriguing question is: did somebody teach Martin right from wrong or did he just know?

Looking back now and talking it over with Pip, our perceptions of what happened and how it happened are identical. When you take on an additional burden something has to give. When one person is needing attention, like Martin, you cannot possibly still do all that you know needs to be done; you have to accept that you can't deal with everything as well as you would want.

*   *   *

Marie, now aged 29, was upset that 'this story makes it sound so easy'. Mark, aged 27, also felt quite angry at 'how easy it all sounds on paper'.

Mark

For example, I've always hated blood, so I really didn't like Martin's dialysis equipment at home. It used to make me shiver even when he wasn't on it, so I hardly ever went into his room at all.

Susie, aged 23 and adopted
It was alright at first, but then when Martin got ill, he took up so much of Mum's time, we found it really hard.

James, aged 20 and adopted
I don't remember thinking of Martin any differently from all the other foster children who came and went in our house. But then I realised Marie was looking after us a lot and I don't think Martin understood how difficult it was for her.

Paul, aged 18 and adopted
I was delighted when Martin came. I was thrilled to bits to have another older brother to play with me and I loved him instantly.

A postscript from Pip
Since this story was put together, Martin had a 'phone call out of the blue from the Immigration Office to say his brother was in the country. He got in touch with him and they arranged to meet the next day in Clapham Junction. Neither recognised the other and they walked round each other for several minutes until Martin made an approach based on what Deyo said he'd be wearing. It is nearly 20 years since they last saw each other. Deyo went to watch Martin dialyse at St. Thomas' hospital and stayed with him in his flat the following weekend. They both came to Sunday lunch and we were all able to meet Deyo. He is a delightful young man, a very talented artist who is hoping to go to college in London and, like Martin, also has severe asthma. He says their parents didn't cope well with his illness either. He hasn't seen them for four years because he has been in the USA but he reports that they and their sister, Fadika, were well when he last heard. It has been a joy for the brothers to meet again and very satisfying for them to get to know each other.

*   *   *

So the story continues, but the last word must go to Martin.

Martin
My family is the best choice I ever made. If there was anyone in my position, I'd tell them to go for it.

11 He even likes Elvis – just like me
Mick and Kevin

Mick is a single man who has adopted two sons with disabilities.

*   *   *

Mick

Looking back on it now, I just wish that I'd known about adoption when I was younger. Kevin's 33 now and he was 14 when I met him, so I was in my early 30s. My sister has two children and I wanted children too.

I can remember seeing Kevin's picture in the *Daily Mail* – there it is over there, and I thought to myself, if I took anyone at all it would have to be Kevin. I'd helped my mum bring up my sister and I thought if I got married now, by the time the kids went to school I'd be an old man so I thought I'd better do it now!

Kevin was advertised for adoption and I thought that fostering was more difficult so I never really thought of fostering him. That was in 1980, I always remember it. I thought to myself if I have Kevin and die at 70 he'll be on his own. Actually I got David eight years afterwards and I did foster him at first because that is what the *Be My Parent* book advertised for. He was 15 when I took him. I've made it clear now to social services that this house is going to be theirs when I go. They are going to make sure that they are all right – just have someone keeping an eye on them. They can cook and clean very well and do the shopping, they just need a bit of help with paying the bills. Mind you, Kevin would have to stop saying he's the boss. Then on top of that I've made my sister the trustee for them. When I die I'll leave them the money and I want to make sure that someone will look after it for them. She will come down and visit them regularly.

I thought the way they prepared me for Kevin was quite good even thought it seemed quick. I worried that someone else might take him. Of course you have to remember that back then single people didn't often adopt and I thought a couple would get him.

I remember that they told me all about Down's Syndrome. I never saw a doctor because Kevin had nothing wrong with him apart from being Downs. We talked about the money side of things and they showed me how to get his allowances. I went with John (local authority social worker) to see his school but of course he had to change schools when he came to live with me.

I know they told me a lot about his parents but if there was a chance of meeting his parents I don't think I would because Kevin would get annoyed. Kevin knows he's got another brother but then again, you don't have one child and put the other away. It's not right. I've got lots of photographs of him when he was little but they were all taken at the Children's Home.

They didn't talk to me much about sexual abuse during the preparations but I remember we talked about calling people names. Kevin had to put up with a bit of it when he was younger but we don't get much of it now. One of the best things PFC did to prepare me was to introduce me to a couple who had a Down's Syndrome boy of their own; we are still good friends although we haven't seen them for a long time now. Kevin always sends them a box of chocolates at Christmas time.

Anyway, when they told me I could have Kevin, I was very relieved. I really thought someone else would get him first and I said to PFC: 'If I can't have him, I don't want anyone else. I only want Kevin.' I felt the same about David too. I was always quite sure what I wanted to do. My mother was quite worried for me I think, perhaps she thought I didn't know what I was doing, or perhaps she didn't know what type of boy Kevin was – but in the end she got used to him. I think my mum used to worry what people would say behind my back. People talk, you know, about a single man taking a boy like that. Kevin himself never got upset about people calling him names and he never gets into fights.

I remember the introductions well too. I used to go and see him at the Children's Home and then John would bring him over to see me. I sent him parcels of drinks and chocolate biscuits – I remember they were called 'Banjos' and Kevin said to me: 'No more Banjos.' I thought that was really funny! He was all right when he was with me but when I left him he got miserable because he thought somebody he knew wasn't there anymore. I got to know him well before he moved in for good.

Settling in problems

As soon as he came I had a lot of trouble with my accommodation. The Housing Department wouldn't give me a house until I got Kevin because they thought I was only getting Kevin to get a bigger place. I was in a tower block then but eventually we moved to a bigger place in Northwest London. Kevin went to a nice school there – he used to like it because they played cricket and had a nice big field for it.

He did have a few problems when he first came to me. The worst one was that he soiled himself but I got him out of that one. He also used to pick at his clothes until he tore them and once he pulled the soles of his trainers so much that they completely came away. I was so mad because he used to cost me a lot in clothes.

School and education

One of the things I am most proud of was when I first got him to do a little bit of reading. When he was at school they said he would never read. I taught him to write a bit too. The other thing I was very pleased about was when he learnt to dress himself properly. He can do all that now and can shave himself too. The only trouble I have with him now is that he has a streak of passivity. If he's upstairs and I call him, I can call and call and he won't answer. It seems as if when he's in his room writing he doesn't like to be interrupted and he won't come.

He didn't have long at school. He left when he was 16. Soon after that we moved to Barnet and he could go to college there because they had courses for the disabled. He wanted to do cooking, that's all he did there, just cooking. He used to go twice a week and they used to make nice things there. I know he can make a cake because he used to do it there. One day he made rock cakes and someone ate 18 of them! He only brought home a few!

He had chances to go on trips and holidays there too but he's never been away from me. He's got a bad hernia at the moment and I'm quite worried what I'll do if he has to go into hospital. He's never been away from me all the time I've had him – even when I was ill and could not move with a bad back – I think I'd go crazy. I think I'd have to move into the hospital ward to be with him.

Anyway, when Kevin left college there was nothing else left for him to do. He did go to the Adult Training Centre for a while but I was really disgusted with it. All they had to do was make coat hangers and garden furniture. I wouldn't let him do it for 20p a day! I said to them: 'Would you let your son work all day and not get any of the profits?' He didn't like it there anyway – he said it was boring. On top of that they used to charge me £2 a day for the transport!

Kevin used to walk a lot when I first had him. I haven't got a car and we used to walk everywhere. For the first year I had Kevin I was still working and during the school holidays he used to walk to work with my Mum. Now he only does the shopping under protest if I'm not well or something. He says he's an old man now and too old to do the shopping! So he stays behind and does the housework. He cleans quite well, the superficial parts, but he won't move the furniture and clean behind. I have to do that. Mind you I say that he doesn't go out but he loves taking the dog for a walk. She gets taken out five or six times a day by Kevin for tiny little walks. Dogs are the best pets to have – we've had everything, fish, terrapins, rabbits, you name it, but dogs are the best for them. The dog is 10 now and she has plenty of walks I can tell you!

When David and I go out to my sisters, Kevin doesn't always want to come so I get him organised to be on his own and give him some money to buy the dog food. I ring him up two or three times to make sure he's all right and I tell him that if anyone else rings up he's not to tell them that his dad is out, he's to tell them that he is asleep. People aren't to know whether I do night work or whatever and perhaps I have to sleep in the day time.

*   *   *

The last five years
The family now lives in a small modern house in a quiet cul-de-sac in a semi-rural area.

*   *   *

Mick
We moved to this house five years ago. We did an exchange through the Housing Association. That was because I had a lot of trouble with the

neighbours who kept complaining – they really complained about everything we did and I just got fed up with it. First of all we had trouble over the garden. I'd particularly asked for a flat with a garden so Kevin could go out there, but the neighbours had taken the garden over, although it wasn't theirs by rights, and were most reluctant to hand it back. Then we had another row because she started saying: 'It's unnatural for men to have boys or be their carers.' I said to her: 'Yes, and you would have a lot more to say if it was a girl, wouldn't you.'

We've got nice neighbours here. Kevin and David are good friends with the man next door but one and we've got a few friends nearby. I don't get a lot of trouble round here with people saying wicked things about me. I don't think you get it from people unless they're dirty minded themselves. People hear that Kevin and David are adopted and they say: 'Oh! Isn't that nice.' Most people don't know that a single person can adopt and I tell them that I went to an agency that specialises in it and that was years back. One woman said to me, 'Oh, you've had him 18 years now,' and I said, 'Yes,' because I'm really quite proud of it.

I belong to the National Carers Association and the Out Workers Group in Brighton. We don't go to many of their coffee mornings and things but they keep us up to do date with the literature.

I used to see my sister nearly every week when I lived in London, but now I see her perhaps every three months or so. We 'phone each other a lot and when we can, we stay at each other's house for a weekend. Her children are 21 and 16 now. We always spend Christmas together and have a good time. When my Mum was still alive, we used to see her every week and Kevin and David used to love her coming. She died five years ago just before we moved here. The boys were very upset and I made sure they went to the funeral.

So now Kevin keeps himself busy. He's crazy about Liverpool Football Club and he watches the videos over and over again. Even more than me because I'm a Liverpool supporter too. You ought to see his room – it's covered in Liverpool stuff, everything's red and the Liverpool duvet cover cost a fortune but he loves it – so there you are!

He'll help me in the garden a bit, especially when the strawberries are ripe, but mostly he says his legs 'need a rest'!

We've got Sky TV and Kevin likes horror movies and a good murder but no love stories. Like me really. He even likes Elvis, just like me! That was one of the things we had in common when we first met.

Kevin and David both have their allowances in their own right. It's payable to me because I'm their appointee. Some of it goes into the bank and some they spend. Kevin's walking about with a heavy leg of £30 worth of £1 coins, it's so heavy he bashes himself on the furniture. The reason I give them coins is because paper money might be dropped and you can't hear it.

Kevin's been very healthy all the time I've had him which is 18 years now. But a few months ago he developed a really bad hernia – it sticks out quite a long way and makes him embarrassed. Anyway, I took him to the doctors and he referred us to a specialist. We waited many months for an appointment at the hospital. When he was finally seen the doctor said as he wasn't in any pain, he wouldn't be doing anything about it. He would only operate in case of an emergency.

Then the following summer, when we got the hot weather, I noticed that Kevin wouldn't take his coat off because he was so embarrassed about his stomach sticking out. So I took him back again and asked if he could be put on the waiting list to have the hernia done. But the doctor refused because he said an operation would only be for cosmetic reasons and he really didn't need to have it done. So I said: 'Well, he can't go round like that. Can you get him a truss?'

Then he asked Kevin if he'd like a truss and of course he said no. So I said to the doctor: 'You shouldn't listen to him, he doesn't know what a truss is and doesn't understand, and he's frightened of things he doesn't know. I know what he needs and you should listen to me.' But the doctor said: 'He's an adult now, so he can make the decisions and if he doesn't want it I can't give it to him.' So of course he's still walking round with this huge stomach and it's not fair on him. It makes me feel dreadful and I'm very angry with those doctors too.

The only other health problem you could perhaps say he's got is that he's overweight. He weighs about 18½ stone and he does put on weight quickly. But again, you see, when I take him to the doctors to get him put on a diet, the doctor asks him if he's happy with the way he is and

Kevin says yes because he doesn't understand that it's bad for his health to be overweight. (Mick himself is overweight and recently managed to lose two stone.) The doctor says he won't put him on a diet because he hasn't got his permission. Kevin really likes his food and he is a big eater.

We get visits from the social services every so often. It's not on a regular basis, it's more when she can fit us in. If there was anything we needed I'd go to her but we don't need any aids or adaptations or things like that. Before her we used to have a good one who was a community psychiatric nurse. She helped me a lot with David by getting grants from the DHSS to help with his clothing. Because he's so big (he weighs 20 stone) he's very heavy on his clothes, they seem to wear out more quickly on him. She said that if I needed any help with Kevin's clothes she'd do the same for him too.

The only health problem I've had since I had Kevin and David was a bad bout of back pain and sciatica a couple of years ago. I couldn't move for about four months. The boys did all the cooking but at first they used to argue about it a lot. I remember one day Kevin was making the tea, David was making the toast and I could hear Kevin saying: 'I'm the boss, I'm in charge,' and David saying: 'You're in charge of yourself!' By the time they'd finished arguing I got stone cold tea and cold toast as well! I always kept plenty of stuff in the fridge to make sure they didn't go without and my sister came down ever such a lot. Social services weren't much help because they said any help they could offer would have to be charged. Like sending someone to go shopping with them would cost money. One thing that made me laugh was that they got a wheelchair for me so that I could go to the shops. I thought David could push me round the supermarket so I could get what we needed. But when I sat in it the damn thing nearly went up in the air! So I said that's it! And I never tried again. I've got diabetes too now and high blood pressure but I take pills for that and I'm all right.

I'm really quite happy with the services I get. As you know, people don't take people like David and Kevin to make money out of them. There's nothing we need. The public transport is good and we can get to Brighton in 15 minutes. I can't drive a car because of my diabetes but we go out a lot. We love going to car boot sales. Kevin and David have got a lot of Liverpool supporters' stuff from them and I collect Dinky Toys. We'd love to go to football matches but we can't because they are too expensive.

I do think that adoption is the best plan for children like Kevin and David, otherwise they'd be in institutions all their lives and never see the outside world. If I was a lot younger I would have liked to adopt about four children with Down's Syndrome. A lot of people find it strange – when I'm out and about with them and I say, 'Come on, son,' to one of them, people wonder what kind of father I am – you can see them working it out in their minds. People often want to know if they are related to each other and I say well they are mine but they are not real brothers. People always want to know how you adopt, where you have to go and what you have to do to get them.

I did try to adopt another child from another agency after I'd got Kevin and before I got David. I was very interested in one particular boy of 14 who had been sexually abused. But even though I'd been all through the assessment by PFC, and gave them my permission to get my Panel report and papers from PFC, they wanted to ask me all these questions all over again and they kept questioning me about the reasons why I wanted to adopt him. It made me so mad. In the end they turned me down and I wrote them a strong letter saying that just because a boy has been abused once, it doesn't mean to say that because I'm a single man I'm also going to abuse him.

If I was giving advice to a single man trying to adopt a child now, I think I'd say that the most important thing is to be absolutely sure you want to do it because they might try and persuade you that it isn't for you. You need to know what kind of disabilities you can cope with and if it's Down's Syndrome, like me, learn all about it. I was always clear in my mind that I couldn't take very young children. But yes, I would say go ahead and do it because it works.

*　　　*　　　*

I talked to Kevin afterwards. He had been there all the time his father had told his story, listening to every word and smiling a lot. He said he could remember coming to the PFC office to see me and two of the chairs broke. They were always breaking! Then he remembered going to meet

Mick from work and helping him to stamp the parcels where Mick worked as a Despatch Manager.

I ask Kevin if he can remember coming to live in Mick's house. 'I love Mick. He's my dad. He's gorgeous,' he says and he strokes Mick's head.

12 Sharon goes to paradise
Sue, Pete and Sharon

Sue

If we're honest, we wanted to adopt an older child because it would have taken too long to wait for a baby. I don't know how we came to PFC.

Pete

You read an article in a newspaper or a magazine and we got in touch from that.

Sue

There's nothing in our background that made us want to take a child with disabilities – it just seemed to happen.

Pete

We didn't want Jody to be an only one. She was a very bright little girl and very easy. We'd had no problems at all with her and we still haven't. She was five at the time and Sharon was eleven – we thought they'd fit in together; she didn't have a lot of disabilities, it was more behaviour problems.

Sue

We intended to have a large family, we're both one of four. We'd probably have adopted more if it hadn't been for the problems that came up with Sharon's illness. We wouldn't have chosen a child with more severe disabilities, not then. Now we might. I think I was too frightened of disability then.

We're different people now. I am a different person because of Sharon. She taught us such a lot – about life – she's tried our patience but we've gained. I wouldn't be doing the job I'm doing now if it weren't for Sharon. I work in a home for disabled adults and I can't imagine ever doing anything else.

Pete
If I finish work, take early retirement as I want, I'd like to put in voluntary work with special needs adults or children. We're contented in a way we couldn't have been without Sharon.

Sue
We might not have said that 15 years ago.

Pete
Well, we wouldn't have. But as you look back, it's worked out fine at the end of the day.

*   *   *

Sue and Pete have always lived and worked in the same area of the West Country. Their home is a detached stone house in a village. Both their large extended families live nearby. They are still young parents although Jody is now 24 and Sharon is 30. Pete's family business has thrived, Sue loves her job, Jody is at university and Sharon is a member of a very special community called Paradise.

*   *   *

Sharon before and after her illness
Sue
We first saw Sharon on video at PFC. We saw videos of lots of children and we both said together: 'What about that girl with the dark hair and the bubbly personality?' So then we just decided to ask more about Sharon and we went on from there.

We knew she was going to have behaviour problems – hopefully ones we could cope with. She was labelled as ESN (Educationally Subnormal) – you were allowed to say that then – because she was born with hydrocephalus – fluid on the brain – and she had epilepsy but the main disability was her behaviour really. She was quite well otherwise.

It was the behaviour that was the challenge and making up for the rejection in Sharon's past. From what we were told, Sharon's Mum tried to look after her until she was about five. She was a very caring person but she wasn't well herself and she was on her own, so Sharon had to come in and out of care whenever Mum had to go into hospital. Then from the age of five she lived in a Children's Home. They tried to have her fostered but it didn't work. When she was nine her Mum agreed it would be better for Sharon to be adopted. She was placed with a couple in the Midlands but it broke down after a few months when the husband and wife separated. Sharon went to stay with friends of theirs but they couldn't keep her.

Instead of meeting Sharon for the first time for a day, we met her for three days because we got stuck in the snow. The road was closed and we had to stay overnight. It wasn't at all like we expected. She was obviously very excited and over the top and we did find that quite difficult to cope with. Within five minutes of meeting her, she was calling us 'Mum' and 'Dad'.

Pete

I found it very hard to accept. It was 'Dad' this and 'Dad' that – an instant dad I seemed to become. It wasn't a very good time, we were stranded up there and worried about Jody down here.

Sue

It was a bit of a disaster really. We didn't fall in love with her, definitely not. But we wanted to carry on. There was lots of talking with PFC and they said it was perfectly natural and normal to feel like that and not to worry about it. And the second time was nowhere as bad.

Pete

The second time she came down here and it was much better. We were more easy because we didn't have the problem of leaving Jody.

Sue

I can't remember it being awful after that. It must have been OK because it was six weeks from the time we met her to the day we were going to take her for good.

Sue

The day before, we had a phone call to say Sharon had been taken to hospital. We were told that she was putting it on and it wasn't serious. She'd bumped her head at school and started to act strangely. So they said: 'Be prepared to come up and collect her from the hospital.'

When we left that day, we still thought we would bring her back with us. It was while we were sat with her that she had that very major fit and then another. She stopped breathing for a time and then she went unconscious. They had to move her to another hospital as an emergency. I went with her in the ambulance.

Pete

And I followed in the car. We had to stay the night again but Jody was with us this time. In the end we had to stay in the hospital because the car got locked in the car park and we were stranded.

Sharon was put in intensive care and they had to operate. They couldn't tell us anything but she was in a bad way. We took Jody home and a friend drove me up again next day.

Sue

I remember you came back saying she wasn't going to pull through. We waited up most of that night expecting the 'phone to ring.

Pete

She was in a coma on a life support machine and they phoned us up to say they were going to turn it off shortly. So I went back to the hospital, with my friend driving, and saw Sharon. They didn't turn the machine off but I came out of there with the impression that there was hardly any chance at all for Sharon.

Sue

We just thought we'd have to wait for another 'phone call to say something had happened to her. The next morning they rang to say her brain had started working on its own. We were all here crying because it really was a miracle and it was totally unexpected. We didn't understand it all but the surgeon from the hospital tried to explain it. This was the end of March and on her 12th birthday in April they did all these tests because they could see she didn't have any movement. A couple of days after that they told us she'd never move; she'd be completely paralysed apart from her face.

Pete

She could talk alright and move her face and that's the time when, in frustration, she bit her lower lip completely off.

Sue

She was paralysed really from March right until June. And that was when her feet were ruined too. Because they didn't think she would ever move again, they neglected her feet. Instead of straightening them out, they left them crunched up and it made her very unsteady.

Pete

While Sharon was paralysed we used to go up every weekend with Jody and stay the night in our caravan. And I used to take the van up once during the week. I had to go to Birmingham for business and it was just another hour to go on to the hospital. Towards the end of June, I remember Sue was giving Sharon a blanket bath and Sharon moved her hand. I said: 'She moved her hand then,' and Sue said: 'Don't be silly,' and I said to Sharon: 'Move your hand and I'll give you a pound.' So then she moved it again. Of course I went rushing to the doctor and he said: 'Don't worry about that, it was just muscle movement,' and I said: 'No it wasn't, she moved her hand.'

Sue

She tried to do it again then but I don't think she could – it was such hard work. But she went on from there. Mind you, it was a long, slow job. We'd booked a holiday because we were so fed up – not with Sharon but because we thought we would never bring her home. By the time we left, she could lie on her front and lift her leg towards her bottom. We gave her the key of our house to look after because we didn't want her to think we were walking out on her.

Pete

Friends and family kept visiting while we were away; they carried on with exactly what we were doing. When we came back a month later, she was walking with a Zimmer Frame.

Sue

We never really found out what it was all about. The only way it was ever described to us was that it was very similar to her having a stroke. It was nothing to do with her epilepsy. She had the fits because she was ill, it wasn't the other way round.

Pete

I still think to this day, that a lot to do with it was another move in her life. The others didn't work out and I think she was worried stiff about what was going to happen to her. It made a bond between her and us. She wasn't ours, it wasn't love – but there was a bond.

Sue

Oh definitely, it just happened while she was ill. If she hadn't been ill, it would have been quite different. It would have been harder maybe. As I've got older, I think things were meant to be. We had thought there'd be problems with Jody and Sharon getting used to each other, but as it was, the first thing Jody felt for Sharon was pity and wanting to look after her and that's how it went on for a long time really.

Pete

We don't know, we just don't know how it would have been without Sharon being ill. And I wonder, if she'd stayed paralysed and gone to a Special Unit, what our relationship would have ended up to be. You don't know what you can do until it happens.

Sue

Whatever happened, we'd have gone on playing a part in her life.

*   *   *

Coming home

Sharon finally came home to her new family nearly six months after the formal placement day. All that time Sue and Pete and Jody travelled 250 miles to see her at weekends and Pete did the same journey again mid-week. When she came, Sharon could still barely walk and she required total care.

*   *   *

Sue

We weren't prepared for what we were going to get, were we? No-one could have prepared us for what we were going to get.

Pete

Let's put it this way: we were thrown in at the deep end. There was never any honeymoon period with Sharon. She wasn't capable of putting on a good show and testing us out later. She just was as she was and she always has been.

Sue

We'd expected bad behaviour problems and we didn't get any of those because by the time Sharon came to us, she was a changed person. She wasn't hyper any longer; she was more wanting to please. She was a totally different child in personality and everything from what she'd been before. Instead of behaviour problems we had physical problems.

Pete

She was a quieter person than she'd been before. No-one has ever had to complain about her. I think she was a nicer person really. Perhaps it was how she was meant to be. All her behaviour problems went away with her illness.

Sue

We didn't know what was going to happen; we thought there might be a recurrence of the illness. It was years, many years before we relaxed. I don't know if we ever stopped worrying.

171

Pete

Truly speaking, you had to block it out of your mind and you carried on day to day. If it was going to happen it would, but you hoped it wouldn't and it didn't. We weren't concerned with much else except what was around the corner. You couldn't plan. We'd go in at night-time just to make sure she was breathing.

Sue

Biting her lower lip off became a habit. She went on doing it when she came home and when they built it up with plastic surgery, she bit that off too. And she did other self-inflicting injuries. She picked her toe nails right off and she picked the operation scar on her head for about ten years. She still has a terrible bump there. It took her a long time to get her feet under the table. Her illness on top of all the moves was too much for her. Her memory went. She remembers everything up to her illness but she can't keep anything in her mind since then. It took a while before we discovered that her memory loss was permanent.

Pete

We got no support locally – nothing. It was shocking. There was no back-up from the hospital either. No documents, no reports. We were told we'd be having a folder with all the medical information in it, but when we finally took Sharon to our doctor, he knew nothing at all about it.

Sue

The local authority worker in London, where Sharon came from, was very caring; she was fond of Sharon, she'd known her for a long time. And we got plenty of support from PFC and we needed it. In the end we saw a neurosurgeon and he said: 'It will take her five years to get over this. Whatever she's like in five years, that's how she'll be.' And he was right.

Pete

He told us to push her because she could vegetate if left alone. He even said she might end up in the corner rocking. Every night we'd sit with her and we'd be pushing her with reading and easy sums. We didn't ever just leave her to get on with things – she wouldn't – she'd just do nothing. I'd give her a newspaper and ask her what time *News at Ten* would be on and it would take her half an hour to find it. She'd go through all the four channels from early morning. It was just to get her brain working a little bit.

Sue

Sharon's loss of memory affected everything. She wouldn't recognise her own clothes or people she knew, although she did always recognise the immediate family. She took up so much of our time.

Pete

You had to make the time to go over and over everything. You had to drop other things to teach Sharon. We'd teach her to go somewhere on her own and to begin with we'd follow her at a distance, even if it was just to the shop down the road. We'd do that for a long time but in the end she managed.

We taught her to get a bus home from the next village when she was older and that took months. I used to hide and watch her get on the bus and then overtake the bus on my push-bike and watch her get off at the other end, which sometimes she didn't. So we taught her to get off at the stop before home, then if she missed it she could still get off and walk back. There's so much hard work there – having to teach her everything again from walking to taking care of herself.

Sue

At the end of the day we got results from all the work that went in. Just getting better over a long period of time was the reward. And she always wanted to help – with anything. If you asked her she'd sweep up all the leaves in the garden.

Pete

Life was a battle for the first few years with Sharon but we laughed more than we cried.

Sue

If Sharon has a chance to get something wrong, she will every time – we laugh about it with her. For my birthday I once had a card from her: 'For You and Your Baby,' and for our anniversary we had a beautiful sympathy card.

*   *   *

Sharon also gets some things right – some of the most important things. When Sue's mother died a few years ago, 250 local people who had known her came to the funeral. But Sue said that it was Sharon who made everyone show their feelings: 'She was so upset, she just sobbed her heart out and got us all going.'

*   *   *

Pete

When Sue's father died earlier, she was also more upset than we thought she'd be. They were very fond of each other and he was always brilliant with her.

Sue

Other than that, the biggest upheaval for Sharon was changing the kitchen around. She still can't find anything and it was done four years ago.

Links with the past

Sue

Now and again Sharon says she wants to know about her "real" mother. I've said we'll write to PFC and ask them to help, but she loses interest.

Pete

If you got Sharon to one side and said: 'Now look, you want to see your mother and we're going to help you,' and you let a few days go by, she wouldn't remember about it. If it meant anything to Sharon to see her mother, I'd pursue it. Ten years ago I wouldn't have wanted to because it would have unsettled her too much, but now I don't think it would. She's stable enough to cope. With any other member of her birth family, it would be the same.

Sue
We're in touch with Beryl, the woman who was going to adopt her, but then her marriage broke up. She really loved Sharon and she writes her a letter every Christmas and sends a present and birthday cards. Sharon says she remembers her but I think it's only a name to her. The same with the people in the Children's Home and other people from the past.

Pete
We took Sharon back to the Children's Home on her 18th birthday because she kept on saying she wanted to go. It wasn't what she thought it was – no-one there knew her and she's never mentioned it again. She got it out of her system and she enjoyed the rest of the day. We took her on an open bus all round London. That's what she wanted.

Adoption or foster care
Sue
We committed ourselves to Sharon when she lay in hospital. We took over complete responsibility for her. We don't ever think of being anything but her parents and Sharon knows we're her family. Love grew very slowly; it took years, but now she feels like our daughter. It was first suggested we foster when she was still in hospital and we were having all those expenses. Then we delayed adoption because we were still scared about what was going to happen.

Pete
They said when she was in hospital on the critical list: 'You know you can still walk away from her.' But we wouldn't have – we couldn't and we didn't. She was only 11 and she had no-one else. We were committed but too frightened to adopt her. We didn't see any difference for Sharon; we got into fostering and we stuck with it. The money never came into it – in fact we asked if we could foster without payment. But they said: 'Why not spend the money on a good family holiday?' And we did. It all worked out for the best. If she'd been adopted, would her London local authority have been as helpful with the charges for Paradise? We know our own local authority doesn't place young people there because it's too expensive.

Sue

The DSS and the London Borough, I suppose, pay the charges between them. We haven't been involved in that side. The London Borough handed over the foster care supervision to our local council but they retained financial responsibility. Unfortunately Sharon was put with the "normal" child care team and they couldn't support us because they didn't know how. We never used respite care. It wasn't made available. Luckily Sharon has always been welcome to stay with family and friends. When she was an adult she was transferred to the special care team which was better.

Pete

Sue would more happily have adopted, it was me that wanted to keep it as it was.

*   *   *

Jody later commented that she didn't know Sharon wasn't adopted until Sharon left home. She said: 'It wasn't ever an issue. My Mum and Dad were her Mum and Dad.'

Sharon's health and development

Apart from her one major illness and her epilepsy, Sharon is described as "fit as a fiddle". She has a shunt in the back of her neck which drains any excess fluid from her brain; the shunt has to be checked regularly to prevent it from becoming blocked but this is simply part of the routine of Sharon's life. She has always had medication for epilepsy.

*   *   *

Sue

She has to take nine tablets a day. We've taught her to fill her little pill boxes herself: she has seven boxes, one for each day of the week, and they each have three compartments. She knows to take three pills three times a day but she still has to be supervised to take them, to make sure.

Mentally Sharon didn't progress after the age of 11 and her illness; physically she didn't change either. She's stayed the same height, about 4' 10", but she's got sturdier. She still takes size 1½ in shoes. She started her periods when she was nine so, by the time we met her, she was already well developed.

Pete

We've worried about someone taking advantage of her when she was out. She'd talk to anyone and, no matter what we said, she could forget everything and go with them. She came home from college once with a great big love bite on her neck. A boy did it while they were watching a video. She didn't really know what had happened but it worried us sick. It's never entered our heads to worry about anything like that happening in Paradise.

Sue

She's interested in boys more like a child. She doesn't show any signs of real interest. She has a boyfriend in the Community, but I think at Paradise they encourage them to live more like brothers and sisters. You never see them holding hands or anything – it's a friendship rather than a relationship. "Boyfriend" is just another word for Sharon.

Sharon's education
Sue

Sharon went to a special school about a month after she came to us – but it was a struggle. She couldn't remember anyone's name or her classroom or where to go.

Pete

That's when the problems started about her being naughty. The teachers didn't understand and Sharon would get in a tantrum because she didn't understand what was wrong either.

Sue

She was at the bottom of the school and she might, at that stage, have done better in a school for more severely disabled children.

Pete
Gradually things improved; they gave Sharon more help and she quite liked being with the other children. She never learned a lot. It was a big effort to make her retain what she knew before her illness. She's never learnt anything since. She can read the simplest of nursery rhyme books; she will take half an hour to read one page over and over, but you ask her straight after what she's read and she can't tell you.

Sue
She stayed on until she was 16 and then there was nothing. We had to insist and fight for her right to have education until she was 19.

Pete
The local education authority started a two year college course for young people with disabilities because of our persistence.

Sue
And Sharon was allowed to go back to school until the course started. It had never happened in our area. In the end she stayed on at college an extra year until she was 19. It was really good for her.

Sharon leaves home
Sharon wasn't becoming an adult at home. She couldn't make any more progress. All she did in the evening was to sit with us or watch television. We wanted a fuller life for her. Jody was becoming independent but Sharon wasn't and we realised she would never be.

Pete
Sharon's local social worker wanted her to go into a residential place when she was 18. We didn't like the place when we saw it and the timing was wrong. Sharon wasn't ready to leave home and she was still at college. I said to the social worker: 'Sharon isn't coming down here,' and she as much as told me that Sharon was fostered and we didn't have anything to do with it.

Sue

This worker put words into Sharon's mouth without even knowing how her mind worked. She said: 'Sharon wants to come here, don't you Sharon?' and of course Sharon said 'Yes' but she didn't know what she was saying 'Yes' to. That's when we got in touch with PFC and they sorted it out.

Pete

We weren't the sort of foster parents the local authority was used fcto dealing with. We were Sharon's parents no matter what we were called. We wanted to make the decision when we knew Sharon was ready.

Sue

We went to look at a Rudolf Steiner Home as a residential place for the future. They said they were starting a Day Centre and we really liked it. They had workshops and a bakery and weaving and they did everything as a community, joining in with the residents. Sharon went there after she finished college. It was a real preparation for communal living. And through them, Sharon got into Paradise.

Pete

By that time we realised that Sharon did better when she was with other young people of her ability and that she really needed the company. Especially when Jody started to lead her own life. We never expected Sharon to be able to leave home or get married and have children, but we did hope she'd be more capable and hold down an ordinary job. She stayed at home until she was 22. But I think now, she's better off where she is.

Sue

We don't have to worry about her. She is not at risk. Paradise House has taken over where we left off. She is more protected living in the Community; there are still people around who can't accept someone like Sharon – which is a shame, but that's how it is.

*   *   *

Paradise

Paradise House was once a manor just outside the village of Paradise. It has been turned into a Rudolf Steiner Community Home for young people with disabilities. In the extensive grounds there are flower, fruit and vegetable gardens, wide lawns and a modest farm. Smaller stone buildings, hidden among the trees, have been dotted around the main house. Paradise House is home for all the people who live there. Everyone, including the carers, contributes what they can to the community in terms of work and support and everyone receives help, clothes and food according to their needs. No-one is paid. The philosophy of Rudolf Steiner is based on the Christian ethic; it enshrines the value of the individual and the mutual support disabled and non-disabled people can give each other to form a strong community. The emphasis is on caring, on creativity and on useful occupation for all. Material possessions and appearances are not a priority and there is no television. Parents are made to feel very welcome at any time and the disabled people, who are called co-workers, are free to visit their families and to take their friends. Locally, and by the people who live there, the Community is simply known as "Paradise".

*   *   *

Sue

Sharon lives in a beautiful place – it's called Paradise and it really is. You can't see any other houses, just fields and their own Community. I think we're very lucky to have it so near us.

There's a few things we don't agree with like the way they dress. They don't worry about how they look, they're completely unmaterialistic and they can seem a bit disorganised. But there's a lot more better things they do for Sharon than things we could criticise. It wouldn't be our way but it suits Sharon and she fits in. They look after her with more love than possessions. They don't mind what she looks like but they give her lots of care and attention.

Pete

Put it another way: when we prepare a meal we make it look good, but they don't care if it's all white as long as it's wholesome.

Sue

As soon as she comes home she says: 'Mum, shall I change?' We spent years teaching her to put clothes together to look nice – now she doesn't care but she knows we do. She'll say: 'Shall I wash my hair today?' and 'What clothes shall I put in the wash?' At Paradise they leave it to Sharon about what she wears and how to keep herself clean and when she tidies her room. She was always so tidy but now her room at Paradise is a mess. Yet she's so happy there, we've got no room for complaints.

Pete

When Sharon comes home and we have a meal, no matter who's here, she'll ask: 'Can I say grace?' and she says it lovely. She can remember her prayers. I'll say that for her, she can't remember much else, but she can remember them. She said the other day: 'I can remember the registration of your last car Dad,' and I said: 'What is it Sharon?' and she said the registration of a car we had 18 years ago when we first met her.

Sue

We don't take Sharon on holiday with us any more. She doesn't really adjust to it. It takes her a week to remember where the toilet is and she's happier on the beach with a bucket and spade. So now we do things she likes on day outings.

Pete

You could take Sharon anywhere nowadays and she wouldn't be noticed – that's very different from how it used to be when she had her chewed up lip and no hair. People used to stare and we didn't like that but Sharon never noticed. I take her to bowls with me and she'll watch when I'm playing a competition – I don't know if she understands it but she talks about it.

Sue

We take her out to eat a lot. We all like our food. There's one pub we go to where they serve "two in one pies" – it's the only thing she can remember and she'll ask for it wherever we go. But she'll eat anything really, only as soon as she's finished she can't remember what it was.

Pete

She never notices the taste of things – not whether it's a hot curry even –
and I think she's got no taste buds.

Sue

When Sharon first went to Paradise, because she appears so capable, they
put her in a chalet to be more independent but that didn't work out. She
couldn't manage and they didn't understand about her memory loss to
begin with, which made it a lot worse.

Pete

She always sounds quite convincing, so people expect more of her; they
may wonder why she's half an hour late and they don't realise she can't remember where she should be or how to get there. It used to make her
moody when she got told off because she would never say: 'I can't
remember.'

Sue

It was better when she moved to the main house and later to the cottage
she's in now. She didn't really have a hard job settling in – she had times
when she wanted to come back but they passed. Sharon isn't able to make
a judgement or a long-term decision about her life. If she has an argument with anybody in the Community, she might ring us up and say she
wants to come home to live and we say: 'Let's talk about it some more
tomorrow.' But by tomorrow she's forgotten all about it. She knows we're
with her, and that we mean it, and that enables her to complain and then
forget about it.

Pete

She keeps in close touch all the time. She phones me at work and she's
talking and talking and after about ten minutes I realise this isn't a 20p
call and I say to her: 'Sharon have you put a pound in?' and she says: 'No
I haven't, I've put in two 50p.'

Sue

For Paradise, we're Sharon's parents, but she lives there and they handle what happens on a daily basis.

Pete

At the beginning we found it difficult to accept that. Because we were saying: '*This* is your home for life, no matter what,' and they were saying: '*This* is your home now.'

Sue

She's safe at Paradise for the rest of her life. That's so important. She has matured, she's as independent now as she can be. There's no need for her to be pushed further. It's a community where everyone's within ten years of each other. Paradise really is their home and they'll grow old together.

Pete

I've always said that I didn't want Jody to be responsible for Sharon if anything happened to us because she didn't choose Sharon, we did. But I know she would always be there for her – definitely.

* * *

Jody's view

Jody added her piece later in London where she is studying. We went to a restaurant she knows which is run by people with disabilities. Jody is taking a degree course in nursing studies and is specialising in mental health.

* * *

Jody

The first thing I remember about Sharon is going to see her in the hospital. We stayed in a caravan and Mum and Dad went to see Sharon a lot; I only went sometimes I think. But I remember seeing her when she couldn't move and when Mum and Dad were called because they didn't think she'd last the night. I knew she was supposed to come and live with us but I was only five years old and I didn't understand really what was happening. I just accepted it. I don't think I was worried by it. We've always had people living at our house, like cousins and friends, and it seemed natural.

When she did come, she couldn't do much. I was probably annoyed because she demanded Mum and Dad's time which I'd had to myself until then. Yet it wasn't a question of before Sharon and after – I can't really remember when she wasn't there. It's always been the two of us; we were brought up together.

The most important thing to say is that when she got better, she became my big sister, although I think I was always quite protective. I don't think I realised then that she was mentally disabled because there were six years between us. I thought she was a bit naughty rather than anything else. She'd play up when one of my older cousins took us both out. And sometimes I felt Sharon caused a lot of problems and arguments. In her teens she used to pinch food out of our cupboards and sweets from the shops and that made everybody cross. She certainly had a great impact on our lives, but I don't feel resentful in the slightest. I don't feel she took Mum and Dad away from me.

By the time I was in my teens, I overtook Sharon and understood what was wrong with her. As I grew older, she seemed to grow younger. If I'm asked, I always say I've got a sister and I introduce her as my sister, but in a way I consider myself to be an only child. I'm very fond of Sharon; I care for her a lot and I still stick up for her but perhaps we're not as close as we would be if she didn't have learning difficulties. We can't share things because we have no common interests.

When Sharon went to live in Paradise, we all took her and my Mum cried all the way home in the car. It hit me how much she meant to Mum and Dad, because although they'd always cared for her, I'd never seen how special she was for them. I felt it was just her leaving home like I would and it was a natural progression. Mum and Dad told me that if anything happened to them, they didn't want me to be responsible for Sharon because I was going to college and having my own life.

I feel happy that Sharon is somewhere where she's so settled. When she comes home she talks about Paradise all the time. I think it's lovely there for her but I think it's been hard for Mum and Dad to hand over responsibility for Sharon and to stand by and see her cared for in a very different way. We taught her a lot of things which have slipped but then they're not as important as her being happy, which she is. I've changed too since I left home.

Sharon came up to London with Mum and Dad to stay with me, but she doesn't understand about my life. In some ways she still regards me as her little sister and she can be quite bossy. But like Mum, I probably wouldn't be doing what I'm doing now if it weren't for Sharon. She's enriched all our lives and made me a lot less selfish than I might have been.

I admire my parents for what they did. Sharon is part of the family and always will be. Because she doesn't live at home any more, people sometimes tend to leave her out when they send Christmas cards or invitations. Mum gets quite hurt – they're both very keen to have her included. She comes home to join in family events and she's part of our lives. Mum and Dad and I were going to travel abroad at Christmas this year, but now we're going after Christmas because we want to celebrate Christmas with Sharon.

*   *   *

Sharon's view
Sharon spoke to me in the living room in Paradise House while her parents chatted to other members of the Community.

*   *   *

Sharon
It's really good. I like living in Paradise. I do the cooking for lunch – that's my workshop, I don't work in the garden any more. I go horse riding on Thursday at half-past nine.

On Monday we have a meeting first, then we go to our workshops. I cook lunch in the morning and I do gardening in the afternoon.

When I came first, I lived in the big house. Then I was put in the cabin where I had to look after myself more – it's more independent. Me and another girl didn't get on very well and it was difficult to be independent. So I moved back to the big house. I was in different rooms. I wanted to move to a smaller house and I moved to Tobias House with three others and the houseparents and their family.

185

I was upset to begin with when I left home. It was all new. The first night I was completely upset, I didn't want to leave home. I kept packing all the time to go home. Then they said: 'You can try again and not keep packing your cases.' I'm not doing it any more because I'm older. I've been here eight years and I'm 30 now. It don't seem it. I still get a little bit upset when I come back here from home, so I'll stay in my room and not come down for supper, and I get over it – I definitely do when I'm on my own.

When I'm home I miss my friends here – definitely – I even miss my boyfriend here. When I'm here I miss the clubs I used to go to: the Phab club and the Gateway Club and my two best friends. When I go home I go to the clubs and I see my friends. I have two homes – but we're told that Paradise is our home and the other is our parents' home. When I came first I got really unsettled because when I said I was going home, they said: 'This is your home now.' Two of the people here don't have another home to go to so we're not allowed to say in front of them about going home. I've settled down now quite a bit.

I remember coming to PFC. I liked it a lot. I liked meeting everybody. I liked having new parents. I say to anybody: 'Go for a family.'

The worst thing was moving from London – that was the worst about it – moving was the worst thing. I had to move when Beryl and Jim split up and then I went to stay with Tony and Lorraine but they were too young to keep me. They would have liked to keep me as their child but they couldn't. Beryl writes every Christmas. I've written four or five letters to her and I've sent them off, but I haven't had a reply as yet.

I can't remember my real mother. Her name is Elizabeth. I want to know how she is. I want to write to her but I haven't got her address. I want to know how I can get her address. I know she's been ill and I just want to know how she is. I want to get in touch with my social worker as well, Ann Cardew (London Borough Social worker). I want to write a letter to her. I haven't got her address to put on the envelope. There's auntie Eleanor and auntie Hilda from the Children's Home, I remember them. I know the address but I haven't written.

When I was ill I just couldn't move and I remember Dad tickling my face with his beard and I couldn't move to scratch it. But it was good. It was nice. I could feel they were there.

I've got a book with my story. The staff have got it in the office. They take care of it. I know a bit of it off by heart. I've put it in the back of my cupboard at home. I'm looking forward to reading my story in this book.

The saddest thing was when one person here died. We had to go to the funeral. But I'm happy all the time really.

Sue and Pete's final view

It's worked out OK for us. It's worked out OK for Sharon. It's worked out OK for Jody. But that's no guarantee for anyone else.

13 I had to learn to fight
Anne and Stuart

How we met

Anne

I was working in a Home for children with severe disabilities and Stuart's social worker and foster carers brought him down for the day to discuss whether he could live there. While they discussed, I looked after him. I remember he ate a banana mashed with bread, like they used to do, and he drank a cup of tea. When they left the matron said to me: 'Shall we keep him?' and I said: 'Yes please.'

When he did come, he didn't bring much with him. I knew there was something between us the first day; I would have taken him home there and then. I would have given up everything to have him but I didn't know what to do about it. I was one of his key workers at the Home. It was a special kind of home – more like a family – we were encouraged to have a close relationship with all the children. Stuart was a lovely little boy, everyone wanted him. I took him on his first holiday; I did everything for him. At the end of the week the people there didn't believe that Stuart didn't belong to me. One year I couldn't go on the holiday and they said Stuart sulked all week.

*   *   *

Stuart was nearly four years old when he moved to the Home where Anne worked. He was a child with profound disabilities due to brain damage. He was placed with Anne and adopted by her three years later. Two other disabled children followed: Reg, who has a congenital disabling syndrome, came when Stuart was 12 and Barbara, also severely brain damaged, is a recent addition to the family.

Anne is a single parent but she is not alone. Kevin has been around as long as Stuart; he is the unofficial other parent although he and Anne choose not to live together. Kevin was present while Anne told their story; he corroborated, reminded, agreed and occasionally elaborated. He also fed Barbara several times, collected Reg from school, gave Stuart his lunch and took him to the hospital in his wheelchair for a routine check-up. Stuart is now 20 years old, Reg is 10 and Barbara is two. Anne and her family have moved to a spacious bungalow with a large garden on the East Coast; Kevin lives two miles away. The local authority has paid to build on an extension with a specially equipped bathroom for Stuart and he has an impressive range of aids and adaptations including a state of the arts bed with clear plastic sides.

*   *   *

Anne

I was born in this town. I was brought up in a hotel – my parents ran it. I didn't like school at all. I knew from a very early age that I wanted to do something with children but I didn't want children of my own. I wanted to work with children. When I was at school they used to tell me if I didn't do sport I wouldn't get a job looking after children. I think I've proved them wrong and I still don't like sport.

When I left school I couldn't get a job with children at the beginning because there was nothing around. So I got a job with a baker making cakes. Then a taxi driver I used to know introduced me to a headmistress of a special school. She was going up to a hospital for disabled children and took me with her to meet the people there. I only went to have a look but I came away with a job! I worked from eight to five, getting the children up and giving them breakfast and then I would go into school with them. But I very often stayed on late in the evening because I loved it so much – I wanted to give them their bath and put them to bed. I was there for a few years and when I left I went to the Children's Home where I met Stuart.

Kevin

Anne is a very caring person. She loves Stuart and Reg and Barbie and I hope she loves me. She'd do anything for the kids, absolutely anything. But she doesn't eat properly herself – you have to make her eat sometimes. She used to be very shy – the only way I got to talk to her was through the children. She was so shy, she was like in her own little world with Stuart and she wouldn't talk to anyone else. She's come out of her

189

shell very much more now. She wouldn't say "boo" to a goose, but now she does.

Anne

I first met Kevin through a holiday for the disabled. I didn't talk to him much. He was a bit afraid of the children to begin with because he hadn't come across children with disabilities before, but as he came down to see them in the Children's Home, he gradually got to care for them. He was a big fellow and I was a bit afraid of him as well – he was all dressed up in his motorbike gear and things – I wasn't used to people like that. There's still times when Kevin has a temper, which I don't like, but on the whole we get on fine and he loves the children and would do anything for them. But we couldn't live together. It wouldn't work at all. After two weeks away on holiday we need a break. I couldn't live with anyone except the children now. On the other hand I do rely on him. There's a lot we do together that I couldn't do on my own. And without Kevin, we couldn't have taken on Barbara.

Kevin

I enjoy doing what we're doing. It's a different life to what I was used to. I was a rough and ready motorbiker and I lived for my motorbikes. I've ridden motorbikes since I was seven years old and I worked in a motorcycle shop when I was still a kid. When I left school I worked as a motor mechanic. I also worked in a youth club and one of the committee members asked if I'd like to help out on a holiday for the disabled. The children really upset me. I went home and started telling my parents about it and I burst into tears. I was still living with my parents in Surrey and I'd come to visit the children in the Home about twice a year and pitch my tent in the garden. Of course the kids all thought that was great. I used to muck in with the staff – another pair of hands sort of thing – and that way I got to see Anne. She wouldn't have let me come up otherwise, she was still too shy. By the time Anne took Stuart, I was coming more regularly but I was still pitching my tent away from her flat. Now I live in the same town, I've got my own home, and we bring up the children together. It's our family but we each need our own space as well. Because I haven't adopted them and I'm not married to Anne, I'm only officially recognised as their volunteer carer.

Anne

Stuart is a multiply handicapped young man now. He has severe epilepsy and learning difficulties, he doesn't walk or talk, he is doubly incontinent, he has tunnel vision with cataracts on one of his eyes and he's still lovely. His disabilities were caused by a non-accidental injury when he was a few months old. He had a brain haemorrhage which left him the way he is.

We let Stuart do what he wants to do. When he's ill we have to plan the day round him. He'll fall asleep absolutely anywhere. If you don't let him sleep when he wants to, then he's more likely to have another fit.

Everything is sort of done at his pace; we don't force him. We try and see what mood he is in the morning as to what we're going to do during the day.

*   *   *

For several hours during this particular day, while Anne talked, both Stuart and Barbara were comfortably curled up on conveniently placed mattresses on the floor.

*   *   *

Applying to adopt
Anne

I vaguely remember, when Stuart came to the Home, that they said it was only short term because they were looking for a family for him. I don't think much was done about it until he was referred to PFC. Then I did start trying to find out how to set about applying for him. I didn't know if I'd qualify being single and living at home at the time. I went up to an interview at PFC and I was invited to an Activity Day. That was difficult for me: I took Stuart up and was looking after him as his residential worker but I was also wanting to have him. And there were other people interested in him. I've spoken to one family who was interested since and they said they laid off because they could see there was a bond between us.

I wanted to give Stuart a permanent home with no fear he could be moved. I wanted to adopt him, I didn't want to foster. After the Activity Day they asked all of us to think about it over the weekend and give a ring if we wanted to go on. I said: 'I don't need to ring, I know what I want, I can tell you now.' But I did ring to make sure.

My family were a bit shocked. They didn't know if I'd cope – but they came round – they had to – and they're still coming round. I had to find somewhere to live and it just happened that my auntie and uncle were moving to a retirement home and we made a private arrangement that I paid their accommodation fees in exchange for living in their flat, and when we sold the flat, I paid them the balance.

I had good preparation for adoption but they did keep telling me that I knew more about Stuart than they did. I knew some of it but you don't know everything when you're working in a Home – like the stuff about his background. I went to see other single parents who'd adopted disabled children and that was very helpful. It was hearing what it was like to be left alone with a child – in the Children's Home there was always someone else around. But it didn't put me off. However hard anyone tried to put me off with all the negatives that could happen, I could always see a positive. In the end the biggest hurdle was the Children's Home. The matron had left by this time and the chairperson and committee of the Home felt it wasn't in Stuart's best interests to be adopted by a single person. They really weren't very nice. PFC came down and sorted it out but we never had any support from the committee. It was: 'If you're going to do it, get on with it.' On the day before Stuart was placed with me, I was left to go backward and forward to move his belongings. They said they'd organise some help but they didn't. Good thing he didn't have too much!

Getting started

I was glad when the day came; not once did I think we'd done the wrong thing. At first it was a relief he was finally here and everyone else was out of the picture. No more asking: 'Can I take him out today?' If we wanted to go out we could go out. But then the first few days he didn't seem himself. There was something not quite right and I began wondering: 'Was Stuart unhappy? Was he missing the company of the other children? Did he want to move? Had I done the right thing for him?' I took him to the doctor and it turned out he had an infection in both ears. We still have to be careful to keep his ears warm. He has suffered from bad colds and earache all his life. Once that was put right we definitely knew we'd done the right thing. Stuart settled in and we just got on with life.

I gave up work at the Children's Home and took a part-time lunch job at the special school where Stuart was going. I couldn't ever bear to leave him alone then. The job didn't last long because Stuart was ill so often and I had to stay home with him. I had to get in tune with Stuart having fits at night. After a time it became automatic. He has a fit, I hear him, I get up to check him and we both go back to sleep. Sometimes he has nights when he sits up and rocks and sings to himself, but you get used to it and doze off. I didn't actually miss work but I was lost in the day time when Stuart was at school. I wanted him to be home all the time. It was lovely in the holidays and at the weekends.

I got the adoption allowance and I'd saved a bit of money which I spent on extras for Stuart and on the flat. I wasn't one to go out much anyway, so I didn't miss the social life. For the rest I managed on Social Security. I had some help from my family: my brother does the painting and decorating at cost and so did my Dad until he retired. And they help in other ways with buying bits and pieces. Sometimes I get upset if I haven't got the money to buy something Stuart needs but that's life. You save up or write to some charity and in the end you will probably get it. What's money when you've got Stuart?

When Stuart was placed I felt 'he's mine, his name is changed, and it's all fine'. But the authorities expected me to be able to do more than if he was born to me. It was like: 'You took him on, you knew what you were doing, so why are you asking for help now?' And that went for everything from the nappy service to respite care. We still come across the same attitude now. Sometimes the local social services have said to us: 'Oh, the local authority that placed him ought to pay for that.' And I say: 'Oh, do you really?' and they say: 'Yes,' and I say: 'Well, he's a child from this county so get on with it.'

Sorting out equipment and benefits has always been a problem. There's been an ongoing issue about how many nappies he should have or could have and we said he needed. It was a question of who was going to supply what for Stuart. He came with a wheelchair and a special bed that had been made for him but he needed a special chair for sitting up at the table, a standing frame, bath aids and a toilet seat. It all took time to sort out and he'd grown out of it before he got his first chair. I had to learn to fight for everything Stuart needed which wasn't the easiest thing to do as I didn't like talking to people.

Early rewards

It was lovely to see Stuart laugh and chuckle. He got one-to-one attention all the time and he was happier and that made me happier. He wasn't made to get up in the morning, especially if he'd had a fit. I had an arrangement with the school that I'd let them know by ten o'clock if he was coming in. He could have a bath when he wanted and his tea when he was hungry – it depended on how he was, not on the time of day. There are times he has to be made to do something, like go to the doctor, but on the whole he's better left at his own pace.

To begin with Kevin didn't get a look in. I was the only person looking after Stuart, I never had a day off, I was there all the time for him and he responded to that. We became even more close. I had to learn to share him with Kevin. Now it's Kevin who'll feed him when we're out and he'll read the menu to him and watch for any reaction and place the order as though Stuart had made the choice. We know Stuart and we know he can't really make a responsible choice – he wouldn't know the difference if you said: 'Do you want to go to a Wimpy or to another kind of restaurant?' Or you could give him a cup of orange juice and he'd turn away and you could try half a dozen drinks before he got the one he wanted. Only he wouldn't know which one he wanted until it was offered. But Stuart has had to learn the rules like everybody has to. When we take him out he can't decide to shout and yell and do. He has to behave.

Birth family contacts

Stuart's grandparents live in Australia and they come to see us every other year when they visit England. They send presents at birthdays, Christmas and Easter and they write letters to Stuart telling him all they're doing. They never talk about his parents or what his mother did

194

to Stuart. He has an older brother who didn't know about him until he went to see his grandparents in Australia. He saw a photo of Stuart and asked. He doesn't want to know any more at the moment but I did say to the grandparents that if he ever wants to get in contact, I don't mind him coming. But he needs to have somebody to talk to him about Stuart before he sees him.

It has taken his grandparents a long time to come to terms with how Stuart is. They used to ask: 'Is he walking yet?' or 'Have you got him talking yet?' They just wanted the best for Stuart but now I think they accept him as he is. I think they should be proud of him.

I'm not really bitter or angry about what happened to Stuart although Kevin is, and I'm afraid he might say something to the grandparents or ask questions. When Stuart was little, I used to look at him asleep and then I'd see other children his age play outside and I'd think: 'Stuart should be doing that,' but then I'd think that if Stuart hadn't been hurt, I wouldn't have had him, I wouldn't have had the opportunity to look after him.

Changes

As long as Stuart's bed and belongings are arranged in the same way as before, he's fine about moving. He needs his routine, he needs to know what's happening. He reacts if you move the furniture around and he isn't confident with new people handling him. He knows people by their voice I think.

When I took Reg, Stuart had to be part of it all the way along – I wouldn't leave him at home. I don't know how much he could understand but he was part of it. I said from the very beginning that if they didn't get on I wouldn't be able to take Reg, but Stuart was quite happy with him. He has days when he doesn't want Reg or anyone else around him except Kevin and me – but that's when he's not feeling well.

The same thing happened with Barbara. Everyone was involved in the planning and introductions. Stuart really likes Barbara. He likes being near her and he's very gentle with her. He's big brother; we tell him to look after her and he seems to respond to that. When they were describing Barbara, they were in a way describing Stuart, because she is also a victim of non-accidental injury.

Stuart at school

There's no choice. If there's a school in your area, that's the one he has to go to. If you want one outside your own area, you have to pay for your own transport which can cost a fortune. Children without disabilities have several schools to choose from. Stuart was in a special class for the most severely disabled children until he was 12. Then they moved him to a class with more able youngsters and he started to have problems because he didn't fit in. After a couple of terms they agreed it wasn't working and they put him back in the special class. Then they decided to split that class and to make a separate class for the older ones. Then they had a new policy and all children over 16 had to go into a further education group – a mixed ability class in the same school. We fought very hard for a special unit in the further education stream for children as disabled as Stuart: they needed a multisensory curriculum. That's when things went wrong. The school told me that's what they were offering but it wasn't what Stuart was getting. The curriculum might have been right but the environment wasn't. The school want parent involvement but they don't want parents who disagree. That's what it seems like. I think the main problem is that Stuart and two others are the only young people with profound disabilities they've ever had to deal with at this age.

Another problem at school was about Stuart's fits. They changed. At school they were saying he was holding his head up and smiling and looking around more but when he came home I could tell he was still having a fit. It was a state he got in and would stay in for a long time and it was dangerous for him to eat or anything. In the end they had a meeting with Stuart's consultant and he explained that they were fits. After that I didn't have the confidence to send him to school. We got to the point of taking him out of school altogether when he became ill – so he hasn't been back since and he's due to leave next month because he's 20.

Stuart grows up

Stuart has grown up; he's grown bigger – he's quite a tall young man – but he hasn't made any other progress. He can be left just to sit and do nothing; he's inclined then to switch off and go to sleep. He needs stimulation and attention and you have to know the difference between

Stuart switching off and genuinely wanting to go to sleep. That's why I don't want him to go to an ordinary Day Centre where he could just be left.

Stuart likes going out but if he's had a fit in the night he doesn't want to get up in the mornings. He'll even stay asleep all day. When he isn't well we don't do much but normally he'll get up about ten o'clock. He has his bath in the morning – he's got a spa bath which he really enjoys. He loves music – natural sounds – birds and water and dolphins. He also likes the loud pop music which I don't.

Stuart has been very ill. He's lost a lot of weight and we still don't know what was wrong with him. He went down seven months ago and we've only gradually got him going again. We've been advised to buy a Light Box because he may be affected by the lack of sunlight in winter like in some Scandinavian countries. So now we're saving up for that. We've always said that Stuart hibernates in winter – perhaps he really does.

Stuart still has a lot of fits and the nature of the fits keep changing. At the moment he has fits that knock him out completely for the day. They used to be at night but now they can come at any time. He has developed sexually and masturbates – we stop him if he does it in the living room but leave him to do it in his bed.

Stuart has got very heavy to lift. Only Kevin can lift him on his own now. When my brother and his girlfriend come to sit with Stuart for a few hours, we can't leave them too long because of the lifting. I miss more than anything being able to do all the things for Stuart I used to do. I can't because I can't lift him if I'm on my own. I have to ring the Christian Care Service and they'll send someone if they can. But even that costs £5 an hour and I might need the help for only five minutes.

When Stuart officially leaves school this summer, he'll come under the adult services. The Adoption Allowance will finish and he'll qualify for Income Support in his own right and we're putting in for Severe Disability Allowance and Invalid Care Allowance.

Stuart likes the circus and he likes going to some shows at the theatre if there is a lot of music. He likes the lights and the noise. He went to an ice show and he enjoyed that. We've taken him to the zoo and he fed the elephants with Kevin. If we go anywhere we take him with us so he joins in everything everyone else is doing. He can go on the rides at the pleasure beach. You've got to have someone strong enough to lift him in and out and you've got to take him on twice. The first time he's getting used to it, the second time he really loves it.

Whatever Stuart can do for himself, you let him do. There's quite a lot he can do. He takes your hand and puts it to his mouth if he wants a drink or is hungry. He can hold a spoon and put it to his mouth but he can't put the food on it by himself. He can drink from a cup with a lid and he's also learnt to drink with a straw which is much better when we take him out because he doesn't have to drink from a baby cup. He can pull his socks off and help to take his arms out of his clothes. He can play with the touch screen on his computer. 'What else can you do Stuart?' Oh yes, he likes going swimming when we've got enough people to lift him. He wears a special life jacket that keeps him afloat and he wants to be left alone and to have his freedom to move round the pool. But someone always has to be with him in case he has a fit.

Who helps?
Up till this year we've never had anything to do with social workers. We've had the occupational therapists when we've needed them but no-one else except the PFC post-adoption worker. Now social services have come to us to do an assessment for when Stuart leaves school. They're still doing it. Most of the time professionals have been a hindrance. They'll come and tell me what I need and I have to say: 'No, I don't need that, I need something else.' Like the ramp to the front of this house. We had loads of arguments about that. I knew what I wanted and they knew better. In the end I've had to pay for some of the work and to sign responsibility for it. But our GP is helpful and the specialist Stuart sees for epilepsy has been very helpful.

We've never had respite care for Stuart. We were linked to another family for shared care but it was only for emergencies and when Stuart got bigger they couldn't manage to lift him. We've had an offer of a link for adult care for Stuart now but we'd have to pay, and for the little we'd use it, it wouldn't be worth it. Holidays are my respite! We used to have two a year: one at Blackpool and one with Holidays for the Disabled. Now we can only afford one because Stuart is an adult and he has to pay as an adult. So we go to Blackpool. When we go away for two weeks we get one good week with Stuart if we string the days together and one bad week with his fits. Still, it's a break – different environment, different things.

The choices for Stuart

They haven't offered anything at the moment, they're still trying to work out a plan. I can see them telling me that Stuart has to be allowed to grow up and make choices and leave home. Like when we were trying to get a special wheelchair for him and they said we were wanting to keep him a baby because we didn't want an ordinary adult chair. I tried to explain that we wanted a chair to be comfortable for Stuart as he is.

We're not even considering residential care and they know it. The only place around here is a kind of hostel where Stuart went to be assessed for his fits. He went in for a week and I went in with him which was against the rules. It was a nice enough place but I didn't feel it was a home and I'd never let him go there.

There are no suitable educational courses for Stuart and there's no kind of occupation, like in a sheltered workshop, that he'd be able to follow. Some local parents got together to get a Day Centre for young people like Stuart but the worker assigned to the project and the organisation behind it went their own way. They seemed to forget about the parents and the Centre that will open will still not be suitable for Stuart. We set out to get a different kind of Day Centre with a person running it who understands the needs of young people with severe disabilities, and where the activities each day would be planned to meet their needs as they arose. For instance, they could go out swimming if the group was well enough that day rather than having to stick to a programme. I wanted a place where Stuart would be safe and belong – his own place to be independent. Social services were willing to buy in to this new Centre for specific timetabled activities and to provide the carers to take him – but that wouldn't make him part of anything. Now they don't think it's suitable for him anyway, and they haven't got the money to do it.

This is Stuart's home and if necessary I'd want carers to come and look after him in his own home. It is hard to think of him as being independent but he's got to get used to other people and not just us doing things for him. What I don't want is for people to come in and take over and think they know best.

Our present and our future

Stuart could live to a ripe old age. There's no medical reason why he shouldn't. We plan to go on being a family for a long time.

I'm trying with the greatest difficulty to make a will in case something happens to me. But every time I come up with something, the solicitor says it can't be done. I want to leave the house to the three children with a guarantee of carers coming in for the rest of their lives. So far I haven't been able to find a way of doing that. I have been told that under all the schemes available they can move the children to another house if they think it best. I'd want Kevin to live here with them while he was able to look after them with other carers as he needed them.

One thing you can't do is think that, because you've adopted, everything will come to you. It won't – you've got to be prepared to go out and get it. I'd not tell anyone not to do it. The rewards you get from the children and the love they give outweigh all the problems along the way. I'd do it again exactly the same. I wish the Adoption Allowance could go on longer. Although you don't do it for the money, they still need the same things as they grow up and the money goes down a lot when they get on Income Support and other benefits. Still it won't stop us getting the best out of life. If we want to do something, we'll find a way of doing it.

A magic wand

Anne

If I had a magic wand, with Stuart, the only thing I'd want to change for his sake, is his fits. Then if we could do anything we wanted and had the money for it, I'd want to have a place for adults with severe disabilities to give them day care.

Kevin

I'd like to give Stuart the power of communication so that he could be understood by other people as well as Anne and me. Only then we'd probably be telling him to shut up all the time!

Anne

If there was another magic wand, we'd start an alternative school for disabled children.

14 Their kind of independence
Chris, Fred, Sarah and Matthew

Chris and Fred are full-time parents to 12 children. Some have left home but they still come and go and they are never far from their parents' minds, even if they are out of their sights. Chris and Fred started their family in a small miner's cottage; each time they moved to have more space they took more children. Their three birth children are not disabled; all the others have a variety of severe disabilities. Four of them were placed by PFC, including Sarah and Matthew who became number five and number seven in the family. They are both black of mixed parentage. Chris and Fred are white. The family now lives in a large, remote house in South Wales with enough ground to keep angora goats and to provide a playing field beyond the garden. Chris has told most of this story but Fred says that she speaks for both of them most of the time.

*   *   *

When Sarah came
Chris
We couldn't have any more children of our own after we'd had three and we did want a large family. We'd always fostered babies and small children short term but we wanted to adopt. We never thought we'd be accepted – we thought you had to be of a certain class and income. We were working class, Fred was a miner and we lived in a three bedroomed council house. We already had two private foster children and we had Ben. I'd said to our local social worker that I wouldn't mind caring for a disabled child because as I'd been a nurse, I felt I'd be able to manage. They placed Ben with us. He was five and a half months old and he weighed five pounds. He had got through open heart surgery but there wasn't much hope for him and he was definitely brain damaged. Ben was not expected to live and the two foster boys were not expected to stay. They did stay, for a time at least, and Ben survived. Sarah came to join us in the middle of it all.

We saw something about PFC on television and came up to the office with our daughter Lorraine. She picked out Sarah from the posters on the wall – we'd wanted a younger child with Down's Syndrome and later we did adopt a baby with Down's Syndrome – but on that day we all homed in on Sarah. She was nine. She'd suffered brain damage as a result of physical abuse and there was a question mark about whether she had also been allowed to take dangerous tablets. Her father was sent to prison for the abuse – her mother had disappeared several years earlier and had a psychiatric history.

Sarah was partially sighted, she also had tunnel vision, spasticity of the legs and arms, mild epilepsy and learning difficulties. When we saw her in the Children's Home for the first time, I do clearly remember that her shoes had no toe caps left because she dragged her feet. She was thin and had the most wild, unkempt Afro hair. She looked like a ragamuffin. We took her to the playground in this massive Children's Home and we said to each other: 'Let's take her home now,' but of course we couldn't. We had to see specialists about her and to get to know her. When she first visited us at home, she thought it was a doll's house. You could see why – the bathroom in the Children's Home was bigger than our living room.

Sarah was black, but race wasn't such an issue 20 years ago. We accepted the child as a child with all her special needs – and she was the child we wanted. We were more bothered about oiling her skin to stop it drying out and knowing how to treat her hair correctly than culture or roots.

The honeymoon

Initially we were over the moon with having Sarah. We were also very nervous, very tense, excited and afraid all in one. When a child comes into the family you're extra careful and conscious about how you handle them; you don't want a child to become distressed about something you have or haven't done without realising. And to begin with Sarah was trying so hard to please. At times we over-compensated for her bad beginning. We felt angry about what had happened to her, we also felt sad about it. Perhaps you go over the top. You try to make it right in terms of loving and being close which she found hard to take because she wasn't ready for that. Then we found it hard to understand why she found it hard. But also on the practical side, we were buying her things because she came from the Children's Home so poorly clothed and with very few possessions. We actually went out of our way to make sure that Sarah had the most expensive doll we could afford and things like that. We felt we were doing the right thing at the right time. In retrospect it wasn't really fair to Lorraine although she doesn't bear grudges and she's been a wonderful sister to all of the children we've adopted. We've sat down since and thought about whether, if we'd handled certain things differently when we were going through problem areas, the outcome would have been different – but it may not have been.

After the honeymoon

I'm not sure, in spite of having been to meetings about what these older children can throw up, that we understood it and took it in. It's not totally relevant until you start living it. You know it's happened to somebody else – but it's always somebody else, not you. Sarah slowly but surely began to accept us – and then she'd throw it all back in our face in very hurtful ways: she hated us, we weren't her real parents, she was running away. She used to pack two carrier bags – one with her underwear and one with her teddies, nothing else. Then she'd put her pyjamas on so she couldn't go out of doors and sit at the bottom of the stairs. Eventually she did go up to bed but she didn't unpack the carrier bags for a week. And then she did and she stayed – until the next time.

One day when she said she was going we opened the door for her and said: 'We can't stop you. If you don't love us, we can't make you. But we love you and this is your home and we are your family.' She didn't actually try to go after that but she went on testing us out. We'd go through great highs and lows with her. She tried out everything in the book: lying, stealing, wetting, soiling, refusing to eat, being unable to walk. Although Sarah can't stand on one leg, when she's in a mood she can kick with both legs! Hell would let loose over the most silly things. There was no reasoning with her. She became aggressive, she damaged her own things and things she knew were precious to other people in the family. Or she wouldn't talk to us for days. She could cut you dead and the intensity of feeling this created, you can't describe. Now looking back, every time she did something or we did something to upset her, we were looking for reasons for her behaviour and finding reasons which were not there. Perhaps we should have gone in like a bull in a china shop and confronted her deep down from the beginning. She has always, from her own point of view, had a love-hate relationship with us and it still remains the same to this day.

Family reactions

Lorraine wasn't that much older and she had a hard time with Sarah. She was very protective towards her. She so much wanted her to be her sister but she often felt let down by her. Kevin and Stephen, our sons by birth, were already teenagers. They have always been very matter of fact about other children coming into the family and their attitude hasn't changed over the years. The two private foster boys left soon after Sarah came but Sarah was always exceptionally caring towards Ben. She saw him as the baby. Whether he posed no threat or she realised he was as ill as he was, we don't know.

*   *   *

Lorraine who was listening to this part of the interview had this to say: 'I've never felt left out. I'd had everything before the others came. Mum always used to sit me down and explain about their special needs and why they were getting things I wasn't. But I already had everything I wanted.'

*   *   *

Getting on with it
Chris

It was difficult to know what Sarah couldn't do because she was failing and what she couldn't do because she was being stubborn. It was always one step forward followed by two steps back. When you're hitting the teenage time, you don't know what's what. So there never seemed to be any break: first it was settling in, then it was testing out and then we were getting near teenage. And by that time they had diagnosed deterioration of her brain.

It was good when she seemed to be really part of the family. She could be very loving, she could get on well with other children and we had a special time together in the evening when we used to sit and help her learn to read and write. She managed to learn both by the time she was 11 and then she slowly but surely lost it. Her language skills have always been good. Her concept of her disabilities is unrealistic. She doesn't consider she's disabled; everyone else is wrong about her. This still causes a lot of problems.

There was no Adoption Allowance when we adopted Sarah. Fred worked overtime doing extra shifts at the pit to make ends meet. We had the Attendance Allowance and nothing else. When the doctor came to see Sarah about the Mobility Allowance she suddenly decided to walk fairly well, so we didn't qualify. Apart from that Sarah ruined her shoes rapidly because she would not wear the National Health special boots – they were for 'handicapped people' she said.

In the early years Fred and me just got on with it, as you do when you're raising a family. My Mum liked the idea of our doing "good works" as long as she wasn't mixed up with it. She used to boast about it to her friends but she never actually visited us. As our own children grew up, they helped – especially Lorraine. We knew we could always talk openly to PFC about all the problems the children presented; they never made us feel inadequate or a failure as parents. We belong to PPIAS – I'm actually the co-ordinator for them in this area – and we've been able to offer quite a lot of support to others.

After the first couple of years Sarah went once or twice a year into respite care. It was a converted police house with six beds in the middle of a council housing estate. As we got more children, we practically filled up the place when they went in as a family group.

Schooling

Schooling became quite a big issue from day one with Sarah. She couldn't attend the school for children with disabilities because it was too far away. She would have had to be residential and that was one thing we would not do. Eventually we persuaded the education authority to let her go to the junior school in the village. She was the only disabled child there. Initially it started off very well – some of the more disruptive boys in the class actually became very good with Sarah. But gradually, Sarah was learning to play the school and home off against each other, and that caused major problems. She became disruptive herself and difficult to teach. On one occasion we flew into the school quite angry when Sarah arrived home escorted by two girls. They were distressed and Sarah was crying because, she said, the teachers had been hitting her. We went straight into school believing everything she was telling us only to be greeted by the teacher saying: 'Oh my God, I'm so pleased you're here.' Sarah had been saying exactly the same at school in reverse: telling the teachers we were hitting her. We talked to Sarah, things calmed down but she didn't learn from this episode. Gradually she was doing the same thing again. In the end she had to leave the school because of her behaviour problems and also because her epilepsy was getting harder to control. In any case, they had already let her stay on in the juniors an extra year.

We were also finding it difficult at home to cope with Sarah full time. When she was 12, we reluctantly allowed her to go to a special boarding school for children with severe epilepsy. Guilt will always remain with us about that. We don't know if we were doing the right thing or whether Sarah felt we were sending her away. She seemed to settle in her boarding school and they had their honeymoon as well. The school helped with the epilepsy and we thought it might be the best option for Sarah. But when school holidays came, it was a stranger coming home. She was making a new life with new friends and when she talked to us, in her head, she thought we knew about everything that was happening to her. But we didn't. We were outsiders again. Looking back on our life with Sarah, a lot of it's been like that: we've been only part of her life. She allows you into her life and then she pushes you out – and we feel at certain times we've pushed her out too.

Again, the same problems started rearing their head at boarding school: playing the teachers off one against the other, lying, stealing, tantrums, the whole lot. We'll never know if we contributed to all that by letting her go. Did she feel rejected? Is that what caused it? At the same time she was still doing it at home. We'll never be sure whether what we did was right or wrong. Sarah stayed at school until she was 19 and then she came home and we started another major episode in our life with Sarah.

*   *   *

While Sarah was at boarding school the family accepted a transfer to a larger house, in the same home county, nearer the sea. Kevin and Stephen grew up and went into the army. Three more children were added to the family according to plan: Lucy the baby with Down's Syndrome, Simon aged eight with the mental age of a toddler and Eddie aged 14 with cerebral palsy. But in between Lucy and Simon, Matthew came to stay.

*   *   *

Enter Matthew
Chris

Matthew came to us unexpectedly. He wasn't a chosen child. He came because his placement with another family broke down. We only meant to keep him for three months while PFC found a new family for him. We would care for him and show him love while he was waiting to move on. Little did we know that he wasn't moving on anywhere. PFC couldn't find a family before Matthew made himself at home with us. When we said that we'd need his bed when Stephen came home on leave, he said: 'That's alright, I'll sleep on the floor.' We wanted to persuade him that another family would be better, they wouldn't have as many children already and they would have more time for him – but he didn't want to know. He made up his mind that he was staying before we did. He was anxious about moving again – he wanted Father Christmas to be able to find him. In the end he did stay and we fostered him because we were still unsure whether we could cope emotionally with his medical problems. After a year and a half we became more confident about him and about ourselves and it just seemed natural to adopt him. Matthew also became more confident: if people stared at him or asked him why he looked as he did – was he burned or something? – he'd look them in the face and say: 'I was born like it.'

Matthew was eight years old, black and very disfigured – weird was the description we used when we first saw him. We'd seen him several times on PFC photosheets and I remember I decided it was a great shame but there was no way I could ever love a child like that. Later on I was to eat my words. Matthew's features were bizarre. He had very large eyes that couldn't close because he had no proper eyelids and where surgery had been done around the eyes it was very dark like on a panda. For a long time we didn't realise that he had no proper expression. You couldn't look at him and say he's happy or he's sad. You couldn't see his mouth move; it was misshapen and quite taut. He couldn't really smile. His nose was very short and turned up without nostrils – more like half a nose. He had ear lobes but not the rest of the ears which gave him a kind of pixie look. He had a little whispy hair on what appeared to be a large head and other bits and pieces wrong with him: webbed fingers, peculiar finger nails, strange toes and chronic eczema all over him which needed constant attention. It all seemed very daunting. Matthew has an extremely rare condition which was first described by a man called Ascot, so it is known as Ascot's Syndrome. When he was born, his black mother and white father abandoned him in hospital and could not be traced. It was thought they went abroad.

Matthew's appearance bothered me quite a bit. It wasn't so much how he looked but how I felt about how he looked. I can remember feeling concerned about touching him, washing him, kissing him, just being with him – yet he was an ordinary little boy. The major obstacle to Matthew becoming secure was my coming to terms with the way he looked. I can't say how long it took, it just happened; one day I realised I wasn't bothered any more. He was just Matthew.

*   *   *

Fred said that he never shared Chris's reaction to Matthew's disfigurement. As far as he was concerned, once they had decided to keep him, he became just another member of their mixed ability, mixed race family.

*   *   *

Chris

The other children accepted Matthew very easily. Sarah seemed pleased to have a black brother when she came home for the holidays. Most friends and neighbours were fine once they got used to him. They'd take a sideways look and try not to stare. There was only one family who told us straight that if we kept Matthew they would stop coming to the house. We thought it was because of his looks but it was because he was black.

Matthew had lived in a hospital for nearly all his life before he came to us so we had very good medical information; we saw all the specialists at the hospital and his plastic surgeon in London. We knew

Matthew would have to have a whole series of operations over many years.

Matthew settles

Matthew's behaviour wasn't described as a problem – only his disfigurement. He was as good as gold when he first came because he was so desperate to stay. Even when he began to relax we found his behaviour quite normal except that he didn't know about family life. He didn't know about money or time – he expected the food trolley when he felt it was time to be fed. He didn't have any ideas about the value of possessions or about family relationships: grandparents, auntie, brother and sister were not within his understanding. He couldn't grasp that people who didn't live with us were part of the family – like the two older boys who had left home and Sarah who was at school. We found at times that he was very self-centred; sharing and thinking of others weren't really Matthew's priorities. Perhaps he felt he had to defend his new territory. He could be quite a bully towards Ben when we weren't watching but when Ben was sick it was Matthew who wanted to look after him and slowly he became a more caring, outgoing boy.

Matthew went through school rather than to school. He went as regularly as his operations allowed. He had a lot of fun and made a lot of friends but academically he came out with nothing. He still has trouble reading and writing and doesn't always understand forms. Soon after Matthew came to us we moved to a new area, to a larger house, and he changed to a Catholic school because the one nearer to us *said* they had no vacancies. Matthew became very religious for quite a long period and it suited him. He needed that kind of commitment. He sang in the choir and he was an altar boy. For a time he wanted to become a priest. He grew out of it but it helped him although we don't know how. It might have been the friendship or it might have been the beliefs. Now he doesn't attend church but he's kept in touch with the friends he made there.

*   *   *

Matthew's struggle

In 1989 Christine wrote a book about Matthew called: *Matthew, My Son's Struggle* (See Further Reading). The following two excerpts about Matthew's physical problems are taken from that book.

*   *   *

Matthew has never complained about his looks or his lot . . . he never asks to have any exceptions made for him although day-to-day life has been hampered for him by his webbed trigger fingers . . . his cracked, dry skin and his lidless eyes which would bleed and water, making his already poor eyesight worse. We tried contact lenses but they dropped out because Matthew's eyes water so much and when the optician devised glasses held on by an elastic band around the back of Matthew's head, his skin bled almost constantly.

. . . even apparently straightforward events, like going to camp with the Cubs, became a major operation . . . The Scout Leader let us pick him up once a day to take him home and bathe his skin in the special cream needed to prevent it bleeding too much. We always got him back for supper and songs round the camp fire . . .

*   *   *

In 1986 Matthew was nominated by his Headmaster for 'The Child Overcoming Adversity' section of Dr Barnado's and Rumbelow's Champion Children Award. He had just had another operation on his ears which had turned out badly, leaving one rather bulbous ear higher than the other. Chris and Fred thought he needed a boost to his confidence. Matthew won the award, together with two other children.

*   *   *

Fred
We weren't satisfied with the results of the plastic surgery Matthew was getting, we always felt there should be something better. Then we watched a TV programme about reconstructive surgery on a boy of Matthew's age and it was Matthew himself who asked if we could take him to America to see that surgeon. We wrote and had a reply to say if we could get him there he'd see Matthew but he couldn't promise anything. Then it was a question of money.

I'd been offered redundancy at the end of the long miners' strike in 1985 and we decided to take it so that I could be a full-time father but it made money tight even without extras. So we started fund raising. With the help of the Scouts, the Firemen, the local church, national television and press coverage and many friends, we raised £190,000 and put it in a trust fund for Matthew. There's still some left and Matthew will have enough for any further operations he will need.

I took Matthew to America for the first time in 1986 when he was 12 years old. Chris stayed at home with Ben and Lucy and Simon and Eddy, who had all joined us by then. Sarah was still at school and Lorraine had left home to start her own family. We got VIP treatment organised by the Fire Service and the Scout movement here and over there. We were invited to Disneyland and Cape Canaveral, Cape Kennedy as it then was.

Matthew was excited when we got to the clinic. He was examined from the top of the hair on his head to his toe nails. The surgeon accepted Matthew but there was more surgery to be done than we had expected. They took some of his skull to make cheek bones, they took his ears off and planted some of the cartilage in his chest to keep fresh, then they re-shaped his ears and put them back on. They put plastic shields under his lower eyelids so that he could close his eyes and protect them from sunlight. They reshaped his nose and mouth. He was in surgery for 16 hours. The operations, the recovery, the physiotherapy and other treatments took seven weeks that first time. We stayed in a kind of hostel run by the clinic for the families of sick children.

Matthew had to go to America twice more and each time the surgeon made some improvements. Chris hates to travel but she came with us the second time. Ben, Lucy, Simon and Eddy went into respite care together, Matthew made a very quick recovery and we were back in less than two weeks. After his three visits to the States, Matthew saw the surgeon whenever he came to England and he had more operations in a private hospital on the outskirts of London.

Chris

We never expected to raise so much money and we didn't expect it to have such an effect on the family. Matthew got quite big headed and arrogant. Poor Ben, who didn't understand any of it and was two years younger than Matthew, went round to the neighbours with a hat to collect pennies so that he could go to America too. Everyone else in the family took a back seat while Matthew became the centre. He was asked to make special appearances nationwide and he became a celebrity. He coped. He coped with the disfigurement, with the operations and all that discomfort and pain, with the publicity and with the gaps in his education so that he was for ever having to catch up. Matthew has always had the ability to talk his way through and out of serious situations. On the other hand, if he cut his finger or had to have an injection he could be a big baby. It was as if those were things he didn't have to put up with. The worst things for us have been Matthew's own disappointments after some of the surgery.

End of school
By the time Sarah left school at 19, Lorraine had a baby and Sarah was determined she would have one too and look after it on her own. She was sexually developed but she was completely incapable of living by herself because of her epilepsy. She could never be left alone. This in turn caused her major frustration. In her own eyes she was able to live independently and everyone else was stopping her.

Sarah came home, she attended a Day Centre and we tried to ease her back into family life. It was difficult for Sarah to accept her own limitations. She didn't want to go to the Day Centre but any employment was out of the question. She felt restricted and created chaos all the way through the family. Social workers were advising us to let her go into residential care but we thought we had a better idea. We were by then living in a ten bedroomed house that had been a seaside hotel and we turned the top floor into a flat for her. We employed people nearer to Sarah's own age than us and we got her to help us interview them to find out who she liked best. Sarah and the helper were completely independent and not answerable to us. Sarah was funded in her own right by social services and her welfare benefits. It was fine for a couple of months – then Sarah didn't like the carer any more and we found a slightly older one. Again it worked to begin with and then Sarah started to complain and to disrupt the situation until the helper left. That's when we realised we'd got to the end of the road. Sarah was 21 and there was no alternative but for her to go into adult residential care.

There were waiting lists for many of the good establishments. Others that we liked or Sarah liked wouldn't take her because one of her many disabilities didn't fit the criteria. Also we were very honest about her disruptive behaviour. Eventually we found a place with a black Head of Home and she stayed there for six years. The setting wasn't ideal but the owner made up for the lack of facilities.

Matthew was fine until he went to college when he was 17. He was doing catering and still living at home. After about a term he wanted to live-in like some of the others. We felt he wasn't emotionally ready but his tutors said he was. So, reluctantly on our part, he moved out. We did explain to them at college that Matthew won't get up in the morning unless you kick him out of bed and alarm clocks aren't of much use. He was a typical teenager but because of his background he was a bit delayed with everything. Then he got into trouble with not attending classes – he either couldn't get up or couldn't be bothered to go. Initially he was being taught in a special department for the disabled where they had extra help in Maths and English to get them up to standard. Matthew didn't like that. So he was integrated into the mainstream courses with still a little extra help.

By this time Matthew knew it all and we knew nothing. That's when we had the grant problems. From the age of 18 Matthew was having his own grant paid directly to him which he promptly spent in a fortnight treating all his friends at the pub. This meant he hadn't paid for his board and lodging or his tuition; as the parents named on the grant papers, we were sent all the bills. That was a shock. We had meetings: Matthew had more chances than most, with us paying out a lot of money. But he wasn't getting what he wanted out of college – he wanted to be a chef straight away. Then one day he was picked up drunk; he was unconscious and the police rang us in the middle of the night. He staggered on at college for a bit longer, subsidising himself by selling all the things we'd been buying for him – like his own TV and stereo. Or if he broke anything, he'd put it in for repair and give our name and address so we'd get the bill. We also got his account from the local taxi driver!

Roots and continuity

When Sarah was a more articulate person than she is now, she had as much resistance to being called black as to being called disabled. She knew that her mother was white and felt that she had more right to call herself white than anyone else had to call her black. When we tried to introduce black issues into the home, she always denied their existence. Even when we had three black children in the family, she didn't seem able to associate race with colour.

We have one photograph of Sarah's father but none of her mother. We all talk about the past and birth families here but Sarah has never wanted to know more. She's always been afraid of her father and for a long time she was afraid of all black men. The court stopped her father having any access to Sarah or any information about her. The black Head of the Residential Home probably helped Sarah as much as is possible with her identity.

We've talked long and hard to Matthew about his roots and his race but it's no big deal for him. He doesn't seem to think that being adopted into a white family has made any difference to him. That's what he tells us – whether he's being kind, we don't know. He mixes easily with black and white and he says he's interested in people not in colour. When he was in his early teens, PFC introduced Matthew to black befrienders. They were a lovely young couple with two children. Matthew used to stay with them for weekends and they took him to the Notting Hill Carnival. It was good but it was misleading – it was black treats and Matthew thought to be black was treats time. Matthew kept it up for a year – then he got more interested in his own friends and community.

While Matthew was going through his difficult phase, we used to ask him: 'Is it because you're adopted? Do you want to know about your parents? You don't have to wait until we're dead, we'll help you.' But he used to say: 'They're not my parents, they had their chance and you're my Mum and Dad' – even if he did kick us in the teeth. He knows that PFC tried to trace his parents before he was placed with us so he also knows that they probably can't be found.

Adults

Matthew left college without finishing his course. He came back home to live and went to work in a local pub, helping in the restaurant and helping at table. He has no worries now about being up front about his appearance. He's never been out of work since he started. He seems to get jobs offered when nobody else does. He stayed in catering and eventually found a live-in job in a hotel and moved out of home for good. But he stayed in roughly the same area of Wales we are now living in.

Then one day, when he was 19, he rang up and dropped a bombshell: he and a couple of his friends were going to live in London. And he went – with little money and nowhere to live except the promise of a friend's floor. Two days later there was a phone call: 'Mum, I've quarrelled with my friends, they're not my friends any more, I'm hungry and cold, can you help?' And we couldn't, we were too far away. I told him to try and make his way to Centrepoint, I'd been watching a TV programme about it. They phoned us from Centrepoint to say thank you and he stayed there until they found him a room and helped him to get a job.

The bills mounted again because it took Matthew a long time to learn how to deal with money – but then he had a lot of time to make up. Matthew is still working in London. He's had offers under the disability quota scheme but he doesn't want that. Like Sarah, he refuses to acknowledge himself as disabled. And he's proving himself right – he isn't disabled although he's disfigured.

Matthew is independent now but completely attached to the family. He brings his friends down – black or white – he belongs, he's one of us for life. Sarah is the same. We can't live together but we couldn't be without each other. Sarah is as attached to us as we are to her but it is still on her terms. Partly she'd like to be at home but deep down she knows it doesn't work.

Sarah is 30 now. Through all the years she's called us Mum and Dad. We're still her family and we're the ones she tells her troubles to. We have now, after all these years, come to the conclusion that Sarah does really need a family, she needed to be adopted, she needs our support but she can't live with us. Whenever she does, she is spiteful, destructive, hurtful and very loving at the same time. We know she can't help it but she's come near to destroying not only her life but our lives as well. Yet we all loved each other. But we also get very, very cross with her. We love her to bits and we wish it could be any other way.

Our plans for Sarah were that she would grow up in the family and that she would remain with the family because of her disabilities. We never envisaged Sarah living permanently away from home though we know that all children eventually do have to leave home. Perhaps we weren't ready for her to go. Maybe if Sarah could have left home to be more independent and if she lived nearer to us, we'd feel better about it. If someone told us that there was anything wrong we'd fight hell and high water to get it put right for Sarah. We'd never let her down. But if you said, 'Sarah has got to come home to live,' I'd run a mile.

Present and future expectations

Sarah's future is an unknown quantity. Physically she is deteriorating quite fast. She can't walk without a Zimmer frame and reluctantly uses a wheelchair outdoors. Mentally she's also regressed but she hasn't lost her stubbornness and determination. She doesn't want to stay in one place for long; she's requested three moves since she's been in residential care. This is a pattern she's likely to keep up until she runs out of options. She arranges her own moves now through social services and because she's an adult they don't have to discuss it with us. We're only informed after the event. We're resigned to it but we have felt resentful at times. There's a lot of conflict with these young people because they are not able to be truly independent or to judge what is best. At the end of the day we're here to pick up the pieces.

Matthew is 23 and he should be able to live a long and fairly happy life. He makes the most of his job opportunities and has matured and learned from his mistakes. He's doing outside catering and deliveries and he's just beginning his training to drive heavy goods vehicles. He no longer expects to be the chef at the Savoy. His health is stable, on the whole, but he will go on having plastic surgery until he feels he's had enough or it's decided that nothing more can be done. He's capable of making his own decisions about that. Matthew had a rough passage in late adolescence but he's turned out a success story.

*   *   *

Lorraine joined us again at this point and had something to add: 'Matthew has turned out to be a really great lad. He's not a timid person any more, he's grown up and gets on with life. I was never shocked by his appearance. When I used to take him out he would put up his hood and hide and I'd say: "Put it down, be proud of yourself," and now he is.'

After the family moved to Wales, they adopted three more older children with severe and multiple disabilities, one of whom has died. Stephen has left the army and is a victim of what has been termed Gulf War Syndrome. Lorraine has two children and Kevin is an active uncle and brother. All three have moved to Wales and live in their own homes a very short distance from their parents.

*   *   *

Chris

Stephen and Matthew are great friends. They share a lot of tastes and Matthew goes to Stephen for masculine advice. Sarah relates most to Ben and Lucy and Eddy. Lorraine's two daughters have grown up with our disabled children and they take them in their stride. We have 11 children now; six of them still live at home. We had 12 but sadly lost one after having him for seven years. We were all broken up but Matthew took it exceptionally badly. All our children are disabled except the three who were born to us. They live a stone's throw away and are in and out of here all the time. We've moved three times, each time to something bigger, so we have plenty of room to expand and we're looking forward to having another son very soon.

If we both died, Sarah would be able to continue the life style she now has. Social services have taken responsibility but she would always have her brothers and sister to call on, like every other adult with a family. The same is true of Matthew although he has become truly independent. He's even become street wise. At times he's still naïve but he's made it as good as most.

218

There's really nothing Sarah and Matthew need now that they haven't got. They're more comfortable than a lot of other people. They don't live on the streets in cardboard boxes or in unsuitable institutions. Matthew has his own place and is making his own way in life. Sarah is cared for and her needs are met as well as they can be. At the end of the road, they've both had years of family life to set them up for their kind of independence.

*   *   *

Matthew has his say
Matthew leads a busy life in London; when he goes home, he brings two or three friends and hardly 'touches ground' according to his parents. He had not had time to read this story so we went through it together in a London pub before he made his comments.

*   *   *

Matthew
I don't like the word "disabled". I never use it about myself – not even to get benefits – I wouldn't ever class myself as disabled. If I was telling my story I wouldn't go into the same depth like my Mum did in her book. I'm not keen on everyone knowing my personal story. But I agree with everything my Mum and Dad have said here, except that I did finish college. I did the three and a half years. I failed the first exam and re-sat it and passed it and I've got my first catering certificate and a food and hygiene certificate as well.

I liked doing practical more than sitting in the classroom and the fact is, I found it hard in the classroom. It wasn't my idea to go to college, it was my parents' – they wanted me to get more education. I didn't choose it but it worked out alright in the long run. Sometimes I still have problems with spelling. I think I didn't concentrate at school and it's more that I'm lazy than that I can't do things. I wish now I'd learnt more at school but I am learning to sort things out more for myself than relying on somebody else.

I left home so soon because both Kevin and Stephen were in the army and they used to come home and talk about different places. So I wanted to get out there as well and be like my brothers. They've lived their own lives since they were 18 and that's what I wanted even though my Mum and Dad were a bit protective – I know they thought I'd fall flat on my face and wouldn't cope in the society that was out there. I've had to prove to myself as well as them that I can cope in society. They didn't really prepare me for leaving home because they thought I wasn't going to. So I've had to find my own way. It's been tough but I'm glad I did it.

I had to leave Wales because there wasn't much work there and the life style was very quiet. I miss my brother Steve – he's gone back to Wales. If I've got a problem I always speak to him first and I phone him up if I need advice. He's coming down to stay with me in my flat. I've lived in it for one and a half years but I haven't decorated yet. Perhaps he'll sort me out.

Colour matters a bit more to me in London when I have to explain to friends why my parents are white. I feel I have been brought up in a white background but now I would say I fit into either culture.

I've always wanted to be like everyone else. When I look at other people with facial disfigurement I feel all my surgery and all the pain has paid off. But I'm still not satisfied. Really when I think about it, it hasn't been me that's said: 'I'll have this done or that done'. It's been my parents. Now I'm going to make my own decisions. At the same time I'm scared that I'll insist to have something else done and it turns out not to be successful. I thought I'd had enough surgery. It's only since this year I've looked at myself and I've thought there's more that could be done. I'm going to see the surgeon here to talk about it and next year I want to go back to America to see my surgeon there.

*   *   *

Matthew has recently left his catering and delivery job at an Exhibition Centre, after three and a half years.

*   *   *

Matthew

I found the hours too unsociable and the money side as well. The work was too unsteady – it depended on when there were exhibitions. I'm still driving; I drive a van for the Borough now. It's a lot better money and it's a full-time job. In a way, I wish my parents lived in London and then I'd still be living at home. I miss my parents a lot – it's the little things, like I've ripped my work trousers and I've got to send them home to my Mum to sew up.

*   *   *

Sarah has her say
Sarah now lives in a family-sized house on the Kent coast. She has a large, airy bed-sitting room with a bathroom next door. Two older disabled people also live in the house; they have lived there for twelve years. The resident carers, Sue and Graham, are a young couple with two small daughters. Sue buys Sarah's clothes and looks after her benefits including a personal allowance of £14 a week with which Sarah buys toiletries and sweets; some of it she saves.

*   *   *

Sarah
This is a family here but it's not my family. I let the girls come up and play with me sometime or I let them watch a video in my room. I miss my Mum and Dad and I miss my brothers and sisters. I want to be part of a proper family. I've written to Mum – and I've posted it – to say I want to come home. It depends on Mum and the family what they decide. I know it was my fault it didn't work out – I can't blame my Mum for that, can I? I'm going home for Christmas and she says we'll talk about it then. I'm really looking forward to Christmas.

I go to work – it's a Day Opportunity Centre. When I first went there you had to put the screws into the holes in rods but now it's got better and we've got more choice. We have students' meetings to say what the students want in the Centre and how they want the Centre run. I do different things on different days. Monday I'm out swimming, Tuesday I have leather-work and woodcraft, Wednesday morning I do the Newsletter. I help other people who can't speak up for themselves because I'm very good at speaking up. I know what I want and how to put it across. Wednesday afternoon I do computers and then Thursday morning I have singing and music and in the afternoon painting. Friday it's computers again and free time in

WHATEVER HAPPENED TO ADAM?

the afternoon. We can watch videos or go into the disco. We get paid £1.50 a week every Thursday.

In the evenings, if it's nice, I ask if we can go out for a walk. It's up to me if I go in my wheelchair or with my walking frame. I never go to the Centre in the wheelchair. If it's not a nice day I come up and play my video game Mum gave me for my birthday or I like listening to my music. On Saturday we go out either to the sea front and we have our dinner out or we go somewhere else or we go to the boating park. Sunday I watch Eastenders.

Lots of things get me fed up I suppose. Sometimes I'll wake up in a bad mood and I'll go to work and come back in a good mood. But if I'm still in a bad mood I'll put my music on full blast. There's some days I won't speak to Graham and Sue but after a couple of days I will. It's like it is with my Mum. I think of my Mum and Dad a lot. I look at their photo over my bed all the time. I just can't wait until I go home for Christmas.

When I went to live with Mum and Dad first, I could talk to both of them. Then after a while I found it hard. Now if me and my Mum are in a room together I find it hard to start a conversation. I don't know how my Mum feels about this, I don't know how it's happened, I don't know. I have a lady come to see me – she's a counsellor – I tell her all my problems really. I find her easy to talk to.

It was alright being adopted when I went to court and that, and meeting the people from PFC and the picnics. The worst thing is now because I'm not with Mum and Dad and I'm to blame a lot. It's just my fault. My attitude should have been different. I should have had more control about what I was doing and saying. I should have thought more about Mum and Dad and my brothers and sisters, how they were feeling. I only thought about myself. I was horrible to my sister. I broke her toys because I was jealous. But I'm beginning to change as I grow up, it's like I was a different person. But I don't suppose my Mum and Dad will ever want to have me back. The other worst thing was being in the Children's Home. I can't remember how many I've been in and I'm glad I'm not there any more.

I'm not black, I'm brown. I accept white people like my Mum and Dad and they accept me.

I don't mind if my Mum reads this but I don't know what she'll think. I don't want to upset her; I don't want to upset the applecart.

*   *   *

Sarah was very interested in what her family had said about her and listened intently as their story was read to her after she had told her own. Occasionally she asked for an explanation. She said she didn't know that 'my Mum and Dad think so much about me'.

When we went to a restaurant to have lunch Sarah was most tolerant of my inexperience with a wheelchair. After I gave her a nasty jolt and apologised, she said: 'Never mind, you're only a learner.'

Sarah asked me to write down everything we had talked about and eaten, so she could tell her friends, because sometimes she forgets things. We agreed that I would send her a copy of her story and that she would read it with Sue. Because, 'If anything has to be written down or read, Sue does it.' Sarah said she would ring her Mum to see what she thought of it.

Sarah went home for Christmas. Everyone said the holiday was a success. Now they are all looking forward to the next time.

*   *   *

On reflection
Chris and Fred

We've coined a saying in our family: 'Very often it's not the children, it's the so-called experts that cause the problems.' The children don't understand the consequences of what they do, but they have this ability to manipulate the situation and to play one lot off against the other. If we believed all the children said, half their teachers and social workers would be under investigation. But too often the roles are reversed and teachers and social workers believe what the children say about us. It doesn't mean that we don't listen to what our disabled children are saying, but we learn to analyse what is happening and professional people don't seem able to do that. A lot of it has to do with lack of communication.

Looking back, we'd do it all over again. We wouldn't be without any of them. It's hard going but it can be fun. These older children come with a damaged past and there's the risk of a very damaged future in adolescence and adulthood. You never know when you take an older child with disabilities what the precise damage is and what the future holds. What you think it holds is not always what it turns out to be. When you take disabled children you think, because they're disabled, they'll be dependent on you and living with you for ever and ever but in the end they need to move on like the next young person – to live their own lives. It's getting that right and feeling right about it which is the problem.

Postscript

It would not be fair to the families who have so generously given their time and shared their experiences to leave their stories behind without learning some lessons and drawing some conclusions.

There are several common threads running through many of the stories. Mothers speak of 'falling in love' with their disabled children while at least two of them say it was definitely not a case of love at first sight but that love grew. Either way, there is an emphasis on the chemistry of attraction. Do placement workers always pay enough attention to how prospective carers intuitively react to a particular child or do we "approve" people for a category of children and expect them to take the child we suggest? It is worth noting in this context that families are not predictable about who will appeal to them: 'We chose the child no-one else wanted,' or 'I asked for the child who was most disabled,' or 'No-one else was interested but me,' are often the reasons given for that first response towards a disabled child.

There were an alarming number of references to social workers who 'don't listen to what parents say,' who 'think they know best,' or 'say we don't count because we only foster'. A few families felt it was necessary to humour social workers: 'If you keep professionals happy, then they'll leave you alone after that.' The most often repeated complaints were made about professionals who advocated the importance of free choice for young adults with disabilities, without really knowing the young person or the risks involved: 'This worker put words into Sharon's mouth without even knowing how her mind worked. She said, "Sharon wants to come here, don't you Sharon?" And of course Sharon said "yes" but she didn't know what she was saying "yes" to.'

Families could feel excluded if social services became involved in the care of their grown up sons and daughters: 'Because she's an adult, they don't have to discuss anything with us – we're only informed after the event.' On the whole, families kept their sense of humour and quietly went on doing what they knew was right for their children, even when they grew up. One adoptive mother put it very clearly: 'Social services kept on saying to me "They've got a choice" but I say to them "Yes, they have a choice but they don't have the intellect to make a choice – someone has to do it for them, and that's going to be me and not you." ' However, decisions on behalf of disabled sons and daughters were not taken lightly; adoptive parents describe vividly how they have agonised over getting it right. In two cases, professional insistence on independence and choice for the disabled young person led to tragic results: Gary died before his foster carer was even informed that he had been ill and Margaret became pregnant without comprehending what had happened to her.

The fear of sexual abuse was widespread among the families who speak out in this book. Some parents have little confidence in adult day care for disabled young people; they say that their special vulnerability is not acknowledged and that there are no safeguards about who is employed. Sexual abuse is always shocking – when people with disabilities are abused it is horrifying. Moreover, when disabled people are abused the perpetrator may not even be charged because people with learning difficulties are often considered to be unreliable witnesses. All parents are aware of the pitfalls when young adults move towards independence, but disabled people are at greater risk of every kind of abuse and that makes it even harder to let them leave home or to be looked after by strangers. The stories of Margaret and Helen reinforce the need for vigilance.

Not all social workers were criticised. Some were highly valued as were some general practitioners, medical consultants and specialists of all kinds including a police surgeon. In general, families appreciated professionals who 'knew what they were talking about': those who knew about a particular disability, understood the problems of a particular family and had taken the trouble to get to know a particular child or young person. Families have to fight for the interests of their disabled children; they want social workers who will be on their side and will not label them as aggressive or unco-operative because they are good fighters.

It will not escape the reader's notice that many transracial placements have been included in this collection. In the early days at PFC there was no firm policy about same-race placements. Although families from minority ethnic groups were sought, none were found and it has to be admitted that ethnicity was seen as less relevant than meeting the needs of disabled children to have a family. It could also be said that nobody looked hard enough or that the agency did not have the right workers for the job. The families and young people who speak in this book have their own views which they have forcibly expressed: 'We are a mixed race family. Mexican and Irish is not the same as Ugandan or English or Iraqi, and the difference does matter, but it is more important for Emily and Firas to have a family than a colour match. You don't sacrifice a family for a child for the sake of an ideal.'

Education is another major theme in nearly every story. Whatever it was that families expected and wanted for their disabled children, very few managed to get it and the provision for disabled young adults has been equally disappointing. Only one young person's college course was described as entirely suitable – and that one had to be fought for. Boarding school was sometimes the only place offered for a child and this led to feelings of guilt about sending children away who could not tell the difference between rejection and leaving home to go to school. Families frequently talked about learning from their own mistakes but they felt that the education system made the same mistakes over and over again.

One of the most intriguing facts to emerge is that the only three young people able to work trained to be chefs and, although they never met, they shared expectations of cooking at the Ritz or the Savoy. The three were placed as older children and comprehended what it meant to have a family – they all speak warmly of their new parents. Is it fanciful to suppose that feeling nurtured at an age when they could appreciate it, they wanted to go out into the world to nurture others? In any case, due to medical problems, all three have had to give up the attempt.

As many as four out of the 14 families represented here, took on children whose disabilities hid a more distressing psychotic condition which was only revealed later. Another four children were found to have more extensive or complex disabilities than had at first been diagnosed. Perhaps it is impossible to do more than prepare families for a leap in the dark to face the unknown and then to support them to do what only they can do. Every story told here cries out for specialised post-placement services, for better funding of existing provision, for more generous disability grants and benefits, for skilled workers in day care, for protection of disabled adults from abuse, for arrangements to suit disabled people when their parents die, and for a greater awareness of the needs of all disabled people.

It is amazing that when families were asked what they would like to do most, nearly all of them wished to do something for other people with disabilities. One mother wants to open an alternative school, another a respite care home, a third would love her own hydrotherapy pool for her own son and others. The largest families simply wanted to add on more disabled children as they moved to bigger and bigger houses. Most of the families already did, or planned to do, voluntary work with disabled people in the community. All the people I interviewed left me feeling exhausted by their seemingly endless energy, staggered by their day-to-day efforts, nourished by their hospitality and inspired by their remaining aspirations. 'How can they do it?' I asked myself every time. 'Can this really be true?' But seeing and hearing is believing.

Although it has long been accepted that single parent families may be the best families for some children, it is salutary to calculate that 12 out of the 20 children in this book have been cared for by eight single mothers and one single father. Two of the mothers were widowed and two couples divorced. The mothers kept the children; two found new partners, one remarried and the disabled young people became part of reconstituted families: 'My children had to accept him as much as him having to accept the children.' The five remaining couples have 36 adopted, fostered and birth children between them (only eight of them are featured here) which is a fair indication that they like being parents. Three of these parents are full-time fathers; they gave up work outside the home because they preferred to look after their disabled children. The other fathers are also involved with the care of their children to an unusual degree.

It is stressful to live with disabled children – not even the most enthusiastic family has denied that – and it has to be a strong marriage to withstand the strain: 'We didn't have time like a normal couple to go out and enjoy ourselves. I like travelling; I still miss it.'

'In a lot of ways adopting disabled children has cemented our marriage. We've had to get through such a lot – it either brings you closer together or it pushes you apart.'

It is gratifying to read how often families describe some horrendous difficulty they have encountered and then dismiss it by saying: 'So we got in touch with PFC and they sorted it out.' My memory is that we offered a listening ear and support for whatever solution they found for themselves. As I read and re-read their stories, I can only salute their achievements. It is a testament to their fortitude, commitment, compassion and above all to their love, that the 20 young people who feature in this book have all remained, in some way or another, permanent members of their "new families".

Hedi Argent
May 1998

Appendix I
Glossary of disabilities

Adrenal hyperplasia describes the increased production and growth of the adrenal gland. The condition requires careful monitoring and life-long medication. It may be accompanied by developmental delay and by a hirsute appearance.

Alports Syndrome is a rare genetic disease which causes kidney failure. The syndrome is associated with deafness and serious eye problems.

Ascots Syndrome is an extremely rare condition which prevents the prenatal development of the eyelids, lips, palate, ears, nose and some internal organs. Babies born with this syndrome require extensive plastic surgery throughout childhood. The facial disfigurement will be a life-long factor.

Autism is a pervasive developmental disorder which affects social and communication skills. There may be other learning difficulties. Characteristic behaviour is obsessive and withdrawn. Children with autism can be exhausting to care for because rules, language and social interaction are incomprehensible to them.

Brain damage before or after birth can cause an unspecified variety of symptoms ranging from mild learning difficulties to complex and profound physical and mental disabilities. Cause and effect may be hard to separate and it is often impossible to make a diagnosis or a prognosis.

Cardiomyopathy describes any chronic disorder affecting the muscle of the heart. There is no specific treatment but the condition can be controlled.

Cerebral palsy is the result of damage to the part of the brain concerned with movement. The effects may be slight or severe and include spasticity (disordered movement control), athetosis (frequent involuntary movements) and ataxia (unsteady gait). Adjacent parts of the brain may also be affected and lead to impaired hearing or sight and learning difficulties.

Cystic fibrosis is a hereditary disease of the glands. The lungs and the pancreas are the most affected. The mucus blocks the airways which are then damaged by repeated infections. The channels of the pancreas also become blocked and cysts are formed leading to fibrosis of the pancreas. Cystic fibrosis is a life-threatening condition but 75 per cent of affected children now survive into adulthood.

Down's Syndrome is caused by a congenital chromosome abnormality. Children who are affected have mild to severe learning difficulties and distinctive features (hence the term "mongolism" which is no longer in use). Up to two hundred ailments, some serious and some quite minor, can be associated with Down's Syndrome; affected children therefore vary enormously in their level of disability as well as in their person-alities.The life expectancy of people with Down's Syndrome has been greatly enhanced by the introduction of antibiotics to fight infection.

Ebstein's Anomaly of the tricuspid valve is a rare heart disease usually found in older people. It causes fatigue and sudden loss of consciousness.

Epilepsy is a tendency to have recurrent seizures due to an excessive or disordered discharge of brain cells. *Petit mal* is a term for minor fits or seizures which are often no more than a momentary break in conscious-ness. *Grand mal* describes major convulsive seizures.

Gunter's Disease is a rare skin condition which reacts to sunlight.

Hydrocephalus is an obstruction to the natural flow of cerebro-spinal fluid which can result in the enlargement of the head in young babies. Usually a shunt (a piece of tubing with a pressure valve) is inserted in the back of the neck to prevent the condition from worsening but some brain damage may be sustained. Shunts can become blocked and cause further damage if not checked immediately symptoms occur.

Meniere's Syndrome is a condition affecting the inner ear in which deafness is associated with vertigo. The attacks of vertigo are sudden and combined with pallor, nausea and vomiting. Between attacks there may be months without symptoms. The cause of the syndrome is not known.

Noonan Syndrome is a genetic condition which is variable in degree but may include heart defects, drooping eyelids and widely spaced eyes, short neck and stature, hearing loss and mild developmental delay.

Spina bifida occurs when the newborn baby has part of its spinal cord and coverings exposed through a gap in the backbone. The resulting disabilities may include paralysis of the legs, incontinence and brain damage from commonly associated hydrocephalus. The extent of the damage depends on the type of spina bifida and on the site of the defect.

Tetraplegia is the paralysis of three limbs accompanied by loss of sensation in the body.

Tuberous sclerosis is a variable genetic disorder which may invade many of the body systems. Typically the brain, skin, heart, eyes, kidneys, bones, lungs and intestines are affected by swellings and hardening of an organ or tissue. Seizures and some degree of retardation are usual; behaviour problems and autistic tendencies are common.

232

Appendix II
Explanatory notes

Parents for Children

Parents for Children's (PFC) philosophy was not to find families without problems but to assess the capacity of potential carers to overcome problems. People came forward in response to the publicised needs of a particular child. There were no conditions regarding age, marital status, income, religion or occupation.

- Videos were made of children referred to the agency and shown to potential carers who expressed an interest in a particular child.

- PFC made a poster with photographs of every child on referral who needed a family. These posters were put up on the walls in the reception area and were seen by all visitors to the agency.

- PFC regularly sends photosheets (a single sheet with a photograph and description of the child) to the families on their mailing list. Some of these families are already adopters or foster carers, others are hoping to foster or adopt and may be at different stages in the preparation process.

- Activity days were organised to enable disabled children and potential families to meet at an early stage. It was thought that the best way to convey information about them was to let the children "speak" for themselves.

- PFC held an annual picnic for their adoptive and foster families in a mansion with extensive grounds, which had been left to a London Borough by a local philanthropist. Everyone put out food to share until the tables were laden; one of the fathers organised archery for all and a variety of care and entertainment was provided for the children and young people. Many families came year after year and supportive friendships developed.

- PFC has always offered a comprehensive post-adoption service. In the early days PFC aimed to place all children for adoption and to support the placement until the child was at least 18. If foster care became the preferred option, PFC would assess the family and prepare the child and family for each other, but the post-placement work was handed back to the child's local authority.

- *Find me a Family* by Hedi Argent (Souvenir Press, 1984) describes the work of PFC in the early days.

Religious organisations

- There are several *Rudolf Steiner* communities in the UK. They are individually managed, but all of them are based on a Christian work ethic and a philosophy of valuing each person's contribution according to their ability and nurturing each person according to their needs.

- *The St Joseph's Centre* is a Roman Catholic church and lay community in Hendon, North London, with special concern for disabled people and their families. The Little House was a Portakabin in the grounds which offered a respite service; it was later taken over by the Crusade of Rescue, a national Catholic child care organisation, and became a larger, permanent provision in Enfield.

- *Jehovah's Witnesses* are a worldwide Christian society of people who actively bear witness to others about Jehovah God and his purposes affecting "mankind". They base their faith solely on the entire Bible, which they believe is the inspired word of God and which they liken to a letter from a loving father. Jehovah's Witnesses are a "brotherhood" of people from all ethnic origins. They are therefore neutral in political matters but show respect for the laws of the land in which they live.

Other organisations

- *Parent to Parent Information on Adoption Services* (PPIAS) is a nationwide adopters' support group. It publishes a quarterly newsletter with photographs and details of children waiting for permanent families.

- *Be My Parent* was a loose-leaf book published by BAAF (British Agencies for Adoption and Fostering). It publicised children from all over the country who needed adoptive parents, with photographs, descriptions of the child and a contact telephone number. Today it is a bimonthly newspaper which features children needing adoption and long-term foster carers.

- *The Independent Living Fund* (ILF) will consider applications for financial assistance to support independent living if a disabled adult is already receiving £200 worth of services from their local authority. The total scheme must not cost more than £500 per week. Some costs are excluded.

- *Community Service Volunteers* is an organisation which can place volunteers in a variety of social aid situations, both in the UK and abroad. Most of the volunteers are students and the placements are time limited. The volunteers are not paid; they must be offered board, lodging and pocket money.

- *Mencap* (national organisation for people with learning difficulties) has a scheme whereby parents can leave their homes to the organisation when they die, in exchange for permanent care for their dependent children with disabilities.

- *Gateway* and *Phab* clubs are a nationwide leisure provision for disabled children and adults.

- *Local authority social services departments* have a duty, under the Community Care Scheme, to make a comprehensive assessment of the needs of every disabled person. Many local authorities employ a welfare rights expert who can help families to sort out their entitlements to allowances, grants and benefits.

Adoption Allowance

- An experimental allowance for adopters could be paid by some local authorities which participated in the scheme under the 1976 Adoption Act. This allowance was attached to the needs of the child and each authority had to submit its own scheme to include rules for awarding the allowance and calculating the amount. The allowance became a statutory benefit under the Children Act 1989. It is still only available for children with special needs; it is means tested, it is generally lower than the allowance for fostering children but it can be paid until the young person is 21.

Adoption procedure
- All adoption and long-term foster placements have to be approved by a statutory panel of people with relevant experience or qualifications.

- Applications to adopt children with foreign nationality have to be made to the High Court. The Home Office automatically becomes a party to the proceedings. British nationality is conferred on the child with an Adoption Order granted to British nationals in the UK.

- Single people of either sex can adopt but if two single people live together, they cannot apply for a joint adoption order. It has become increasingly common for single women to adopt but it is still quite rare for single men, and many social workers are unfamiliar with the practice.

- Young people cannot be legally adopted after their eighteenth birthday.

- A guardian *ad litem* is an independent social worker appointed by the court to act on behalf of the child to investigate all the issues leading to an adoption. Since 1984 it has not been necessary to appoint guardians *ad litem* in uncontested and uncomplicated cases.

Education
- All children who have special educational needs have the right to be assessed and to have their identified needs met by the education authority. Parents or guardians must be fully involved in the process (often called "statementing") and the resulting Statement of Educational Need has to be agreed by them.

- BSL (British Sign Language) is a full, visual language system used by people who are deaf. It is usually only taught in schools for deaf children. Makaton is a more simplified sign language used by people with a variety of communication problems; it is generally taught in special schools for disabled children.

Appendix III
Further reading

Argent H, *Find me a Family*, Souvenir Press, 1984

Argent H and Kerrane A, *Taking Extra Care: Respite, shared and permanent care for children with disabilities*, BAAF, 1997

Macaskill C, *Against the Odds*, BAAF, 1985

Learoyd C, *Matthew: My son's struggle*, Macdonald Queen Anne Press, 1989

Morris J, *Gone Missing? A research and policy review of disabled children living away from home*, The Who Cares? Trust, 1995

Unequal Opportunities: Children with disabilities and their families speak out, National Children's Home, 1994

A free publications catalogue listing a range of books and periodicals on adoption, fostering and child care issues is available from BAAF Publications, Skyline House, 200 Union Street, London SE1 0LX.

Appendix IV
Parents for Children

Parents for Children (PFC) was founded in 1976 to find families for children who at that time were considered unplaceable. Initially the children referred to PFC were physically and mentally disabled. Most of the children the agency has worked with and placed in the past five years, however, have been children who are older, often boys over the age of seven, and who are seriously distressed as a result of experiencing physical, mental and sexual abuse.

To work effectively with some of the very damaged children that need permanent families, we must have a team of professionally trained, highly supported and well paid foster carers and adoptive parents. To that end, PFC set up a bridge fostering scheme in 1997 in the belief that children should come into the scheme in a planned way and move on in a planned way as well as allowing for some children to stay put. We also have a small but highly effective respite service. There is family to family respite and, in addition, trained volunteers go into the family's home. This gives fun-time to the children and helps the parents get on with other chores such as medical appointments or school visits.

PFC has also found new ways of keeping families in touch with each other and, over the past three years, has developed telephone conferencing. We use the conferences as support meetings and regularly have experts leading telephone seminars on a range of topical and pertinent issues.

At Parents for Children we specialise in:

- Finding families for older children with complex needs

- Finding families for mentally and physically disabled children and children who have suffered abuse

- Providing support services for the new families for as long as they need it

We are committed to finding families for children to meet their racial, religious, cultural and emotional needs.

Services

- Our highly skilled team of social workers and consultants undertakes assessment of complex child care cases and advises on planning for children.

- We work with children to prepare them for placement, using creative programmes specially tailored for the individual child's needs.

- We supervise the child on behalf of the local authority once he or she has joined the new family.

- PFC was the first adoption agency in this country to offer comprehensive post-placement and post-adoption support. Support and counselling are available to the families as and when they want it. We offer a rolling programme of training and study days for our families.

- We are now working in partnership with the Post-Adoption Centre in London and After Adoption in Manchester to extend the services we offer to children and families.

Information supplied by
Parents for Children
41 Southgate Road
London N1 3JP

May 1998

Could you be my parent?

There are lots of children who need new mums and dads.
Single, married, black, white, young or older,
someone right for each of us.

That someone could be you

If you are thinking about adopting or long-term fostering,
either for the first time or if you have some experience,
Be My Parent can help.

**B
A
A
F**

Be My Parent is a bimonthly family-finding newspaper
published by BAAF, which carries news and articles and
contains a supplement featuring hundreds of children of all
ages and backgrounds who need new permanent families.
Subscription is open to anyone interested in adoption or
long-term fostering.

If you would like to see a free copy of the *Be My Parent*
newspaper and receive a free information pack;
then please ring:

0171 593 2060

BAAF registered charity 275689

1998 editions of guides on adoption

Adopting a Child

A guide for people interested in adoption

Prue Chennells and Chris Hammond – revised by Jenifer Lord

BAAF's bestselling guide has been comprehensively revised in light of legislative changes in England and Wales and Scotland and other significant developments. This fifth edition looks at the reasons why people adopt, the kind of requirements adoption agencies make, the different types of children that need adoption, adopting a child from a different ethnic and cultural group and from overseas, the legal requirements, the costs involved, what happens after adoption, and how to go about fostering a child. *Adopting a Child* also tells you how to get in touch with adoption agencies throughout the country, and gives details of useful organisations and a list of useful books.

Agreeably presented and brought to life with attractive drawings and the experiences of people who have been through the adoption process themselves, this guide is the only book of its kind in the UK and essential reading for anyone considering adopting a child.

104 PAGES PAPERBACK   ISBN 1 873868 54 5   £6.50

Talking about adoption to your adopted child

Prue Chennells and Marjorie Morrison

This new and comprehensively revised edition outlines the whys, whens and hows of telling the truth about an adopted child's origins. It is rich with practical ideas for children of all ages, including those with disabilities and children who come from a different country or are of a different ethnic background.

Talking about Adoption contains useful information simply presented on why telling is so important, what and when to tell your child, how adopted children and birth parents feel, and where you can get more help. Illustrated throughout, the book contains the experiences of adopted people and adoptive parents told from different perspectives as well as useful tips and recommendations.

104 PAGES PAPERBACK   ISBN 1 873868 55 3   £6.50

B
A
A
F

Order copies from BAAF Publications, British Agencies for Adoption and Fostering, Skyline House, 200 Union Street, London SE1 0LX
FAX 0171 593 2001   *Charity Registration 275689*